Barcodes with iOS

Barcodes with iOS

BRINGING TOGETHER
THE DIGITAL AND PHYSICAL WORLDS

OLIVER DROBNIK

MANNING
Shelter Island

For online information and ordering of this and other Manning books, please visit www.manning.com. The publisher offers discounts on this book when ordered in quantity. For more information, please contact

Special Sales Department
Manning Publications Co.
20 Baldwin Road
PO Box 761
Shelter Island, NY 11964
Email: orders@manning.com

Manning Publications Co.
20 Baldwin Road
PO Box 761
Shelter Island, NY 11964

Development editor: Sean Dennis
Copyeditor: Andy Carroll
Proofreader: Katie Tennant
Typesetter: Gordan Salinovic
Cover designer: Marija Tudor

ISBN 9781617292156
Printed in the United States of America
1 2 3 4 5 6 7 8 9 10 – EBM – 20 19 18 17 16 15

brief contents

contents

preface

When Apple released the first beta of iOS 7 at WWDC 2013, I scoured through the API changes looking for anything out of the ordinary. That's when I noticed the unexpected addition of new APIs pertaining to barcodes.

At that time, barcodes were little more than visual noise to me, a necessity of modern commerce but of no value to me as a consumer or app developer. Why would Apple devote precious resources to implementing functionality for *that?*

Several third-party libraries for barcode scanning were available at that time. Some were commercial offerings too expensive for casual use. Others were open source projects requiring a great deal of work to understand or implement in your own apps. By adding support for barcodes within the iOS SDK, Apple made the technology accessible to all developers equally. Apple was sending a message: *barcodes are important to us.*

This paradigm shift inspired me to learn all I could about barcode technologies. I began to research the barcode types supported by iOS and their capabilities and limitations, and all the new related iOS APIs.

A mere month after WWDC 2013, I was contacted by Manning. They'd found me via my blog (cocoanetics.com) and inquired if I would be interested in writing an iOS book for them. They could not have contacted me at a more perfect moment! I was willing, able, and inspired to write, for more than a year, the book you're now holding.

June 2014 marked the 40-year anniversary of the first barcode being scanned at a point of sale. In other words, barcodes are a nearly ubiquitous, mature technology. The UPC you'll find on all products sold in your supermarket was just the beginning.

Just look at any Apple product box. You'll find several barcodes on the stickers offering additional information such as the device's serial number.

Since October 2013, all iPhones can be used to scan barcodes. Together with always-on mobile internet and built-in device sensors, this enables a new breed of product-centric apps that weren't feasible before.

After reading this book, you'll be able to build the exciting new apps that are bringing together the digital and physical worlds.

acknowledgments

I am thankful to ...

Erica Sadun, who—four years ago at a developer conference in Seattle—put the notion into my head that someday I could be a book author too. When I got the opportunity to provide technical feedback for several of her books, I found that my commentary was both welcome and highly relevant. This has inspired my writing ever since.

Scott Meyers, for asking me on behalf of Manning if I would consider writing a book. He supported my idea of writing a "vertical book," slicing through several different technologies, as opposed to writing a "horizontal book," covering only a single technology. I could have chickened out at several points before we signed the book contract, but Scott's trust in me—which was entirely based on a few blog articles I had sent him as samples—kept me in the game.

Bert Bates at Manning, who taught me how to shift from writing blog articles to designing instructive book chapters. I had arrived at my own "tutorial style" over several years of writing blog tutorials at cocoanetics.com, and initially there was doubt that my style would work for a Manning book. Bert believed in me and convinced the powers that be that my style was perfect for an advanced-level Manning book. He also gave me a ton of instructional tools that I am using to this day, even in blog posts.

Sean Dennis, my development editor at Manning, who guided me through giving the book a professional structure and feel. Often he would play dumb and nagged me to explain something better. At first I cringed, but after having made the changes, I always found that Sean's suggestions had made the book much better as a whole. It was also Sean who suggested I use Discogs for the networking chapter's sample app, being an audiophile himself.

The people who contributed to BarCodeKit: Andy Qua, Jaanus Siim, Brendan Duddridge, and most importantly Geoff Breemer. BarCodeKit is the key ingredient that made chapter 5 possible. I also thank Geoff Breemer for migrating this book's sample source code to Swift. This book's code listings are all in Objective-C, but because of Geoff's work you get the free bonus of seeing how it looks in Swift, too.

All the other people at Manning who helped polish this book into its published form, in particular Andy Carroll, my copyeditor, and Katie Tennant, my proofreader, for making me sound like a brilliant native English speaker. Also my technical proofreader, Gregory Hill, for helping me eliminate several embarrassing mistakes in the source code.

The following reviewers, who read the manuscript at various stages of its development and who provided invaluable feedback: Arif Shaikh, Brent Stains, Chris Davis, Emre Kucukayvaz, Gavin Whyte, Jim Amrhein, Jim Matlock, Johan Pretorius, Mark Janssen, and Subhasis Ghosh.

René Swoboda and Roland Moser, who believed in me when I pitched them the ProductLayer.com product information service for a startup, the idea for which came to me as a result of researching barcodes. Their enthusiasm made me realize that I wasn't alone in my vision: mobile apps that interact with physical products via barcodes will be highly relevant.

My colleagues Stefan Gugarel (cameo in figure 3.1) and René Pirringer, for taking on the majority of client consulting work in our company while I was working on this book. They allowed me to concentrate on building sample apps and writing book chapters while sitting next to them in our basement office, which I lovingly started to refer to as "the mine."

My father, Klaus Drobnik, for passing on to me a passion for engineering, structured analysis of complex topics, and teaching. And, of course, for all the other things he did for me, growing up, that I could never thank him enough for. In his role as head of our family business, I thank him for having my back while writing has kept me from contributing to our company's bottom line.

Last but not least, I wish to thank Apple, Inc. The iPhone SDK and the subsequent App Store revolution allowed me to reinvent myself as a full-time self-employed software developer and blogger of technical tutorials. And now I'm even a published author! *Apple enabled me to boldly go where I had never gone before.*

about this book

This book is intended for *intermediate-level* iOS developers who know their way around Xcode and have built a few apps already. This allows me to provide instructions in a terse, tutorial-like style, as readers of my blog, cocoanetics.com, have come to appreciate. By focusing on a more experienced audience, I don't have to waste your time with iOS development basics that are well covered in other books.

Roadmap

The topic of barcodes serves as the common thread running through the chapters of this book, but you can dive into specific chapters to learn about particular technologies. Here's a quick overview of what you will find in each of the chapters.

Chapter 1 introduces you to the barcode types that are natively supported starting with iOS 7. You'll become a barcode guru and be able to hold your own in any conversation about barcodes, their promises, and their limitations. If you like a good story, flip to appendix A, which recounts the curious history of the mother of all barcodes: the UPC.

Chapter 2 gives you a solid introduction to AV Foundation media capture. You'll become familiar with the components of this framework, which we'll use to build a camera app.

Chapter 3 introduces you to the metadata detectors for scanning barcodes, building on the camera preview from chapter 2. At this point, you'll have a reusable barcode scanner that you can employ in all your apps.

Chapter 4 deals with Apple's main reason for pushing forward with barcode support in iOS: Passbook. You'll learn how to generate Passbook tickets with Ruby and how to validate them in an iOS app without the need for server infrastructure.

Chapter 5 looks at how you can generate your own barcodes for display on devices and how you can print them to physical media via AirPrint. You'll learn about the use of Core Image for generating QR Codes and BarCodeKit for all kinds of 1D barcodes.

Chapter 6 dives into retrieving metadata for scanned barcodes, in particular how to use `NSURLSession` for creating a web service wrapper. The second half of this chapter is about creating a custom `NSURLProtocol` and how to stub network requests for unit testing without the need to call an actual server over the internet.

Chapter 7 then rounds out the book by adding contextual information about the user who's scanning barcodes. Core Location and iBeacons let you magically adapt your app's UI to your user's needs.

Three appendixes provide additional background and other useful information.

Code conventions and downloads

All source code in listings or in text is in a `fixed-width font like this` to separate it from ordinary text. Code annotations accompany many of the listings, highlighting important concepts. In some cases, numbered bullets link to explanations that follow the listing.

Source code for all working examples in this book is available for download from the publisher's website at www.manning.com/BarcodeswithiOS.

Author Online

Purchase of *Barcodes with iOS* includes free access to a private web forum run by Manning Publications, where you can make comments about the book, ask technical questions, and receive help from the author and from other users. To access the forum and subscribe to it, point your web browser to www.manning.com/BarcodeswithiOS. This page provides information on how to get on the forum once you are registered, what kind of help is available, and the rules of conduct on the forum.

Manning's commitment to our readers is to provide a venue where a meaningful dialogue between individual readers and between readers and the author can take place. It is not a commitment to any specific amount of participation on the part of the author, whose contribution to the book's forum remains voluntary (and unpaid). We suggest you try asking the author some challenging questions, lest his interest stray!

The Author Online forum and the archives of previous discussions will be accessible from the publisher's website as long as the book is in print.

about the cover illustration

The figure on the cover of *Barcodes with iOS* is captioned "Girl from Split, Croatia, Dalmatia." The illustration is taken from the reproduction published in 2006 of a nineteenth-century collection of costumes and ethnographic descriptions entitled *Dalmatia* by Professor Frane Carrara (1812–1854), an archaeologist and historian, and the first director of the Museum of Antiquity in Split, Croatia. The illustrations were obtained from a helpful librarian at the Ethnographic Museum (formerly the Museum of Antiquity), itself situated in the Roman core of the medieval center of Split: the ruins of Emperor Diocletian's retirement palace from around AD 304. The book includes finely colored illustrations of figures from different regions of Croatia, accompanied by descriptions of the costumes and of everyday life.

The girl on the cover is wearing a richly embroidered vest over a white linen shirt, and an embroidered apron over a long, colorfully striped skirt. She is holding a fan in her hand, and a kerchief on her head and coral beads around her neck complete the outfit. The elaborate and colorful embroidery on her costume is typical for this region of Croatia.

The author chose this illustration for the cover because the vertical lines on the girl's skirt reminded him of a barcode pattern. That's what happens when you research and write about barcodes for a prolonged period of time: you start seeing barcode patterns everywhere!

Dress codes have changed since the nineteenth century and the diversity by region, so rich at the time, has faded away. It is now hard to tell apart the inhabitants of different continents, let alone different towns or regions. Perhaps we have traded cultural diversity for a more varied personal life—certainly for a more varied and fast-paced technological life.

We at Manning celebrate the inventiveness, the initiative, and, yes, the fun of the computer business with book covers based on the rich diversity of regional life of two centuries ago, brought back to life by the pictures from this collection.

1 Barcodes, iOS, and you

This chapter covers

- Why the nexus of barcodes and mobile technologies is creating new, exciting opportunities for app makers
- The barcode symbologies in iOS you should know about
- The distinctions between 1D and 2D barcodes
- A brief history of the UPC/GTIN, the mother of modern barcodes

In the past, if you wanted to add barcode scanning to your apps, you had to either fight your way through open source projects or license a commercial barcode-scanning library. None of those projects were written in Objective-C, documentation was lacking, and commercial solutions required payment of license fees for each downloaded copy of your app. All of these issues made barcode scanning impractical for all but the most skilled iOS developers, and too expensive to make economic sense for free or low-cost apps.

When Apple added Passbook to iOS 6, they built in the ability to display barcodes on Passbook passes. With iOS 7, Apple made these APIs public and added the ability to scan barcodes. This allowed them to add barcode-scanning functionality to several of their first-party apps:

- The *Passbook app* lets you add new passes to your device by scanning special QR Codes.
- The *iTunes app* has the ability to redeem iTunes credits by scanning a voucher.
- The *Apple Store app* has an in-store UI that lets you scan the barcodes of accessories for unassisted checkout (see figure 1.1).

In June 2014, the mother of all barcodes, the UPC, celebrated its 40th anniversary. This makes it an incredibly well understood and ubiquitous technology. Throughout these four decades, different usage scenarios prompted the development of a variety of barcode symbologies that were more or less all informed by the UPC. Apple selected from these the most prevalent and useful kinds of barcodes to support in iOS 7. Support for a few additional barcode symbologies was added in iOS 8. To grasp the full potential of these differing symbologies—as they're relevant to you in iOS app development—you'll learn which purposes they're best used for.

This introductory chapter will give you a solid understanding of barcode technology. Seeing how the multitude of symbologies relate to each other should alleviate any anxiety you might feel right now. You'll no longer shiver in fear from not knowing the difference between UPC, EAN, GTIN, Code 25, Code 39, Code 93, and Code 128. A brief

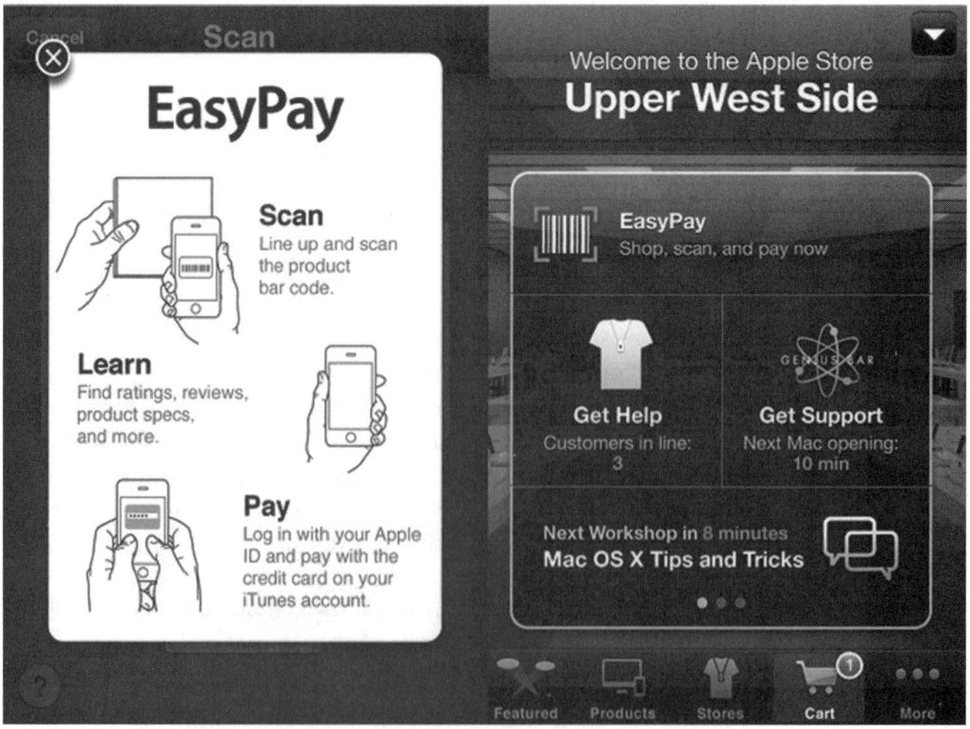

Figure 1.1 Barcode scanning in the Apple Store app

history of the UPC/GTIN will prove illuminating. Not only has its long history been quite amusing at times, this background will aid greatly in your appreciation of the current state of the GTIN. You'll become a barcode guru and be able to hold your own in any discussion about barcodes.

In order to appreciate the power of the barcode, we'll first take a look at how they evolved. Beginning with the UPC, more and more barcode symbologies evolved over time because their predecessors had been designed to solve very specific problems. If you know how to tell them apart—just from glancing at them—you'll know if you're looking at an opportunity for a new app.

1.1 The evolution of barcodes

The first barcode in wide use was the *Universal Product Code* (UPC), combining the semantic meaning of a 12-digit number with a machine-readable scheme for representing this number as a series of bars. It was designed only for automated handling of physical products and was therefore limited to representing numerical product codes. Appendix A will walk you through the history of the UPC and how it became the GTIN, as it's referred to nowadays by people in the know. Figures 1.2a and 1.2b show some examples of how barcodes have changed over the years.

1952
Bull's-eye code is the spiritual ancestor of the UPC
1972
12345678901234
Interleaved 2 of 5 code is invented for marking corrugated shipping containers and casino tickets
1973
8 88462 04074 7
0 425261 4
UPC is announced by the Ad Hoc Committee, UPCC formed to oversee it
1974
Barcodes!
Code 39 boasts ability to encode alphanumeric characters
1977
9 781617 292156 >
< 9638 5074 >
EAN adds additional leading digit to UPC to support multiple countries outside USA
1978
Japan adopts the EAN and calls it JAN
1981
Barcodes!
Code 128 supports full ASCII out of the box
1982
Barcodes!
Code 93 improves on Code 39, not quite reaching the versatility of Code 128

Figure 1.2a Timeline of barcodes

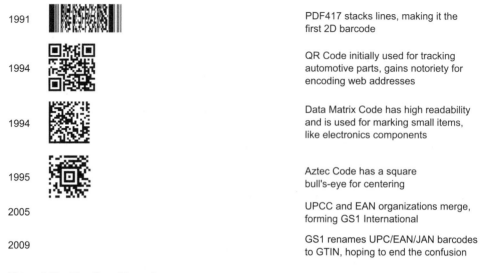

1991	PDF417 stacks lines, making it the first 2D barcode
1994	QR Code initially used for tracking automotive parts, gains notoriety for encoding web addresses
1994	Data Matrix Code has high readability and is used for marking small items, like electronics components
1995	Aztec Code has a square bull's-eye for centering
2005	UPCC and EAN organizations merge, forming GS1 International
2009	GS1 renames UPC/EAN/JAN barcodes to GTIN, hoping to end the confusion

Figure 1.2b Timeline of barcodes

Having overcome the hurdle of enabling a machine to recognize visual markings with a laser beam, a plethora of other kinds of barcodes started to appear, all with more-or-less specific fields of application. For example, the post office found that adding markings to mailed items would allow them to automatically sort the items. Luggage for airline travel was similarly tracked with numeric codes. Other industries had their own standards that worked better for them.

A combination of several bars that make up an individual character or digit is often called a *symbol*. The set of symbols available for a specific barcode standard is referred to as its *symbology*. All these different symbologies can be read with a laser beam.

1.1.1 One dimension: laser

Think of a laser beam as cutting out a horizontal slice of the vertical code bars. As the beam moves over the symbol (see figure 1.3), it measures the relative time it spends scanning dark bars and light spaces. A lookup table is then used to decode individual characters from those times.

The line of the laser beam is also the reason why these kinds of barcodes are referred to as being *one-dimensional* (1D).

If you have more-complex encoding schemes, you can also represent letters and special characters. Some 1D barcode types were created to represent short texts.

The long-recognized major advantage of 1D barcodes is that they can be decoded extremely reliably even when the items

Figure 1.3 A laser needs to cross all bars of a 1D barcode for scanning

tagged with such codes are moving at high speed. Some schemes even employ checksums to recognize when something is misread and increase this reliability.

The second advantage of 1D barcodes is cost. Because the technology has been around for 40 years now, the necessary components (laser diode and decoding electronics) have become cheap and reliable. This makes them ideally suited for high-volume deployment as well as for use in environments where you need to scan a great many codes in quick succession.

1.1.2 Two dimensions: CCD

The *charge-coupled device* (CCD) was invented at AT&T Bell Labs by Willard Boyle and George E. Smith in 1969. This is the chip at the heart of any kind of digital camera. Curiously, the technology for CCDs was invented around the time the first 1D barcode was introduced, but it took decades to develop CCDs to the point where they could compete with the accuracy of their technically much simpler predecessors.

A CCD is essentially a matrix of pixels that reads different binary values for each pixel depending on the light intensity shining on it. As a result, a CCD can read barcodes just like a laser beam can if you have a sufficient number of pixels (a.k.a. resolution). Because the CCD pixels are laid out in two dimensions, CCDs are also able to recognize a new kind of barcode, the *two-dimensional* (2D) barcode.

Freed of the limitations of one dimension, 2D barcodes usually consist of small rectangles laid out to form a square grid. Figure 1.4 shows such a barcode.

Initially CCDs didn't have the necessary resolution, nor did CPUs have the decoding power, required for barcode recognition. A CPU essentially needs to look at each individual frame of video coming from the CCD and look for patterns that constitute a code. Significant advances in electronics and computer vision were necessary to be able to do that.

Figure 1.4 A CCD camera can "see" the squares that make up a 2D barcode.

As with all computer technology, Moore's Law worked its magic on CCDs to eliminate these hurdles over time. Modern smartphones have resolutions measured in megapixels, which are more than sufficient for scanning 1D and 2D barcodes.

There are only two reasons why laser-based scanners are still more widely used at supermarket checkouts than CCD-based scanners: First, CCD hardware is more complex and expensive than laser scanners. And second, CCDs were limited in how many frames per second of video they could capture. If you moved the scanned code too quickly, all a decoder saw were blurred images, and it would be unable to recognize any barcodes. Modern CCDs are capable of sufficiently fast shutter speeds that the blurriness of individual frames is much less of an issue.

1.1.3 Versatility is winning

Imagine setting up a competition for accuracy and speed between laser- and CCD-based scanners, of course using the latest and greatest models. The test scenario is a checkout stand at a supermarket. The contestants are professional cashiers with years of experience scanning products. Whoever scans 1,000 products first, distributed among 100 shopping carts each, will be the winner.

Who do you think will win? Laser or CCD?

I'd still bet on the laser winning this race because of its history and the fact that it's been optimized for exactly these kinds of high-speed scenarios. But any relevant difference in technical ability or cost will continue to melt away in the coming years.

One disadvantage of laser-based scanners remains: they will never be able to scan 2D barcodes, whereas CCD scanners are more versatile. There are many scenarios where versatility trumps speed. Consider yourself and your cellphone: you're never going to compete for speed with a professional cashier, but having the ability to scan barcodes might be a very welcome function in your pocket.

All modern smartphones have a camera built in for taking photos. With a bit of software intelligence, all those cameras gain the ability to scan barcodes at no extra cost.

1.1.4 Where are the bars?

You might wonder why I'm referring to the two-dimensional technology as "2D barcodes" even though there are no bars in sight. All 1D barcodes really do have bars representing a code; most 2D barcodes have small squares. It would be grasping at straws to argue that squares are really bars that are very fat and not very tall.

This technical inaccuracy is why the hyper-precise Apple engineers refer to these codes as *machine-readable codes*. But despite the logic of this term, nobody so far has suggested a term for 2D barcodes that has stuck and found wide usage.

Other terms you'll sometimes hear—like "QR Code"—refer to a single member of the family of 2D barcodes and thus are just as inaccurate. If you wanted to be extra-precise, the correct technical description would be something like "machine-readable codes that use markings forming a matrix grid."

You'll probably agree that "2D barcode" is still the best option, however inaccurate it may be. It simply rolls off the tongue better.

1.2 Barcode symbologies in iOS

There are far too many types of 1D and 2D barcodes to cover all of them in this book. This book is about Apple's support for barcodes, so we'll only look at the types of barcodes that the operating system actually supports. Apple added general barcode support in iOS 7 and added support for a few more symbologies in iOS 8. Figure 1.5 gives a categorized overview of all supported symbologies in iOS.

We won't go into the details of how the individual symbologies are constructed. This overview will give you the basics you need to understand the supported barcode types, their abilities, and where they're primarily used.

Figure 1.5 Barcode types supported in iOS

1.2.1 *1D barcodes in iOS*

Barcodes are said to have one dimension if there's a single line (such as a line traced by a scanner's laser) that can cross all lines of the symbol. iPhones don't have a built-in laser for scanning, but the single-line scanning can be emulated with the camera. The AV Foundation framework scans multiple horizontal and vertical lines on the images coming from the camera and recognizes a 1D barcode as soon as one scan line crosses all bars of the code.

THE GTIN FAMILY

The first commercial barcode, the Universal Product Code (UPC), was announced—after much deliberation—in a press release in April 1973. The first-ever product carrying a UPC code in its packaging was scanned in June 1974. It was a 10-pack of chewing gum, now on display at the Smithsonian in Washington, DC. If you're interested in the curious history of how this came to be, please turn to appendix A, where I tell the whole story.

The GS1 organization (www.gs1.org) maintains the standards related to the *Global Trade Item Number* (GTIN). There are several symbologies that belong to this family, all of them representing a product code and all using the same kind of barcode symbols:

- *UPC-A*—The classic first product barcode (12 digits). GS1 refers to it as GTIN-12.
- *UPC-E*—A narrower version for compressed product numbers (8 digits).
- *EAN-13*—The classic European barcode with a thirteenth digit; in Japan it's referred to as the *Japanese Article Number* (JAN) (13 digits). GS1 refers to it as GTIN-13.
- *EAN-8*—A narrower version of the EAN for compressed product numbers (8 digits). GS1 refers to it as GTIN-8.

These variations are illustrated in figure 1.6.

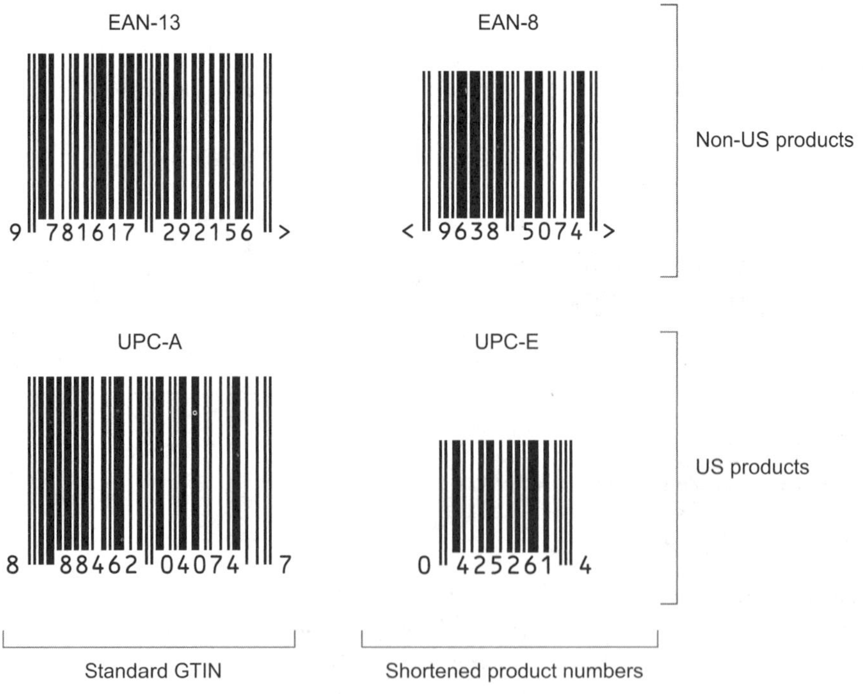

Figure 1.6 The four members of the GTIN family of barcodes

For the narrower symbologies, product numbers that contain several zeros in the middle can be compressed by suppressing the string of zeroes. This requires a manufacturer prefix that ends in zeroes (by special request from GS1) as well as a product number that's prefixed with zeros. Manufacturers love to use these for products with little space on the packaging.

All product codes represented by barcodes of the GTIN family expand to 13-digit numbers. UPC-A (the "classic" code used in the USA) just gets an extra zero as a prefix. Uncompressing UPC-E and EAN-8 to 13 digits is slightly more complicated, but still possible.

> **NOTE** Paper magazines often have an additional barcode next to the GTIN. This is used to encode the issue number with EAN-2 or the price with EAN-5. Those extra barcodes are currently not supported by iOS and are ignored when scanning the EAN-13.

Of these 13 digits, the rightmost is the *check digit*. After scanning, the check digit must match a calculation based on the other numbers; if it doesn't match, the scan is considered corrupted.

The first digit is not directly encoded as bars, but is represented by a certain pattern of odd and even bars. Thus US GTINs always use the same pattern, tied to the prefix 0, whereas international GTINs have 9 other patterns to choose from. When scanning a barcode, the scanner infers the leading digit from the pattern of odd and even symbols.

The left half of GTINs contain the *manufacturer prefix*, which is assigned by GS1. The organization responsible for the manufacturer's country assigns those prefixes based on the table reproduced in appendix A. For example, a company located in Taiwan would have its manufacturer prefix assigned by GS1 Taiwan, and it would have a 470 prefix.

After that, each manufacturer decides on the numbers they assign to their products. If they were to assign a very low number, with several leading zeroes, this would allow for the number compression in UPC-E and EAN-8.

The *International Standard Book Number* (ISBN) is a variant of the GTIN-13 used for books and book-like publications. In this case, the fixed prefix 978 or 979 replaces the manufacturer prefix, and the remaining digits are assigned by national ISBN agencies. ISBNs have their own check digit, which is calculated differently than the one in the GTIN.

The *International Standard Music Number* (ISMN) is a unique number for the identification of all notated music publications from all over the world. It uses a fixed prefix of 9790. ISMNs are also assigned by national agencies.

The third kind of special GTIN-based numbering scheme is the *International Standard Serial Number* (ISSN), used for printed or electronic periodical publications. They share the 977 prefix and are assigned by national centers of the ISSN organization, which is independent of GS1.

Figure 1.7 Netgear combines a UPC with three Code 39s to simplify adding this router device to a corporate tech inventory-tracking system.

> **NOTE** There are several additional GTIN prefix ranges used for products that are packaged in stores, like cheese or meat. Also, you can infer the country that a product manufacturer is located in from these prefixes. For more details, refer to the table "GTIN-13 prefixes" in appendix B.

CODE 39 AND CODE 39 MOD 43

Code 39 was developed by Dr. David Allais and Ray Stevens of Intermec (now a subsidiary of Honeywell Scanning and Mobility) in 1974 to overcome the limitation of the just-released UPC-A, which was only able to represent digits. They saw the promise of automating identification and data capture, but wanted to be able to represent letters as well.

Code 39 is also known as Alpha39, Code 3 of 9, Code 3/9, Type 39, USS Code 39, and USD-3. Its name derives from it initially being able to represent 39 different characters (plus a symbol to represent start and stop)—generally only uppercase letters. With the help of control characters, it can also represent the full ASCII set of characters.

Another advantage that Code 39 has over GTIN is that it can be used for any length of text. But as the number of characters increases, so does the width of the barcode representation. Figure 1.7 shows several Code 39 examples that represent a device model number and its serial number in scannable form.

The plain version of Code 39 doesn't have a checksum to detect scanning errors. A variant of Code 39 does have such a check digit, involving a modulo 43 operation; it's referred to as *Code 39 mod 43*. iOS supports both variants.

A human-readable version of the represented text is usually displayed beneath the code, with an asterisk representing the start/stop character.

> **NOTE** Because Code 39 is as old as the UPC, virtually all existing barcode scanners are able to read Code 39 codes.

CODE 93

Code 93 is a descendant of Code 39, developed by Intermec eight years after its predecessor, in 1982. Its design goal was to reduce the horizontal space required to represent the text and improve error detection by adding a checksum. Figure 1.8 shows examples of the two codes.

Code 39

BARCODES

Code 39 mod 43

BARCODES

Code 39 (full ASCII)

Barcodes!

Code 39 mod 43 (full ASCII)

Barcodes!

Code 93 (full ASCII)

Barcodes!

Code 93

BARCODES

Figure 1.8 Code 93 is an optimized version of Code 39, developed by the same company, Intermec.

The origins of the name are unknown—there's nothing in the standard with the number 93. Maybe it's just a play on the name of its predecessor. By placing the 9 in front, it sounds newer, bigger, and better. That's marketing for you.

Code 93 at its core has 43 characters and 5 special characters. Like Code 39, it can represent all 128 ASCII characters with the help of control characters. This feature was tacked on to Code 39 by reusing codes, but in Code 93 dedicated control characters are used.

The main benefit of Code 93 is that if you scan such a code with iOS, you get the ASCII characters decoded, whereas with Code 39 you have to find the control sequences and do the decoding yourself.

CODE 128

Code 128 was developed in 1981 by Computer Identics Corporation, and its name references the fact that it can represent the full 128 characters of the ASCII code.

Data density in Code 128 is comparable to Code 93, and the features are quite similar. Figure 1.9 shows a sticker from an Apple product box where you can see two Code 128 symbols representing supplementary information about the device.

Code 128 has a more sophisticated mechanism for extending the range of characters—it uses three different sets of character codes specified by control characters. Those character sets are referred to as 128A, 128B, and 128C.

Code 128 has a mechanism that allows it to save horizontal space. The 128C symbol set allows two neighboring digits to be encoded in one code symbol. This compression

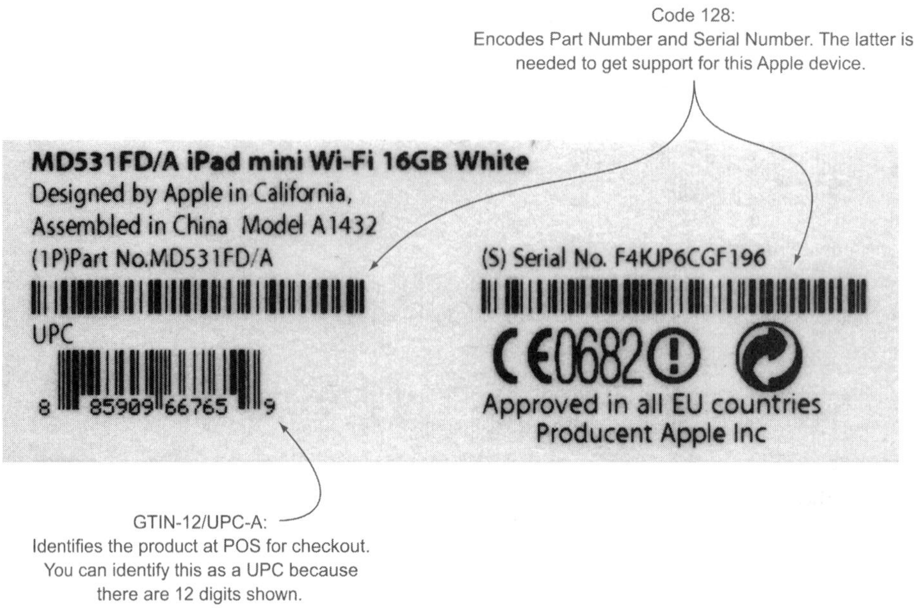

Figure 1.9 Apple prefers to use Code 128 for supplementary information.

mechanism was added to reduce the distance that the laser would have to travel when scanning such a code, which could become rather long.

This code was adopted by GS1 to represent supplementary product information like product weights, dimensions, expiration dates, and so on. Multiple pieces of information like this can be contained in a single barcode. When used in this context, the concrete application of the Code 128 specification is referred to as GS1-128.

This standard defines multiple "application identifiers" to specify the meanings of values following them. The full list of identifiers is reproduced in appendix C. In human-readable captions, GS1-128 barcodes indicate application identifiers by enclosing them within parentheses. This is how you can easily identify a GS1-128 barcode.

CODE 25 AND ITF-14

Dr. David Allais invented Code 25 at Intermec in 1972, before the previously mentioned Code 39 and Code 93, also credited to him. This makes Code 25 the oldest barcode symbology supported by iOS. In 1998 Eastman Kodak Company patented the use of Code 25 for marking film canisters for automatic processing in film development machines.

The barcode can only encode pairs of digits. The first digit is encoded in five bars, and the second digit is encoded in five spaces interleaved with the bars. There are two widths for bars and spaces. The encoding table is constructed such that there will always be two wide spaces and bars for one pair of digits. It's because of this that the code got its original name: *Interleaved 2 of 5*, sometimes abbreviated as *ITF* and more commonly referred to as *Code 25* (see figure 1.10).

As one of the oldest barcode types in use today, Code 25 has a few flaws. Besides being limited to encoding only even numbers of digits, it doesn't have marker bars to indicate to a reading device where the bars start and where they end. This can cause incomplete reads. Also, there's no built-in error checking or correction.

12345678901234

Figure 1.10 An example of an Interleaved 2 of 5 code

Despite those flaws, Code 25 was chosen by GS1 to represent 14-digit GTINs. The predominant use is for marking shipping boxes that contain multiple identical products. Because there are always 14 digits to be represented, the even-numbers-only limitation is a non-issue. A check digit adds protection for incorrect scans. As an additional measure for battling incomplete scans, so-called *bearer bars* were added. Those are meant to abort the scan if the scan line doesn't cross all bars, for example, if the scan angle is too steep.

For printing on labels, only the horizontal bearer bars (above and below) are required by the standard. For printing on corrugate boxes, vertical bearer bars (left and right) are also recommended to even out the printing plate pressure. Figure 1.11 shows an ITF-14 barcode with both vertical and horizontal bearer bars.

GS1 International refers to this scheme as *ITF-14* and lists it as an important standard on equal footing with its other standards. It's probably for this reason that Apple added support for both ITF-14 and "classic" Code 25 with iOS 8.

1 06 14141 99999 3

Figure 1.11 An example of an ITF-14 barcode

1.2.2 2D barcodes in iOS

A problem of barcodes encoding text strings of variable length is that there's a maximum useful width for the markings, which is dictated by what they're printed on. You can't put a longer string onto an envelope than fits on the paper. The obvious solution for this, represented by PDF417, is to wrap the single scanning dimension onto multiple lines. Such a stacked linear code can be read by specialized (and thus more expensive) laser-based scanners.

When there's no single line that can cross all parts of a barcode in one scan, the code is referred to as 2D, and as a rule of thumb you need a camera to read this digital content. Several barcode symbologies were designed to form two-dimensional squares, most notably QR and Aztec.

Apple added support for the PDF417, QR, and Aztec barcode types to iOS so it could represent modern digital boarding passes and tickets in Passbook.

PDF417

PDF417 was invented by Dr. Ynjiun P. Wang at Symbol Technologies in 1991. This company was founded in 1975, a mere two years after the initial UPC was announced, with a primary goal of pursuing the blooming retail- and inventory-management market.

The name PDF417 is in no way related to Adobe's Portable Document Format (PDF), which uses the same acronym. This similarity in name often confuses people first dealing with it. In this case, PDF417 is short for *portable data file.* The barcode consists of symbols that contain 4 bars and spaces each, with each symbol being 17 units long, hence the *417.* An example is shown in figure 1.12.

Figure 1.12 An example of the PDF417 2D barcode

The greatest advantage of PDF417 is that you can decide how wide and how high each individual line should be. And although it's being patented, PDF417 is fully in the public domain and is thus free of all usage restrictions, licenses, and fees. Thanks to these features, PDF417 has become the 2D barcode of choice for a great variety of use cases.

PDF417 is one of the formats accepted by the United States Postal Service for printing postage. More than 200 airlines have settled on using it as the Bar Coded Boarding Pass standard since 2005. It's also used by package services and on ID cards.

QR CODE

You've probably seen a QR Code before: a large square made up of small squares, with larger squares in three of its corners. See figure 1.13 for an example. Those squares are used by scanners to align themselves on the code and determine its orientation.

In contrast to PDF417, the QR Code never had roots in the one-dimensional space—it was designed from the ground up to be read by CCDs. Toyota's subsidiary Denso Wave, an automotive components manufacturer, invented the QR Code in 1994 for tracking parts around car factories.

Figure 1.13 An example of a QR Code

QR Codes can represent any kind of data with great density. As the length of encoded data grows, so does the square area of the code, or the individual squares inside the code shrink. This means that the data density is only limited by the resolution of the scanner camera. The individual squares making up a QR Code are also referred to as *modules.*

The QR Code gained popularity outside of the auto industry when it was used to encode website addresses, mostly in print media and advertising. For a long time it was derided as being a Japanese fad, but now almost all phones have the ability to read QR Codes.

Because QR Codes can represent any data, use cases range from encoding vCards to audio files. For example, a QR Code sticker on a box could contain an audio recording of verbal instructions for visually impaired people.

There's no universal standard for how certain kinds of complex data should be represented in a QR Code—it's agnostic to what data you want to put in it.

QR Codes embed multiple error-correction symbols, which make them extremely resilient. See chapter 5, section 5.1.2, for an explanation.

AZTEC CODE

The Aztec Code was invented in 1995 by Andrew Longacre, Jr., and Robert Hussey. It was published by Automated Industry Machines (AIM) two years later. Its original purpose inside this company is not publicly known.

You can differentiate Aztec Codes from QR Codes by looking at the number of concentric squares. Aztec has one square in the center (see figure 1.14), whereas QR Codes contain multiple squares (see figure 1.13).

The name of the code derives from the central square bull's-eye being reminiscent of an Aztec pyramid. Of course, the Aztec Code has built-in error correction as well.

This code is also one of the three barcode types that can be used on boarding passes following the Bar Coded Boarding Pass standard. (The two others are QR Code and Data Matrix.) On top of that, the Aztec Code is used by a great number of railway companies for digital train tickets.

Figure 1.14 An example of an Aztec Code

Just like with the QR Code, you can represent any kind of data with Aztec Codes, so it's a matter of developer preference which of the two you use to represent your data.

DATA MATRIX

Dennis Priddy of International Data Matrix, Inc., invented the Data Matrix barcode in 1994 and submitted it as a public domain standard to AIM (Association for Automatic Identification and Mobility) to promote widespread use.

Data Matrix is a very compact code that retains a high scan rate even if printed very small or with low contrast between dark and light blocks. The US Electronic Industries Alliance (EIA) recommends using Data Matrix for labeling small electronic components.

Similar to QR Codes, there are data redundancy and error correction provisions built into the specification. Because of this, Data Matrix symbols with scratches, tears, holes, and stains can be successfully read without data loss, even if more than 20% of the symbol were to become damaged and unreadable.

Data Matrix can be read at lower contrast ratios than most barcode symbologies, which is a helpful feature for environments where symbols may be obscured by grease, dirt, paint and chemical coatings, and when the symbology is applied to metal and other reflective surfaces (see figure 1.15).

GS1 International promotes the use of Data Matrix in labeling health care products. The same application identifiers that were defined for Code 128 (see appendix C) can also be used in Data Matrix Codes, but will take up less space due to compaction and the use of two dimensions.

Apple added support for scanning Data Matrix Codes in iOS 8.

Figure 1.15 An example of a Data Matrix Code

1.2.3 So many choices: which barcode should I use?

Out of the large number of different barcode symbologies, Apple chose to support the ones that make most sense for mobile applications. If you're building apps to read existing codes, it's very likely that one of the barcodes we've already discussed has you covered:

- *Physical products, all items that are scanned at the point of sale:* GTIN family
- *Relatively short alphanumeric texts, serial numbers:* Code 93 or Code 128
- *Digital tickets, boarding passes, loyalty cards, PassKit:* PDF417, QR Code, or Aztec Code
- *Arbitrary data in a square space:* QR Code or Aztec Code
- *Arbitrary data using less height than width:* PDF417

iOS, beginning with version 7, can generate bitmaps of all the 2D barcodes we've discussed, and it provides scanning ability for all the 1D and 2D barcodes we've covered. To fill the niche of generating 1D barcodes, I created a library dubbed BarCodeKit. This commercial library is available to readers of this book at no charge. You'll find all the details about this in chapter 5, which covers generating barcodes for display and print.

1.3 Summary

2014 marked the 40-year anniversary of the first widely used barcode, which eventually became the GTIN. Its original goal was to increase the efficiency of the grocery industry by enabling automatic product identification at the point of sale, and it fulfilled this goal many times over as the entire world adopted it. Most barcode symbologies are ISO standards at the lowest technical level; GS1 is in charge of defining the semantic meaning of content represented as GTINs and Code 128.

Other industries had different needs, and this led to the development of barcode symbologies that could represent alphanumeric characters. Code 39 is the oldest among the barcode types supported by iOS; Code 93 and Code 128 are more advanced symbologies.

The advancements in digital image processing gave rise to a new kind of barcode using more than one dimension. Small, inexpensive cameras on a chip, called CCDs, were able to scan 2D barcodes as well as the older 1D barcodes, which initially could only be scanned with a laser beam. As it became standard for smartphones to have a camera built-in, this put a potential barcode scanner in everyone's pocket.

Before the rise of the mobile phone, barcodes were only useful in places that had scanning equipment installed. Point-of-sale (POS) systems had bulky cash registers with built-in laser scanners and a database for looking up price information. But these technologies are now available in modern smartphones. Not only can users now scan barcodes with a device they're already carrying with them, but always-on internet connectivity and device sensors detect the user's current context and add degrees of utility that have never been possible before.

These are the key takeaways for this chapter:

- Barcodes are a tried-and-true technology, with the most widely used form—the UPC—being more than 40 years old.
- Previously barcodes required laser-based scanners found in factories or at the point of sale. Today camera-equipped mobile phones are able to read them with ease. This opens up new usage scenarios with app users being able to interact with the physical world.
- One-dimensional (1D) barcodes encode numbers or alphanumeric characters on a single line. Two-dimensional (2D) barcodes are able to encode arbitrary data on a grid forming a square.
- The international GS1 organization oversees the semantic implementations of barcodes in the context of commerce. See appendixes B and C for details of the semantics that they manage. GS1 unified the previously used UPC, EAN, and JAN codes and numbering schemes into the GTIN.
- Apple began to integrate barcode technologies in iOS 7, adding only a few barcode-related APIs to iOS 8. Beginning with iOS 7, you don't need any third-party software to add barcode scanning to your apps. This book will equip you with all you need to know to create barcode-enabled apps.

2 Media capture with AV Foundation

> ***This chapter covers***
> - Introducing media capture in AV Foundation
> - How video frames flow through the AV Foundation components to a preview layer
> - Configuring cameras and toggling device features
> - Implementing autofocus and tap-to-focus
> - Capturing still images
> - Handling UI rotation

To be able to scan barcodes with the iPhone camera, you need to understand two things: AV Foundation's *media capture* functionality and its *metadata detector*.

Most iOS developers have little reason to familiarize themselves with AV Foundation. The usual kinds of apps have no need to capture audio or video. Even less often do developers need to manipulate or compose media. But this knowledge is a requirement for the barcode scanning this chapter is devoted to, so we'll run through a tutorial on AV Foundation and its components pertinent to media capture.

Chapter 3 will build on this foundation and add the actual barcode scanning via AV Foundation's metadata detector.

2.1 Introducing AV Foundation

AV Foundation is Apple's framework for working with audiovisual media. Initially it contained only functions for dealing with audio media, most notably `AVAudioPlayer` and `AVAudioRecorder`, which are still available today. The earliest traces of AV Foundation date back to iPhone OS 2.2 and OS X 10.7.

When iOS 4 was released in the summer of 2010, Apple added a plethora of new APIs for handling video media. AV Foundation rests on the lower-level frameworks Core Audio, Core Media, and Core Animation (see figure 2.1). Of these, both Core Audio and Core Media are C-based; Core Animation and AV Foundation provide comfortable Objective-C APIs that make working with them an order of magnitude more convenient.

These additions for video content found their way into OS X 10.7 (Lion), which was first unveiled at an event Apple titled "Back to the Mac" in the fall of 2010. This suggests that Apple made media handling on the mobile platform a priority but also gave developers on OS X access to the rich media functionality. Why wouldn't they?

AV Foundation is vast. As of iOS 7 there are 78 public headers. With its richness and multitude of applications, AV Foundation is deserving of a book in its own right, but much of it is outside of what you'll need for barcode scanning.

> **PRO TIP** Cmd-click on any class name or constant in your code to jump straight to the header file where it's defined.

We're only interested in the parts of AV Foundation that let you access the camera and scan barcodes, so we'll focus on `AVCapture` functionality in this chapter. In the next chapter, we'll add `AVMetadataOutput` for barcode recognition.

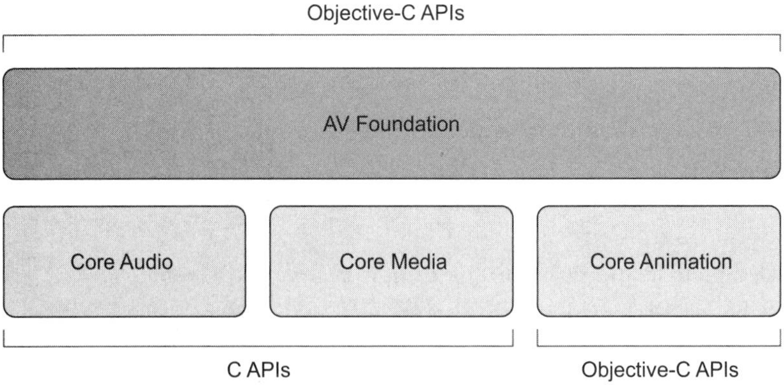

Figure 2.1 AV Foundation rests on three lower-level frameworks.

Dual platform: iOS and OS X

Apple is developing AV Foundation in parallel on OS X and iOS, with only minor differences between the two. For example, on OS X you can find a class to grab video from your desktop display, including mouse clicks. So far Apple hasn't felt it necessary to provide similar functionality for iOS. This class is visible in the AVCaptureInput.h header file, but it's marked as not available on iOS.

Apple provides exactly the same headers for AV Foundation on both iOS and OS X, and the `NS_AVAILABLE` macro is used to mark items available for the individual platforms. If a class is not available, it's marked as NA; otherwise you'll see the minimum OS version supporting it.

For example, the `AVCaptureSessionPresetPhoto` constant is available beginning with iOS 4.0 and OS X 10.7, as you can see in this excerpt from AVCaptureSession.h:

```
AVF_EXPORT NSString *const AVCaptureSessionPresetPhoto
NS_AVAILABLE(10_7, 4_0);
```

This is the quickest way to determine whether something is available for iOS or OS X, should you ever want to check for a specific constant, class, or method.

2.2 Building a camera app

Imagine you're tasked with building the next awesome camera app for the iOS App Store. Building it will give you a solid understanding of AV Foundation's media capture functionality.

NOTE This chapter's sample project works on iOS 6 or higher. Because the iOS simulator doesn't have any camera devices, you'll need to run it on a physical iOS device.

Your camera app (see figure 2.2) will have the following features:

- Show a live preview of the camera image
- Support interface rotation as you rotate the device
- Switch between multiple camera devices (if available)
- Ask the user for permission to access the camera (if required)
- Take a picture and save it to the camera roll
- Toggle the torch (video light) on and off
- Select a focus point by tapping
- Switch back to continuous autofocus if subject changes

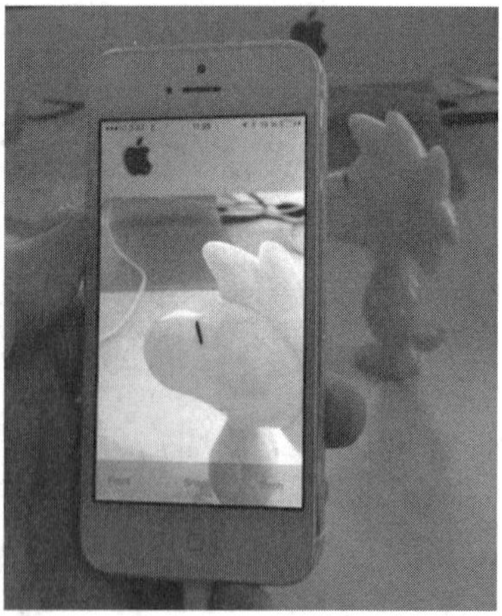

Figure 2.2 The finished camera app

To build this app, you'll use classes and methods of AV Foundation that support media capture, whose names are collectively prefixed with `AVCapture`. Figure 2.3 shows an overview of the basic building blocks at your disposal.

You'll start by selecting a camera device, for which you'll create a device input. This will be added to a capture session. To get a live preview of the camera image, you'll add a preview layer. Finally, to take pictures, you'll add a still image output. The `AVCaptureSession` acts as a central manager that establishes and controls the connections between its inputs and outputs.

The number of moving parts involved in capturing media might seem daunting, but you'll see how it all fits together as you build the camera app.

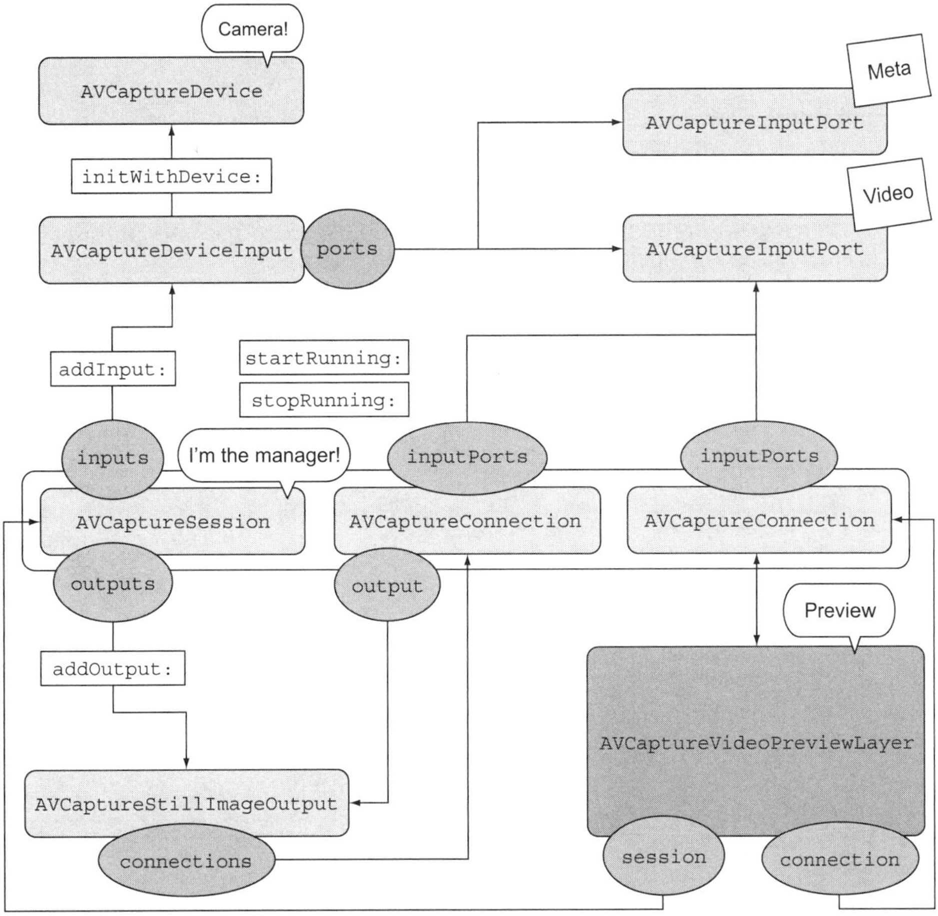

Figure 2.3 AV Foundation components involved in media capture

2.2.1 AV Foundation setup

Some initial setup is required before you can dive into media capture:

1. Create a new app project from the Single View Application template.
2. Rename the root view controller to `DTCameraPreviewController`.
3. Link in the AV Foundation framework.
4. Add the AV Foundation framework header import to your precompiled header.
5. Add private instance variables to hold onto references for often-used AV Foundation objects.

Let's look at each of these steps in detail.

First, create a new app project by selecting File > New Project and choosing the Single View Application template (see figure 2.4). This template has the fewest unnecessary files while still having a storyboard for you to customize.

Next, rename the `ViewController` class to `DTCameraPreviewController`, and adjust the class name in the storyboard. Make sure that it still builds and runs.

> **PRO TIP** The fastest way to rename a class is to select the class name in the source file while it's open in the editor and then select Edit > Refactor > Rename from the menu bar. This renames the .h and .m files and updates all interface builder files referencing them.

The third step is to link in the AV Foundation framework. In your app target, under Build Phases, add `AVFoundation.framework` (see figure 2.5). This is a dynamic

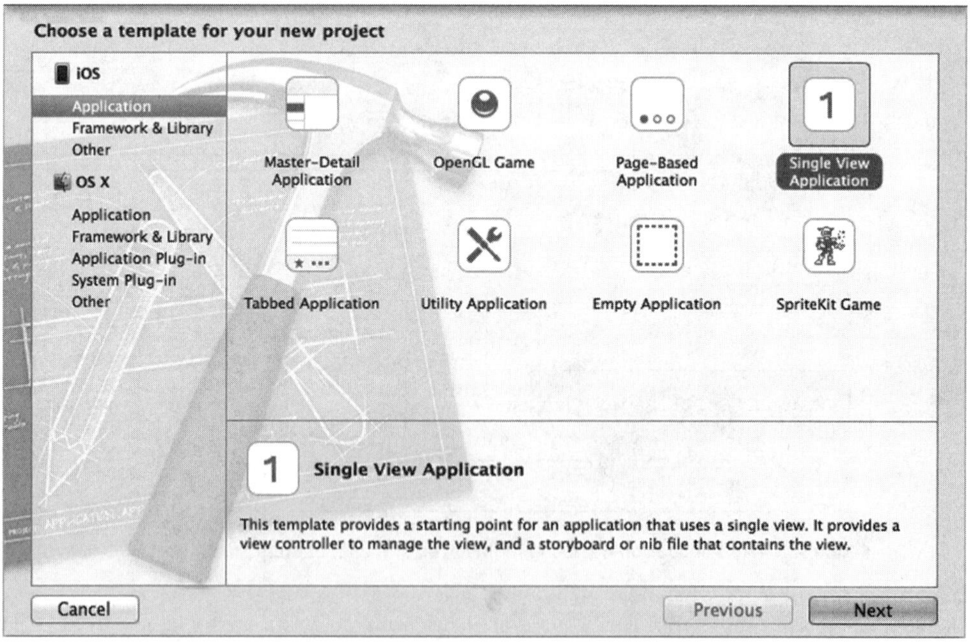

Figure 2.4 Creating a new single-view application

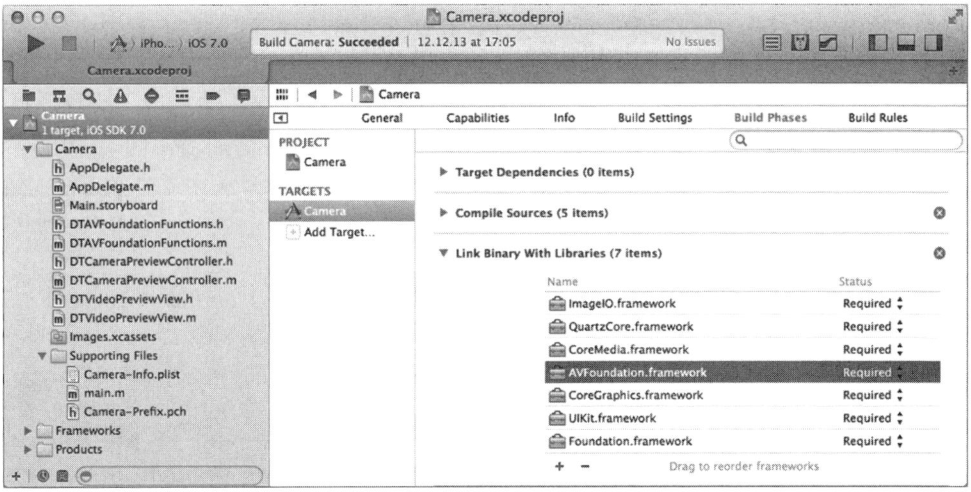

Figure 2.5 Linking the target with `AVFoundation.framework`

framework (as you can tell from the yellow toolbox icon) that's preinstalled on all iOS devices. Adding this in the Link Binary With Libraries build phase allows the linker to resolve references to AV Foundation symbols at link time.

Next you need to add the AV Foundation framework header to your precompiled header (PCH) file. Xcode optimizes the building of the app binary by creating a fast index of the precompiled header contents; during the build, it uses this index to quickly look up system symbols, classes, and methods.

This way, you don't have to repeat the same imports for system headers in all the source files where you make use of the symbols. There's less to type, your code is shorter, and builds go much faster ... isn't that great?

Add the import for the AV Foundation header to your Camera-Prefix.pch, as follows:

```
#ifdef __OBJC__
   #import <UIKit/UIKit.h>
   #import <Foundation/Foundation.h>
   #import <AVFoundation/AVFoundation.h>
#endif
```

You can also safely remove the UIKit and Foundation imports from class headers that you create via Xcode templates. Those imports are redundant, and besides cluttering up your source files, they slow down your builds, because Xcode has to compile these headers every time it encounters an import for them.

Finally, you need to add several instance variables to `DTCameraPreviewController` to give you easy access to the AV Foundation instances you're currently using. Put them in the implementation file to make them private. Classes outside of the preview controller never need to access these variables, and this way of hiding them from the outside world makes for simpler and cleaner headers. You can prefix them with an underscore to visually mark them as internal:

```
@implementation DTCameraPreviewController
{
    AVCaptureDevice *_camera;
    AVCaptureDeviceInput *_videoInput;
    AVCaptureStillImageOutput *_imageOutput;
    AVCaptureSession *_captureSession;
}
```

Current capture device
Video input for the device
Still image output
Capture session manages connections between inputs and outputs

With this setup in place, you're ready to dive into media capture with AV Foundation.

2.2.2 Building the camera UI

Now that you've created a single-view app, you have an empty `Main.storyboard` file. You next need to set up a few basic user interface (UI) elements that will allow you to interact with the example camera app. The UI calls for a camera preview that covers the entire display. Layered on top of it, there should be a dimmed bar that contains three buttons: Switch Cam (to switch cameras), Snap! (to take a picture), and Torch (to toggle the torch on and off).

You haven't created the specialized `DTVideoPreviewView` yet, so leave the base view empty for now. An empty class string for the base view means that it defaults to `UIView`. The shaded bar at the bottom is 60 pixels high, and it has a black background color with 20% alpha. This creates a good contrast between the button text and the background, so that the user can more easily recognize the buttons.

Add three buttons to the shading bar and name them Switch Cam, Snap!, and Torch, from left to right (see figure 2.6). Add sufficient autolayout constraints to the buttons and the shaded bar to keep the bottom of the bar aligned with the bottom of the view and all buttons in their relative places. The UI layout should survive device rotation later in this chapter.

Connect the three buttons to one action and one outlet each.

It's good practice to do a quick test of the actions after connecting them like this. Add an `NSLog` statement for each action handler and launch the app:

```
- (IBAction)snap:(UIButton *)sender {
   NSLog(@"Snap!");
}

- (IBAction)switchCam:(UIButton *)sender {
   NSLog(@"Switch Cam");
}

- (IBAction)toggleTorch:(UIButton *)sender {
   NSLog(@"Torch");
}
```

If everything is connected correctly, then tapping the individual buttons will log the corresponding text.

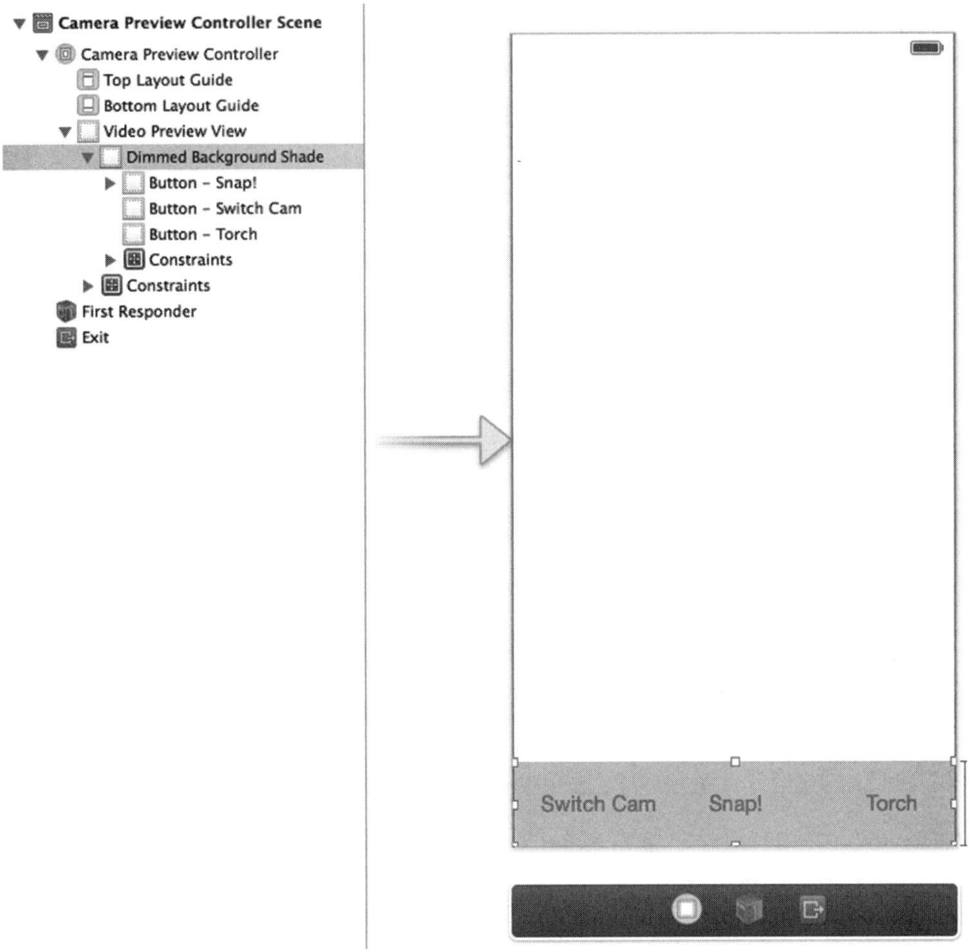

Figure 2.6 Camera UI storyboard

2.2.3 *Selecting capture devices*

The `AVCaptureDevice` class provides class methods for retrieving media capture devices for a given media type. You specify the media type with the `AVMediaTypeVideo` or `AVMediaTypeAudio` constants. Other media types are also defined in the AVMediaFormat.h header, but they aren't used for media capture.

NOTE Never rely on your assumptions about the capture hardware available for specific devices. Use the methods to query the system for what devices are actually available.

Quickly adding action and outlet connections

The fastest way to create an `IBAction` and `IBOutlet` for UI elements in Interface Builder is by enabling the assistant editor. In automatic mode (while showing a storyboard in the left pane) the assistant editor shows the header of the matching view controller class in the right pane. Ctrl-drag the UI element from the left canvas to the right editor, and choose whether to create an action or an outlet as shown.

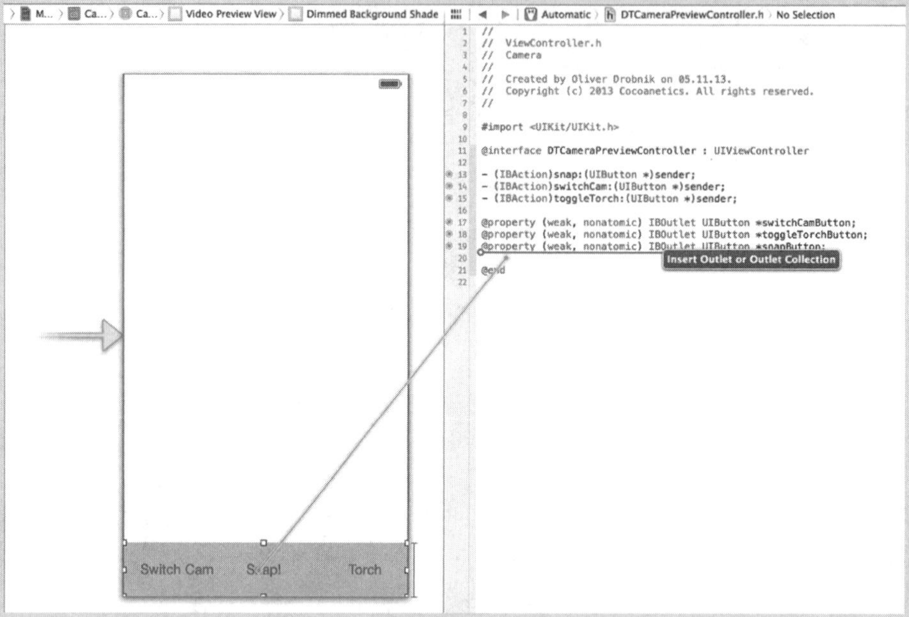

Ctrl-drag to create outlet or action

Current iOS devices provide devices for capturing video or audio media. The iPhone 5, for example, provides an `AVCaptureDevice` for both the front- and back-facing cameras and the microphone. For the camera app, we'll use only the video capture hardware.

Open the DTCameraPreviewController.m implementation file. This is where you'll add most of the code for interacting with AV Foundation. You need to add a `_setupCamera` method to set up the media capture stack. This will contain code for initializing various components of AV Foundation for media capture.

First, you need code to retrieve the default capture device for the `AVMediaTypeVideo` media type. Usually this will be a camera pointing away from the user. Add this code to `_setupCamera`:

```
_camera = [AVCaptureDevice defaultDeviceWithMediaType:
                            AVMediaTypeVideo];
```

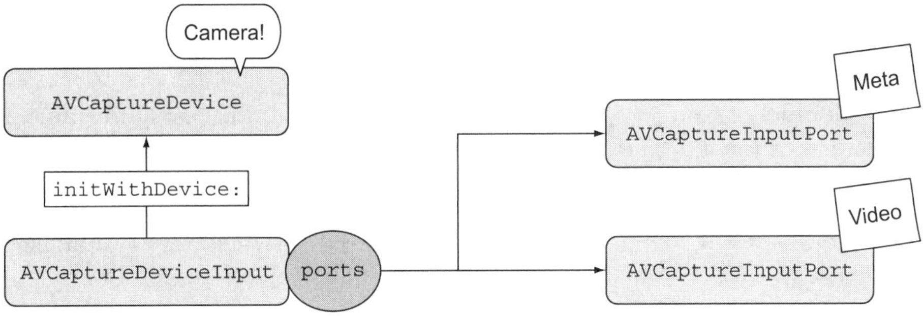

Figure 2.7 The capture device is plugged into the device input.

The preceding code will retrieve the AVCaptureDevice, which you can think of as the camera hardware itself. In order to use it with your system, you have to connect it somehow, like you'd connect a physical camera via a USB cable. The job of the cable is taken on by AVCaptureDeviceInput (see figure 2.7).

To create a device input for the default camera, you initialize it with the device. The following code should also be added to _setupCamera:

```
NSError *error;
_videoInput = [[AVCaptureDeviceInput alloc]
                initWithDevice:_camera error:&error];

if (!_videoInput) {
   NSLog(@"Error connecting video input: %@",
         [error localizedDescription]);
   return;
}
```

Variable receives a reference to error object if there's a problem

Create a device input for camera

Bail out of setup method if there's a problem

Plugging device input (the cable) into the device (the camera) might not always work, as evidenced by the existence of an error parameter. On OS X this fails if an app tries to access the iSight camera while another app is already recording video from it. On iOS devices, such a scenario is extremely unlikely, because iOS lets only the foreground app access media devices. Still, it's safer to deal with the error case. If the connection fails, the result is nil and the error variable will be filled with the reason for the failure. The preceding example simply aborts the setup, but in a production app you might want to inform the user about the failure, possibly providing a way to retry later.

There's no other (publicly visible) link between the capture device and the device input besides passing the camera in the -initWithDevice: method. Calling this method causes the device input class to set up the available *ports*. You can think of ports as strands in the metaphorical USB cable. Each port can transport a single stream of media data. On the iPhone 5, one input port provides an `AVMediaTypeVideo` stream and another provides an `AVMediaTypeMetadata` stream, regardless of which camera device you inspect.

In practice, you'll probably never need to deal with the ports individually. The system hands you a device that it knows supports the media type you're interested in, so you can simply rely on that.

PRO TIP Code defensively. If a method provides an `NSError **` output parameter, check the result and handle the potential problem gracefully.

2.2.4 Media capture session

The `AVCaptureSession` class is the central manager for a media capture session. Typically you only need a single one. It has `inputs` and `outputs` to plug in devices, and it takes care of connecting compatible inputs and outputs (see figure 2.8).

Some input or output objects might not be suitable for a session, so you have to ask it for permission to plug in the object with the `-canAddInput:` method. Add this code to `_setupCamera`:

```
_captureSession = [[AVCaptureSession alloc] init];

if (![_captureSession canAddInput:_videoInput]) {
   NSLog(@"Unable to add video input to capture session");
   return;
}

[_captureSession addInput:_videoInput];
```

- Create media capture session (using default AVCaptureSessionPresetHigh)
- Check if input can be added to session
- Bail out of setup method in case of problems

When you add any input or output to a capture session, it checks which connections are reasonable and establishes these as instances of `AVCaptureConnection`. It would make little sense, for example, to connect an output writing a video file with the metadata stream from a camera, so that connection wouldn't be made.

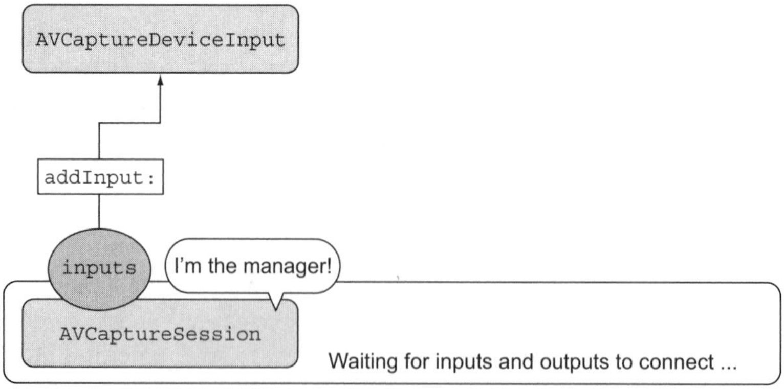

Figure 2.8 The capture session manages everything.

For the most part, you can rely on these automatic connections on iOS. But should you feel the need to establish these manually, `AVCaptureSession` provides the `-addConnection:` and `-removeConnection:` methods.
Any `AVCaptureConnection` has multiple `inputPorts` and a single `outputPort` or `videoPreviewLayer`. The output port and preview layer can never be connected at the same time.

So far, there's no video preview, nor is there any output capture device. That also means there are no connections yet in the session.

2.2.5 Showing live video preview

Apple provides the `AVCaptureVideoPreviewLayer`, which taps into the internal video stream from the camera and displays a high-fidelity video preview. Because it's a `CALayer` subclass, the preview layer is the one item that AV Foundation gets from Core Animation. In order to make the preview layer play nicely with the other `UIView` hierarchy, you can wrap it in its own `UIView`. This lets the preview layer work much better with autoresizing masks and autolayout.

To set this up, create a new `DTVideoPreviewView` class deriving from `UIView`. In the header, define a property allowing access to the video preview layer:

```
@interface DTVideoPreviewView : UIView

@property (readonly) AVCaptureVideoPreviewLayer *previewLayer;

@end
```

Wrap AVCaptureVideoPreviewLayer so that it plays nicely with UIKit frame animations and autolayout (annotation on `@interface`)

Creates an accessor to receiver's main layer, typecast to correct class for convenience (annotation on `@property`)

The implementation of this class sets a black background and specifies an autoresizing mask so that both dimensions follow the superview's lead. The `+layerClass` method is overwritten to return an `AVCaptureVideoPreviewLayer`. This makes sure that the layer class backing this view will be a video preview layer instead of the default `CALayer`. The `-previewLayer` method simply passes the reference on, typecast for future convenience:

```
@implementation DTVideoPreviewView

- (id)initWithFrame:(CGRect)frame {
   self = [super initWithFrame:frame];
   if (self)
   {
      [self _commonSetup];
   }
   return self;
}

- (void)awakeFromNib {
```

Called if instance is created from code (annotation on `initWithFrame:`)

Called when loaded from NIB file (annotation on `awakeFromNib`)

```
    [self _commonSetup];
}

+ (Class)layerClass {                                     <-- Specify use of video preview layer class
    return [AVCaptureVideoPreviewLayer class];
}

- (void)_commonSetup {                                    <-- Setup performed when view is created in code or when loaded from NIB
    self.autoresizingMask = UIViewAutoresizingFlexibleHeight |
    UIViewAutoresizingFlexibleWidth;
    self.backgroundColor = [UIColor blackColor];
    [self.previewLayer
     setVideoGravity:AVLayerVideoGravityResizeAspectFill];   <-- Specify aspect fill to avoid side bars on iPad
}

- (AVCaptureVideoPreviewLayer *)previewLayer {            <-- Pass through typecast for convenient access
    return (AVCaptureVideoPreviewLayer *)self.layer;
}

@end
```

Having `DTVideoPreviewView` in your project lets you add the live video preview wherever you can put a view in Interface Builder. Note that the `_commonSetup` method is executed regardless of whether this object is instantiated from code via `initWithFrame:` or from a NIB.

Now open your storyboard and set the class of the `DTCameraPreviewController` root view to `DTVideoPreviewView` (see figure 2.9).

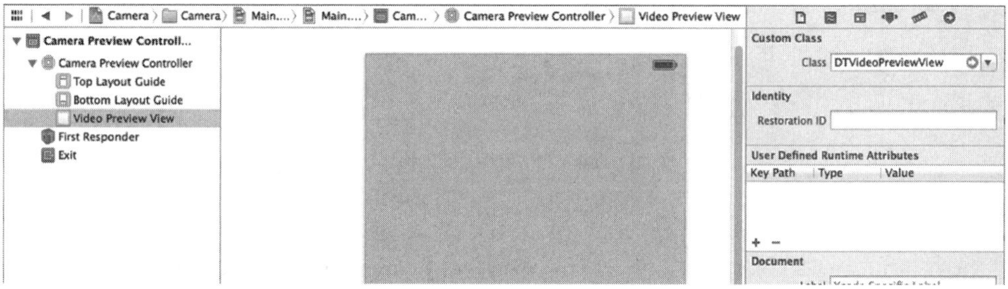

Figure 2.9 Changing the root view to be a video preview

In `DTCameraPreviewController`, add the following `-viewDidLoad` method, which sets a new instance variable (`_videoPreview`) to a `DTVideoPreviewView` reference after the view hierarchy is loaded from the storyboard:

```
- (void)viewDidLoad {
    [super viewDidLoad];

    NSAssert([self.view isKindOfClass:[DTVideoPreviewView class]],
             @"Wrong root view class %@ in %@",
             NSStringFromClass([self.view class]),         Assert that you have
             NSStringFromClass([self class]));             correct root view class
```

```
    _videoPreview = (DTVideoPreviewView *)self.view;      <-- Save reference to preview view into a new instance variable
    [self _setupCamera];                                   <-- Call camera setup method
}
```

With this in place, you can now add the final piece to `_setupCamera` to connect the preview layer to the capture session:

```
_videoPreview.previewLayer.session = _captureSession;
```

Now you have the first `AVCaptureConnection` established, connecting the video port of the `AVCaptureDeviceInput` with the preview layer (see figure 2.10).

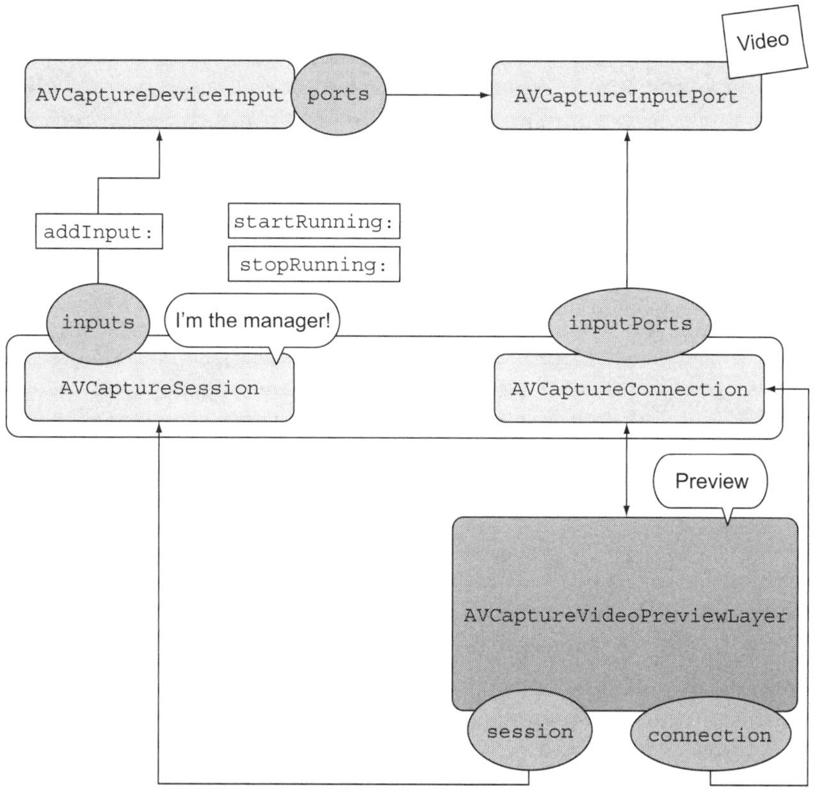

Figure 2.10 The first connection between a video input port and the preview layer

To start the flow of data, you call `-startRunning` on the session when the view controller is presented. To make your app a good iOS citizen, add a corresponding `-stopRunning` when the view controller is dismissed:

```
- (void)viewWillAppear:(BOOL)animated {
    [super viewWillAppear:animated];

    [_captureSession startRunning];      <-- Start session so that you see video instead of black rectangle
}
```

```
- (void)viewDidDisappear:(BOOL)animated {
    [super viewDidDisappear:animated];

    [_captureSession stopRunning];
}
```

Stop session when view controller disappears

Run the app on your iOS device, and you should see a live video feed ... unless you're testing on a device that was sold in China. There the law requires that the user consent to any app accessing the camera.

2.2.6 Authorizing camera access (or not)

There are some situations where camera access might require user authorization, or access to the camera might have been disabled through device restrictions. You have to take charge of the authorization process as part of your app's user experience. Failure to do so might leave your app unusable and only display an empty rectangle where the user might expect the video preview.

Disabling camera access

The most common way to disable access to the camera is via Settings > General > Restrictions > Enable Restrictions.

For configuring multiple iOS devices in a school or business environment, there's also the Apple Configurator utility (https://itunes.apple.com/us/app/apple-configurator/id434433123). This tool builds a profile specifying available device features for "supervised" devices. This has the same restrictions available on a single iOS device, along with a plethora of additional configuration options.

Authorization for audio input is necessary on all iOS devices. Up until iOS 7, authorization for access to video input was only required for devices sold in China. Apple figured that it would be beneficial for users' privacy to extend this requirement, so beginning with iOS 8, apps require user authorization to access the video camera as well. The authorization request dialog looks the same as the requests for accessing the user's location or microphone (see figure 2.11).

You don't have to do anything about this—the dialog will be presented in any case. But because the user might disallow camera access, you should be aware that this will probably make some functionality in your app impossible. You should disable functionality that won't work without the camera and inform the user that it's their choice. If you don't disable camera functionality when camera access is denied, your code will progress without a problem but all video images will be black.

Figure 2.11 Camera+ asking a Chinese iOS 7 user for camera authorization

Add a new method that's called from `-viewDidLoad` instead of `-setupCamera`. This checks the authorization status first, and only sets up the camera once the authorization status has been determined:

```
- (void)_setupCameraAfterCheckingAuthorization {
    if (![[AVCaptureDevice class] respondsToSelector:
      @selector(authorizationStatusForMediaType:)]) {
        [self _setupCamera];

        return;
    }

    AVAuthorizationStatus authStatus = [AVCaptureDevice
    authorizationStatusForMediaType:AVMediaTypeVideo];

    switch (authStatus) {
        case AVAuthorizationStatusAuthorized: {
            [self _setupCamera];
            break;
        }

        case AVAuthorizationStatusNotDetermined: {
            [AVCaptureDevice requestAccessForMediaType:
             AVMediaTypeVideo completionHandler:^(BOOL granted) {
```

❶ For iOS 6, assume authorization

Request status of authorization

Access granted; set up camera

❷ Access status unknown; request access

```
            dispatch_async(dispatch_get_main_queue(), ^{
                if (granted) {
                    [self _setupCamera];

                    ...

                    [_captureSession startRunning];
                } else {
                    [self _informUserAboutCamNotAuthorized];
                }
            });
        }];
        break;
    }

    case AVAuthorizationStatusRestricted:
    case AVAuthorizationStatusDenied: {
        [self _informUserAboutCamNotAuthorized];
        break;
    }
  }
}
```

3 The completion handler is called on a background thread. This dispatches execution back to the main queue.

Update UI buttons

Start capture session

4 Access not granted; inform user

This code also works on iOS 6. The `AVCaptureDevice` doesn't have an `-authorizationStatusForMediaType:` selector in that version, so you can skip right to camera setup in that case ❶.

If the authorization status is `AVAuthorizationStatusNotDetermined`, you request access for the video media type ❷, and only if the completion handler comes back with a positive result do you set up the camera.

If access is restricted or denied, or the completion handler comes back negative, you need to inform the user that their choice makes camera functionality not possible ❹. An `-_informUserAboutCamNotAuthorized` helper method displays an alert view to that effect.

Note the `dispatch_async` to the main thread ❸. This is needed because the completion handler will be called on a background queue, but you want the methods contained in the dispatch block to be executed on the main thread.

If the authorization status is restricted or denied, there's nothing you can do about that from inside your app. All you can do is inform the user that this app requires authorization to be granted from the Settings app. If you call the access request method with the status being restricted or denied, the completion handler will be executed right away with `granted` being `NO` and no authorization dialog being shown. The dialog asking for permission only appears if the current authorization state is undetermined.

2.2.7 Toggling the video light

Video capture devices have a number of features that might vary quite a bit between devices and device generations. In this section you'll add a video light, a.k.a. "torch," to your camera. A torch isn't a typical feature for a still image camera, but adding one will demonstrate how to query available features from a capture device. Also, in chapter 3 you'll find the light useful for scanning barcodes in dimly lit places.

The AVCaptureDevice has a -hasTorch method that you can query, and you can use this to hide the Torch button on cameras that have no LED flashlight, like the user-facing camera. The following method adjusts the visibility of the Torch button based on the currently selected camera. Note the use of the Torch button outlet that you connected earlier:

```
- (void)_setupTorchToggleButton {
   if ([_camera hasTorch]) {
      self.toggleTorchButton.hidden = NO;
   } else {
      self.toggleTorchButton.hidden = YES;
   }
}
```

Capture device tells you if there's a torch available

In section 2.2.2 you added a dummy implementation for the three actions linked with three buttons in Interface Builder. Now you need to add the actual code to toggle the torch feature. This method demonstrates how to query for the availability of a device feature as well as how to lock it while making configuration changes:

```
- (IBAction)toggleTorch:(UIButton *)sender {
   if ([_camera hasTorch]) {
      BOOL torchActive = [_camera isTorchActive];

      if ([_camera lockForConfiguration:nil]) {
         if (torchActive) {
            if ([_camera isTorchModeSupported:AVCaptureTorchModeOff]) {
               [_camera setTorchMode:AVCaptureTorchModeOff];
            }
         } else {
            if ([_camera isTorchModeSupported:AVCaptureTorchModeOn]) {
               [_camera setTorchMode:AVCaptureTorchModeOn];
            }
         }

         [_camera unlockForConfiguration];
      }
   }
}
```

Capture device knows if torch is active

Need to lock capture device for changing settings; without this there's an exception

Toggle torch on if supported

Toggle torch off if supported

Unlock configuration when done

Your camera app now doubles as flashlight app! If you tap the Torch button, you turn on the video light. Tap it again to turn it off.

> **Beware of AV exceptions!**
>
> You *must* lock a capture device before and unlock it after making configuration changes to it. Trying to change the configuration without locking will cause AV Foundation to trigger an exception.

(continued)

Trying to set an unsupported value on a property of the capture device is equally bad. For every configuration property `foo`, there's a corresponding `-isFooSupported` method, which you can find in the SDK documentation.

Exceptions are bad for the user experience: they terminate your app.

2.2.8 Taking pictures to the camera roll

Now you get to take pictures! Let's fill in the action method for the Snap! button.

To take pictures, you need to add an `AVCaptureStillImageOutput` class to your capture session. This is the last piece to the video capture puzzle (see figure 2.12).

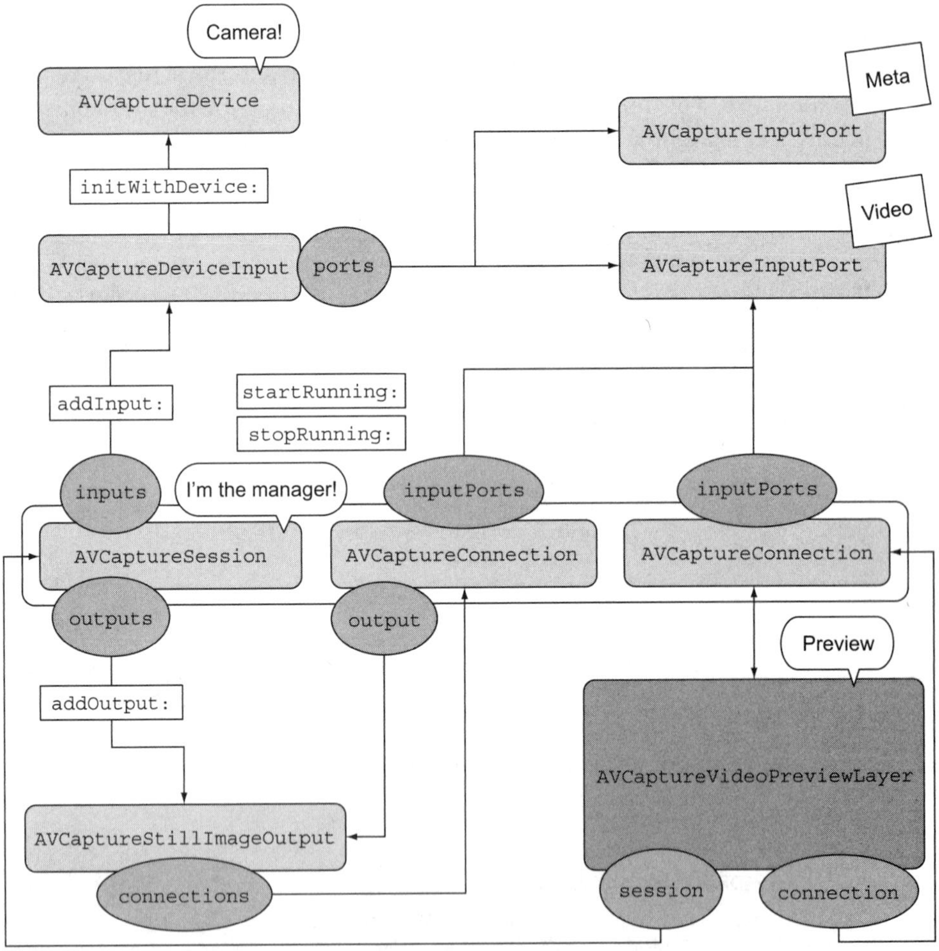

Figure 2.12 The completed AV capture puzzle

In figure 2.12 the media streams from the capture device (top left) and flows through the device input into the capture session. The session manages the capture connections between inputs and outputs. At the bottom, the media data flows into the still image output as well as the video preview layer.

The following code shows the complete `_setupCamera` implementation containing all the previously explained camera setup steps. It also adds a still image output to the capture session:

```
- (void)_setupCamera {
   _camera = [AVCaptureDevice
             defaultDeviceWithMediaType:AVMediaTypeVideo];

   if (!_camera) {
      [self.snapButton setTitle:@"No Camera Found"
                       forState:UIControlStateNormal];
      self.snapButton.enabled = NO;
      [self _informUserAboutNoCam];
      return;
   }

   NSError *error;
   _videoInput = [[AVCaptureDeviceInput alloc] initWithDevice:_camera
                                                        error:&error];

   if (!_videoInput) {
      NSLog(@"Error connecting video input: %@",
            [error localizedDescription]);
      return;
   }

   _captureSession = [[AVCaptureSession alloc] init];

   if (![_captureSession canAddInput:_videoInput]) {
      NSLog(@"Unable to add video input to capture session");
      return;
   }

   [_captureSession addInput:_videoInput];

   // [self _configureCurrentCamera];

   _imageOutput = [AVCaptureStillImageOutput new];

   if (![_captureSession canAddOutput:_imageOutput]) {
      NSLog(@"Unable to add still image output to capture session");
      return;
   }

   [_captureSession addOutput:_imageOutput];

   _videoPreview.previewLayer.session = _captureSession;
}
```

Method to configure current camera will be implemented later

Add still image output

Ask capture session if input can be added

Bail out if there is problem

Connect still image output

Set session to be previewed

You need a reference to the current capture connection to take a still image. This helper method finds and returns it:

```
- (AVCaptureConnection *)_captureConnection {
   for (AVCaptureConnection *connection in _imageOutput.connections) {
      for (AVCaptureInputPort *port in [connection inputPorts]) {
         if ([port.mediaType isEqual:AVMediaTypeVideo]) {
            return connection;                          <- Returns connection of first video input port
         }
      }
   }

   return nil;                 <- Returns nil if no capture connection was found
}
```

With this setup in place, you can fill in the -snap: action. This is the second method you need to replace in the previous dummy implementation from section 2.2.2:

```
- (IBAction)snap:(UIButton *)sender {          <- Method called when Snap! button is tapped
   if (!_camera) {
      return;                                  <- No camera, so no photos possible
   }

   AVCaptureConnection *videoConnection = [self _captureConnection];   <- Get capture connection from helper method

   if (!videoConnection) {
      NSLog(@"Error: No Video connection found on still image output");
      return;
   }                  <- No connection found, so there's no video connection to capture still images from

   [_imageOutput
    captureStillImageAsynchronouslyFromConnection:videoConnection
    completionHandler:^(CMSampleBufferRef imageSampleBuffer,
                        NSError *error) {          <- 1 Asynchronous image capture
      if (error) {
         NSLog(@"Error capturing still image: %@",
               [error localizedDescription]);
         return;                        <- Bail out of completion handler if there's a problem
      }

      NSData *imageData = [AVCaptureStillImageOutput
                           jpegStillImageNSDataRepresentation:
                           imageSampleBuffer];     <- 2 Convert sample buffer to JPEG image data
      UIImage *image = [UIImage imageWithData:imageData];   <- 3 Create an image out of the data blob
      UIImageWriteToSavedPhotosAlbum(image, nil, nil, nil);   <- Save image to camera roll
   }];
}
```

For capturing still images, you need a reference to the `AVCaptureConnection` that's feeding your still image output. `AVCaptureSession` doesn't provide a method to get connections, so you have to iterate through the image output connections, as demonstrated by the `_captureConnection` helper method shown earlier. Capture connections have multiple inputs, so you're looking for the one that has the video stream.

The actual photography occurs when you call the awkwardly named `-captureStillImageAsynchronouslyFromConnection: completionHandler:` ❶. After a few milliseconds, the completion handler will be called, providing a reference to a sample buffer.

Camera sound

The still image capturing method also makes a camera-shutter sound. Apparently there have been incidents of people sticking their camera apps where they don't belong, so some governments mandate that you shouldn't be able to disable the camera sound on mobile phones. If you can, you should abide by these rules, but if you absolutely need to eliminate the sound, there's a way to do that: you can employ `AVCaptureVideoDataOutput`, which lets you grab individual video frame sample buffers and then convert them to images.

The CM prefix of `CMSampleBufferRef` tells you that it's coming from the depths of Core Media, which AV Foundation rests on. This sample buffer contains the actual pixels of a frame of the video stream.

You don't need to worry about converting this buffer data into a JPEG image—that's taken care of by the `+jpegStillImageNSDataRepresentation:` class method of `AVCaptureStillImageOutput` ❷. This gives you the actual JPEG data, which can easily be transmuted into a `UIImage` for saving to the user's camera roll ❸.

NOTE `UIImageWriteToSavedPhotosAlbum` asks for user permission the first time it's called, much like camera authorization. The additional function parameters let you specify a callback method to handle the user's response. If you were to make a real-life photo app, you'd also have to deal with the user taking a picture but then denying access to the camera roll.

2.2.9 *Supporting rotation of device and UI*

If you run the camera app at this point, you should be able to take pictures. The default setting for iPhones is to support both landscape orientations and the one portrait orientation where the home button is at the bottom. But if you rotate to landscape, you'll find that both the preview image as well as the photos taken aren't rotated with the interface orientation as you would expect. To fix this, you also need to update the video connection orientation when the phone is rotated.

In real life, you'll probably want to keep the system default of `UIInterfaceOrientationMaskAllButUpsideDown` for iPhone and iPod touch, and `UIInterfaceOrientationMaskAll` for iPad. For demonstration purposes, let's override `-supportedInterfaceOrientations` to allow all orientations, even upside-down portrait:

```
- (NSUInteger)supportedInterfaceOrientations {
    return UIInterfaceOrientationMaskAll;
}
```

AV capture connections allow you to specify a video orientation, and you'll want to set this in sync with the current view controller's interface orientation. Because interface orientation and video orientation are two different enums, you'll need to implement a function to convert between them. In the sample code, you'll find this function in DTAVFoundationFunctions.m:

```
AVCaptureVideoOrientation
   DTAVCaptureVideoOrientationForUIInterfaceOrientation(
      UIInterfaceOrientation interfaceOrientation) {

   switch (interfaceOrientation) {
      case UIInterfaceOrientationLandscapeLeft:
         return AVCaptureVideoOrientationLandscapeLeft;

      case UIInterfaceOrientationLandscapeRight:
         return AVCaptureVideoOrientationLandscapeRight;

      default:
      case UIInterfaceOrientationPortrait:
         return AVCaptureVideoOrientationPortrait;

      case UIInterfaceOrientationPortraitUpsideDown:
         return AVCaptureVideoOrientationPortraitUpsideDown;
   }
}
```

The following method iterates through the video connections and updates the `videoOrientation` where relevant, using the preceding helper function to determine the correct video orientation for the given interface orientation parameter. Grouping these updates together in a helper method allows you to call it where necessary, like before a rotation and after switching cameras:

```
- (void)_updateConnectionsForInterfaceOrientation:
      (UIInterfaceOrientation)interfaceOrientation {
   AVCaptureVideoOrientation captureOrientation =
      DTAVCaptureVideoOrientationForUIInterfaceOrientation(
         interfaceOrientation);                                   // Convert interface orientation into video orientation

   for (AVCaptureConnection *connection in _imageOutput.connections) {
      if ([connection isVideoOrientationSupported]) {
         connection.videoOrientation = captureOrientation;        // Update orientation on all video connections
      }
   }
```

```
    if ([_videoPreview.previewLayer.connection
            isVideoOrientationSupported]) {
        _videoPreview.previewLayer.connection.videoOrientation =
            captureOrientation;
    }
}
```

Update orientation for video preview

The update method in the preceding code iterates over all capture connections of the still image output object to update the video orientation where possible. The same is done for the view preview layer's capture connection. Note the repeated pattern of inquiring `-isVideoOrientationSupported` and only making the change if the answer is `YES`.

Finally, you need to call the orientation update method right before a rotation animation occurs:

```
- (void)willRotateToInterfaceOrientation:(UIInterfaceOrientation)
                                        toInterfaceOrientation
                                duration:(NSTimeInterval)duration {
    [super willRotateToInterfaceOrientation:toInterfaceOrientation
                               duration:duration];

    [self _updateConnectionsForInterfaceOrientation:
        toInterfaceOrientation];
}
```

Now you can launch the app to see that the video orientation stays in sync with the interface orientation.

Orientation and performance

Changing the video orientation of a capture connection has no impact on performance. AV Foundation avoids rotating sample buffers and instead adds metadata to the video streams indicating the video orientation. Apple says so in Q&A QA1744 (https://developer.apple.com/library/ios/qa/qa1744/).

The same is true for pictures saved to the camera roll and for images that users upload to websites. The orientation information is stored in an EXIF header in the image file. If you encounter user-uploaded images on the web that are awkwardly rotated by 90 degrees, this is often because the website didn't properly handle the EXIF orientation value.

2.2.10 Switching between camera devices

You'll be hard pressed to find a current iOS device that has only a single camera. At the time of writing, only the fifth-generation iPod Touch has a single FaceTime camera. All other devices supported by iOS 6 and up—except for the Apple TV—have two cameras.

The process for switching cameras is similar to the process for configuring devices. You have to call `-beginConfiguration` up front and end the configuration activities with `-commitConfiguration`.

Let's implement a helper method to determine if there is indeed an alternative to the current camera available:

```
- (AVCaptureDevice *)_alternativeCamToCurrent {
   if (!_camera) {
       return nil;                                      <- No current camera
   }

   NSArray *allCams = [AVCaptureDevice
                        devicesWithMediaType:AVMediaTypeVideo];

   for (AVCaptureDevice *oneCam in allCams) {
      if (oneCam != _camera) {
         return oneCam;          <- Return first camera different from current one
      }
   }

   return nil;                                          <- No alternative cameras present
}
```

To inform the user about which camera is currently selected, you can update the text on the camera-switching button accordingly:

```
- (void)_setupCamSwitchButton {
   AVCaptureDevice *alternativeCam = [self _alternativeCamToCurrent];

   if (alternativeCam) {
      self.switchCamButton.hidden = NO;

      NSString *title;

      switch (alternativeCam.position) {
         case AVCaptureDevicePositionBack:
            title = @"Back";
            break;
         case AVCaptureDevicePositionFront:
            title = @"Front";
            break;
         case AVCaptureDevicePositionUnspecified:
            title = @"Other";
            break;
      }

      [self.switchCamButton setTitle:title
                            forState:UIControlStateNormal];
   } else {
      self.switchCamButton.hidden = YES;
   }
}
```

The action method for switching cameras is called whenever the user taps on the camera-switching button. This is the third and last of the action methods you need to replace from section 2.2.2:

```
- (IBAction)switchCam:(UIButton *)sender {
   [_captureSession beginConfiguration];

   _camera = [self _alternativeCamToCurrent];

   // [self _configureCurrentCamera];

   for (AVCaptureDeviceInput *input in _captureSession.inputs) {
      [_captureSession removeInput:input];
   }

    _videoInput = [AVCaptureDeviceInput deviceInputWithDevice:_camera
                                                        error:nil];
    [_captureSession addInput:_videoInput];

    [self _updateConnectionsForInterfaceOrientation:
             self.interfaceOrientation];

    [_captureSession commitConfiguration];

   [self _setupCamSwitchButton];
   [self _setupTorchToggleButton];
}
```

Lock running session for making configuration changes

Method to configure current camera will be implemented later

Remove all old inputs

Commit changes to session configuration

Helper methods for updating buttons for capabilities of newly selected camera

Just like you had a method for showing the Torch button only when a torch was available, you also have such a method for the camera switch button, albeit one that's slightly more complex. The `-position` property of a camera lets you update the button title to read "Bottom" or "Front" to match the camera position. This is done in the `_setupCamSwitchButton` helper method (see sample code).

Switching the camera involves removing all previous `-inputs` from the capture session, adding a new input for the alternative camera, and updating the resulting video connections for the current interface orientation.

Both the `_setupCamSwitchButton` and `_setupTorchToggleButton` methods for updating the UI buttons need to be called in multiple places so that the UI always reflects the capabilities of the current camera. The sample code (in DTCameraPreviewController.m) calls these methods in `-_setupCameraAfterCheckingAuthorization` and `-viewWillAppear:` in addition to the `-switchCam:` action. If you aren't sure where to add these, check the sample code.

NOTE If you turn on the torch on a back-facing camera and switch to a front-facing camera, the torch is disabled automatically, because the video light would be facing the wrong direction. There is no flash/torch for the front-facing camera.

2.2.11 Implementing autofocus and tap-to-focus

The last feature of this chapter's camera app to implement is tap-to-focus coupled with automatically switching back to continuous autofocus if the subject area changes.

The default capturing cameras on iOS devices—cameras pointing away from the user—generally support autofocus. The FaceTime camera—the camera pointing toward the user—doesn't. There are three autofocus modes:

- `AVCaptureFocusModeContinuousAutoFocus`
- `AVCaptureFocusModeAutoFocus`
- `AVCaptureFocusModeLocked`

The continuous autofocus mode is the default; in this case the camera focuses automatically when needed. The noncontinuous option will focus on the current focus point; once focus has been found, it changes to the locked mode.

To enable subject-area change monitoring, there's a new method (shown in the following code snippet) to configure the current camera. This method is called from `_setupCamera` and `_switchCam:`, and it enables this feature if it's supported. Enabling subject-area change monitoring is a rare exception to the rule of having to inquire about an ability before using it—in this case, there's no method available to do that. Monitoring the video stream for significant changes is not a function performed by the video capture hardware but rather is done by the OS itself:

```
- (void)_configureCurrentCamera {
   if ([_camera isFocusModeSupported:AVCaptureFocusModeLocked]) {
      if ([_camera lockForConfiguration:nil]) {
         _camera.subjectAreaChangeMonitoringEnabled = YES;

         [_camera unlockForConfiguration];
      }
   }
}
```

Helper method to configure current camera

Subject-area change monitoring makes sense only if autofocus lock is supported by camera

Enable subject-area change monitoring on current camera device

Once subject-area change monitoring is enabled, iOS sends an `AVCaptureDeviceSubjectAreaDidChangeNotification` whenever there's a substantial change of what's visible to the camera. You can subscribe to this notification in `-viewDidLoad`, as this is where you already put some setup code previously. At the same time, you can install a tap-gesture recognizer for detecting a tap-to-focus gesture:

```
- (void)viewDidLoad
{
   [super viewDidLoad];

   NSAssert([self.view isKindOfClass:[DTVideoPreviewView class]],
         @"Wrong root view class %@ in %@",
         NSStringFromClass([self.view class]),
         NSStringFromClass([self class]));
```

```
    _videoPreview = (DTVideoPreviewView *)self.view;

    [self _setupCameraAfterCheckingAuthorization];

    UITapGestureRecognizer *tap = [[UITapGestureRecognizer alloc]
                                   initWithTarget:self
                                   action:@selector(handleTap:)];
    [self.view addGestureRecognizer:tap];

    NSNotificationCenter *center = [NSNotificationCenter defaultCenter];
    [center addObserver:self
               selector:@selector(subjectChanged:)
                   name:AVCaptureDeviceSubjectAreaDidChangeNotification
                 object:nil];
}
```

Install tap-to-focus gesture

Subscribe to subject-area change notification

The code to unsubscribe from the subject-area change notifications goes into the class `dealloc` method:

```
- (void)dealloc {
   [[NSNotificationCenter defaultCenter] removeObserver:self];
}
```

The method that's called on the notification sets the autofocus mode back to continuous, if supported:

```
- (void)subjectChanged:(NSNotification *)notification {
   if (_camera.focusMode == AVCaptureFocusModeLocked) {
      if ([_camera lockForConfiguration:nil]) {
         if ([_camera isFocusPointOfInterestSupported]) {
            _camera.focusPointOfInterest = CGPointMake(0.5, 0.5);
         }

         if ([_camera isFocusModeSupported:
                        AVCaptureFocusModeContinuousAutoFocus]) {
            [_camera setFocusMode:
                       AVCaptureFocusModeContinuousAutoFocus];
         }

         NSLog(@"Focus Mode: Continuous");
      }
   }
}
```

Only switch back to continuous mode if AF is currently locked

Restore focus point of interest to center ❶

Switch back to continuous AF

Note the `focusPointOfInterest` property on the camera device, which gets set to a point `(0.5, 0.5)` ❶. The reason for this is that the focus point needs to be specified as a percentage rather than in points. The default setting is the center of the video image: 50% of the width and 50% of the height.

You can use the preview layer's -captureDevicePointOfInterestForPoint: method to convert the tap coordinates from the preview layer's coordinate system to the capture device's point of interest:

```
- (void)handleTap:(UITapGestureRecognizer *)gesture {
   if (gesture.state == UIGestureRecognizerStateRecognized) {
      if (![_camera isFocusPointOfInterestSupported] ||
          ![_camera isFocusModeSupported:
                      AVCaptureFocusModeAutoFocus]) {
         NSLog(@"Focus Point Not Supported by current camera");
         return;
      }

      CGPoint locationInPreview =
         [gesture locationInView:_videoPreview];
      CGPoint locationInCapture =
         [_videoPreview.previewLayer
            captureDevicePointOfInterestForPoint:locationInPreview];

      if ([_camera lockForConfiguration:nil]) {
         [_camera setFocusPointOfInterest:locationInCapture];
         [_camera setFocusMode:AVCaptureFocusModeAutoFocus];

         NSLog(@"Focus Mode: Locked to Focus Point");

         [_camera unlockForConfiguration];
      }
   }
}
```

Require both focus point and autofocus.

Convert tap location from layer coordinates to capture device coordinates.

Sets new focus point. This change doesn't yet trigger focusing.

This focuses once and then changes to locked mode.

You don't need to remove the tap gesture recognizer when switching the current camera. Instead, the tap-handler method checks whether tap-to-focus is possible by looking for the availability of both the focus point and the focus-once-then-lock mode AVCaptureFocusModeAutoFocus.

With this code in place, the camera app launches in continuous autofocus mode. If the user taps on the screen, the default focus point in the center of the screen is moved to the tap location. The device will focus on this point and then lock focus. If the subject area changes—causing the subject-area change notification to be sent—then autofocus is switched back to continuous mode.

NOTE The built-in iOS camera app makes a distinction between a normal tap and a long press. Try to emulate this behavior as an advanced exercise.

2.3 Summary

Your camera app now has all the features promised at the start of this chapter. There are many more configuration properties available on AVCaptureDevice that you could use to further enhance your photo app. You could try adding support for the available flash modes, depending on which ones the current camera supports. An advanced exercise would be to capture video instead of still images. For this you'd need to use

AVCaptureMovieFileOutput to send video output to a file, and you'd need to add an audio input so that your videos have sound as well.

There are several key takeaways for this chapter:

- Start a capture session with -startRunning. A corresponding -stopRunning doesn't hurt if the view controller goes away.
- Enclose configuration changes for a running capture session between -beginConfiguration and -commitConfiguration.
- Enclose setting changes for capture devices in -lockForConfiguration: and -unlockForConfiguration.
- Always inquire from the device whether a setting is supported before setting it.
- Camera focus points are specified as percentages and they relate to the capture device's coordinate system. Use the provided methods (such as -captureDevicePointOfInterestForPoint:) to convert from view coordinates to device coordinates.

You've now learned how to fit together the pieces of AV Foundation necessary for capturing media. This gives you a solid basis for adding barcode recognition in chapter 3.

3 Scanning barcodes

This chapter covers

- How to scan barcodes with AV Foundation's metadata detector
- Optimizing scanning performance and user experience
- UI considerations for different kinds of barcode-scanning scenarios
- Navigating around common barcode-scanning pitfalls

The previous chapter introduced you to capturing media with AV Foundation. You learned about the components of AV Foundation that allow you to take a video stream from the device's cameras and display it in a preview layer and capture media to files.

In this chapter you'll learn how to add the AV Foundation metadata detector to this video stream, and have it report back about barcodes it has detected.

Figure 3.1 One face and two barcodes (2D on left and 1D on right) detected and marked

3.1 Metadata detection in AV Foundation

In chapter 2 you built a camera app and encountered one kind of AV capture output, `AVCaptureStillImageOutput`. Other outputs allow you to write to audio or video files, and they're set up the same way as the still image output.

For scanning barcodes, you'll use the `AVCaptureMetadataOutput` component. As you can infer from the name, this is also part of AV media capture, it's an output, and it has something to do with metadata. This isn't data that describes actual pixels or audio samples. Rather it's metadata *about* the picture, describing things that you can see in the video image.

iOS 6 was the first iOS version supporting such metadata, and the first kind of metadata to be delivered by AV Foundation was information about human faces found on video frames. iOS 7 added the ability to read barcodes via the same mechanism. You can configure one metadata output to simultaneously detect barcodes and faces, although I have yet to see a sensible use case for that, apart from producing illustrations for this book (see figure 3.1).

Next you'll add a barcode detector to the camera app from the previous chapter.

3.2 Building a QR Code scanner

Your project for this chapter is to build a scanner app for deciphering 2D barcodes. If the decoded code contains a web address, the app will switch to Mobile Safari to show

Figure 3.2 The finished QR Scanner app

the web page. This will teach you how to set up and configure a metadata output to plug into the media capture stack from the previous chapter.

Your QR Scanner app (see figure 3.2) will have the following features:

- Functions from the camera app: switch cameras, toggle the torch, live preview, tap-to-focus
- Detect and decode PDF417, Aztec, and QR Codes
- Visually mark boundaries of detected codes
- Limit the active scanning area with a viewfinder
- Find URLs in the decoded barcode data and open them with Mobile Safari
- Optimize the video stream for better detection performance

Figure 3.3 should remind you of figure 2.3, with a couple of differences: In the lower-left corner of this figure, `AVCaptureStillImageOutput` has been replaced with `AVCaptureMetadataOutput`. Additionally, you specify a `metadataObjectsDelegate` to receive callbacks whenever metadata objects (such as barcodes) are detected.

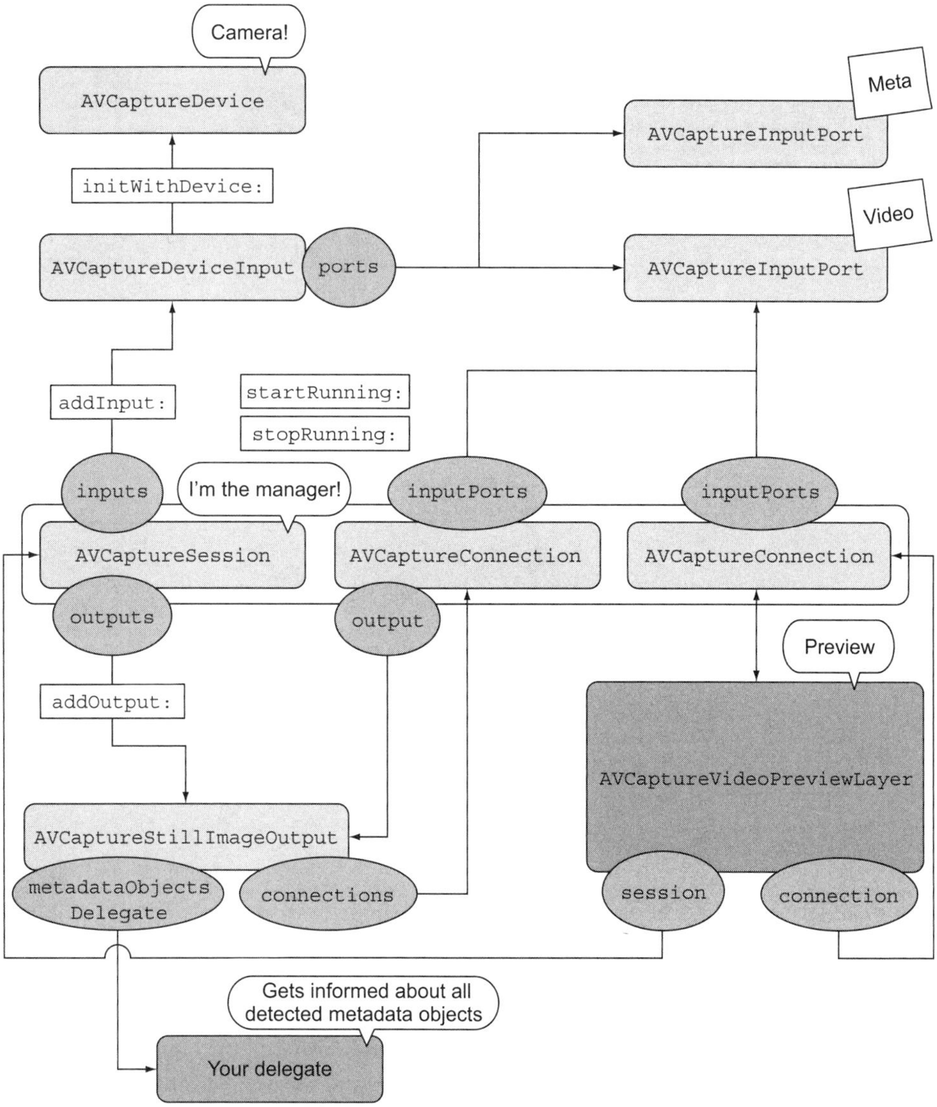

Figure 3.3 AV Foundation components involved in barcode scanning

3.2.1 Reusing camera code

Almost all the code you wrote in chapter 2 for the camera app can be reused as a starting point for this project. Start a new project—again a single-view application—and copy the following files to it:

- DTAVFoundationFunctions.h and .m
- DTCameraPreviewController.h and .m
- DTVideoPreviewView.h and .m

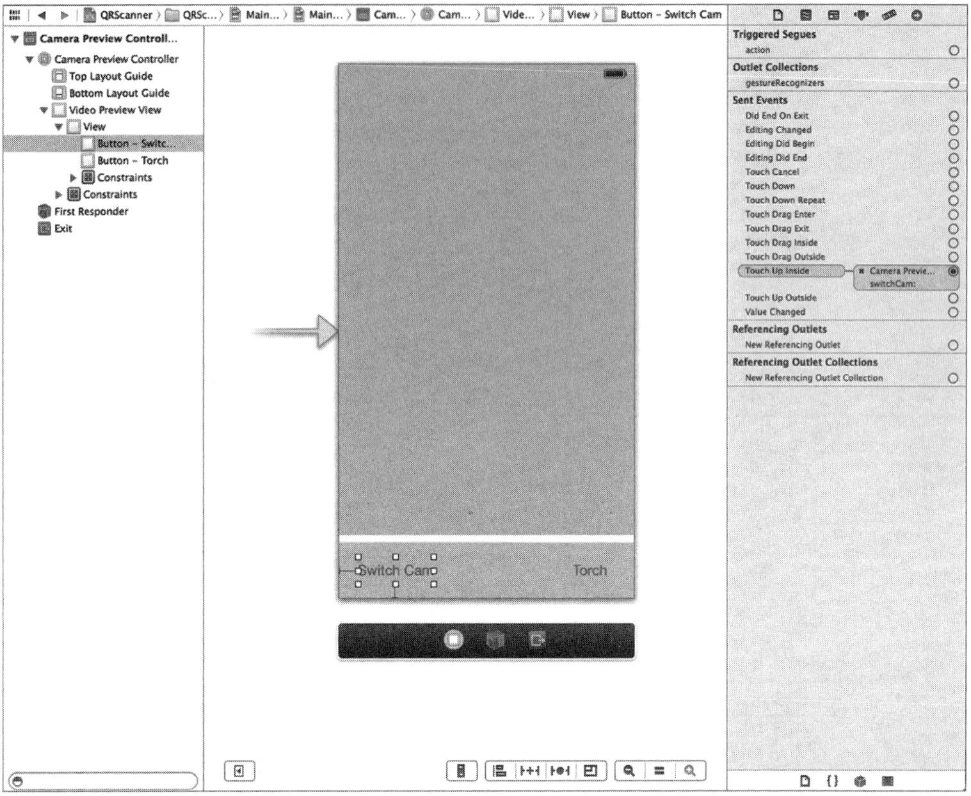

Figure 3.4 QR Scanner storyboard setup

You'll use `DTCameraPreviewController` as the root view controller of your app. You can delete the `ViewController` generated by the template because you won't be using it. To set up AV Foundation, add the AVFoundation.h import to the PCH file, and add AVFoundation.framework to the Link Binary with Libraries build phase.

In the storyboard, change the root view controller's class name to `DTCameraPreviewController` and the root view's class name to `DTVideoPreviewView`. The app will be a full-screen video preview. Add buttons for toggling the torch and switching the camera, as in the previous chapter, and make the appropriate connections to the view controller header's outlets and actions (see figure 3.4). A couple of constraints will keep the buttons in place if the device is rotated.

After these setup steps, the app should build and run showing a full-screen preview of the camera video. You should be able to switch cameras and toggle the torch if you hooked up the buttons correctly. Tap-to-focus should work as before: tap to focus on a point on the preview, and move the device to unlock the focus and switch back to continuous autofocus.

3.2.2 Creating and configuring the metadata output

The next thing you need to do is add a setup method for the metadata output to DTCameraPreviewController.m. This setup method will create a barcode scanner and configure it to look for specific types of barcodes. This method will ensure that all the barcode types you're looking for are also reported by `availableMetadataObjectTypes` as being supported:

```
- (void)_setupMetadataOutput {
   _metaDataOutput = [[AVCaptureMetadataOutput alloc] init];
   _metaDataQueue = dispatch_get_main_queue();
   [_metaDataOutput setMetadataObjectsDelegate:self
                                          queue:_metaDataQueue];

   if (![_captureSession canAddOutput:_metaDataOutput]) {
      NSLog(@"Unable to add metadata output to capture session");
      return;
   }

   [_captureSession addOutput:_metaDataOutput];

   NSArray *barcodes2D = @[AVMetadataObjectTypePDF417Code,
                           AVMetadataObjectTypeQRCode,
                           AVMetadataObjectTypeAztecCode];
   NSArray *availableTypes = [_metaDataOutput
                             availableMetadataObjectTypes];

   if (![availableTypes count]) {
      NSLog(@"Unable to get any available metadata types, "\
            @"did you forget the addOutput: on the capture session?");
      return;
   }

   NSMutableArray *tmpArray = [NSMutableArray array];

   for (NSString *oneCodeType in barcodes2D) {
      if ([availableTypes containsObject:oneCodeType]) {
         [tmpArray addObject:oneCodeType];
      } else {
         NSLog(@"Weird: Code type '%@' is not reported as supported "\
               @"on this device", oneCodeType);
      }
   }

   if ([tmpArray count]) {
      _metaDataOutput.metadataObjectTypes = tmpArray;
   }

   _metaDataOutput.rectOfInterest = CGRectMake(0, 0, 1, 1);
}
```

Create a new metadata output

GCD queue on which delegate method is called

Set self as delegate, using the specified GCD queue. The main queue is used for simplicity.

Connect metadata output if possible

1 Connect metadata output to capture session

The 2D barcode types to detect

Extra sanity check; there should be metadata types available

Extra defensive coding; only adds supported types, logs unsupported

Only types reported as available are scanned for

Default rect of interest is entire video (you'll reduce this later)

You can call this `_setupMetadataOutput` method as the last statement in your `_setupCamera` method, which you've copied as part of DTCameraPreviewController.m from the camera project. This ensures that the entire AV Foundation media capture stack is set up before you add the metadata output to it. You don't need to do anything about the `AVCaptureStillImageOutput` that's also set up there; it doesn't hurt to have both outputs active.

> **NOTE** While I was writing this book, I forgot to call `-addOutput:` on the newly created metadata output ❶, so `-availableTypes` was `nil`. The available types depend on what kind of content is available on the capture device's input ports. It's better to have too much sanity-checking code in your apps than too little.

3.2.3 Wiring up the metadata objects' delegate

You already specified that `self` should be acting as the metadata objects' delegate and also set the GCD queue on which the delegate method will be executed on. The delegate method will be called multiple times per second to deliver recognized metadata objects. To simplify this example, the GCD queue is set to be the main queue.

> **PRO TIP** If you plan to do more extensive work inside the delegate method, you should create and use a private background queue for delegate messages to be delivered on. Don't forget to `dispatch_async` back to the main queue for all interactions with UIKit and code that's synced via the main thread. Proper thread behavior is critical for a well-behaved app.

The `AVCaptureMetadataOutputObjectsDelegate` protocol contains only a single method. As of iOS 7, two kinds of metadata object classes are supported, both subclasses of `AVMetadataObject`:

- `AVMetadataFaceObject` represents a human face.
- `AVMetadataMachineReadableCodeObject` represents a "machine-readable code": a barcode.

For scanning barcodes, you'll deal with only the latter subclass.

Both subclasses derive common properties from `AVMetadataObject`, such as `bounds`, which describes a perpendicular box around the metadata object. For the most part, you'll want to get at the properties that are added in the `AVMetadataMachine-ReadableCodeObject` implementation, which necessitates a typecast.

The following snippet demonstrates iterating over the metadata objects and logging-encountered barcode objects. Here you can see object polymorphism in action—all metadata objects derive from `AVMetadataObject`, but individual instances can be either of the concrete subclasses of that:

```
- (void)captureOutput:(AVCaptureOutput *)captureOutput
   didOutputMetadataObjects:(NSArray *)metadataObjects
      fromConnection:(AVCaptureConnection *)connection {
   for (AVMetadataObject *obj in metadataObjects) {     <-- Iterate over all detected metadata objects
```

```
    if ([obj isKindOfClass:                                  ← Check if it's a barcode object
          [AVMetadataMachineReadableCodeObject class]]) {
       AVMetadataMachineReadableCodeObject *barcode =
             (AVMetadataMachineReadableCodeObject *)obj;     ← Typecast to gain access to specialized properties of barcode objects

       NSLog(@"Seeing type '%@' with contents '%@'",
             barcode.type,                                   ← The type string of the barcode, such as org.iso.QRCode
             barcode.stringValue);                           ← The string value of the barcode, such as http://www.cocoanetics.com

    } else if ([obj isKindOfClass:
                [AVMetadataFaceObject class]]) {
       NSLog(@"Face detection marking not implemented");     ← Ignore face metadata objects
    }
  }
}
```

Detecting faces and barcodes simultaneously

To detect faces and barcodes simultaneously, you add `AVMetadataObjectTypeFace` to the `metadataObjectTypes` array.

iOS delivers both kinds of metadata objects on *separate calls* to the delegate method. This means the calling class has to determine which of these calls it's dealing with each time: faces or barcodes. Otherwise it would wrongfully assume that no longer having a face object in the passed array meant that the face had disappeared. If you were marking the metadata objects on screen, you'd see those shapes flicker as the markings switched repeatedly between faces and barcodes.

iOS is able to detect up to four QR or Aztec codes in parallel. PDF417 is considered to be a stacked linear code and is grouped with the other 1D codes in the detection engine. Even if there are multiple 1D barcodes visible to the scanner, you only get one delivered to the delegate method.

You can configure the metadata output to detect 1D and 2D barcodes at the same time, but the preceding limits are unaffected by this. In this case, you get 0 or 1 1D barcodes, plus 0–4 2D barcodes in the passed array.

In practical use, you won't be interested in getting the entire list of all detected barcodes multiple times per second. Rather, you'll want to be able to set a scan delegate and have this be notified when a new barcode appears in view for the first time.

3.2.4 Creating a barcode scan delegate

To ensure that the scanner view controller is reusable in subsequent chapters, as well as in your own apps, you need to avoid putting any app-specific logic into it. Rather, you want to create a delegate protocol that defines the methods that will notify the object you designate as the delegate. This protocol definition goes above the `@implementation` in DTCameraPreviewController.h:

```
@class DTCameraPreviewController;

@protocol DTCameraPreviewControllerDelegate <NSObject>
@optional
- (void)previewController:(DTCameraPreviewController *)
                              previewController
               didScanCode:(NSString *)code
                    ofType:(NSString *)type;

@end
```

Define class name so it can be used in the protocol (`@class DTCameraPreviewController;`)

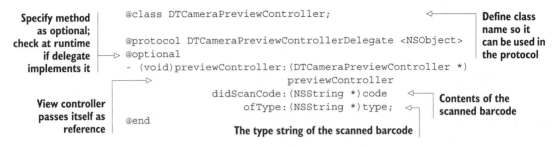

Specify method as optional; check at runtime if delegate implements it (`@optional`)

View controller passes itself as reference (`previewController`)

Contents of the scanned barcode (`didScanCode:(NSString *)code`)

The type string of the scanned barcode (`ofType:(NSString *)type;`)

A delegate property goes with the protocol definition; it can be any `NSObject` as long as it's tagged as implementing the protocol mentioned in the angle brackets:

```
@property (nonatomic, weak) IBOutlet
                     id <DTCameraPreviewControllerDelegate> delegate;
```

iOS doesn't keep track of individual barcodes, like it does for faces. Instead, each time the metadata objects' delegate method is called, each visible barcode is represented by a new instance of `AVMetadataMachineReadableCodeObject`. To keep track of individual barcodes, you'll have to create identifiers for them. Otherwise, you might end up calling your delegate every time a particular barcode is encountered, whereas you really only want to know about the very first time (see figure 3.5).

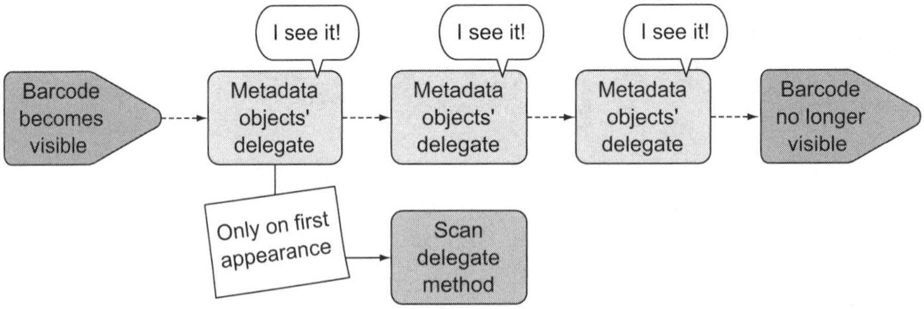

Figure 3.5 The scan delegate should be called only once.

You can use the following items to create an identifier:

- *The* `type` *property*—The type string of the barcode
- *The* `stringValue` *property*—The decoded contents of the barcode in string form
- *A sequential number*—To keep track of multiple barcodes with the same type and contents

The following snippet shows a variant of the metadata objects' delegate method that's able to keep track of multiple barcodes and report when they appear and disappear. `_visibleCodes` is a new private instance variable that preserves the reported barcodes from one call of the delegate method to the next:

```
- (void)captureOutput:(AVCaptureOutput *)captureOutput
   didOutputMetadataObjects:(NSArray *)metadataObjects
       fromConnection:(AVCaptureConnection *)connection {
   NSMutableSet *reportedCodes = [NSMutableSet set];
   NSMutableDictionary *repCount = [NSMutableDictionary dictionary];

   for (AVMetadataMachineReadableCodeObject *obj in metadataObjects) {
      if ([obj isKindOfClass:
           [AVMetadataMachineReadableCodeObject class]]) {
         NSString *code = [NSString stringWithFormat:@"%@:%@",
                           obj.type, obj.stringValue];

         NSUInteger occurencesOfCode = [repCount[code]
                                        unsignedIntegerValue] + 1;
         repCount[code] = @(occurencesOfCode);
         NSString *numberedCode = [code stringByAppendingFormat:@"-%lu",
                                   (unsigned long)occurencesOfCode];

         if (![_visibleCodes containsObject:numberedCode]) {
            NSLog(@"code appeared: %@", numberedCode);

            if ([_delegate respondsToSelector:
                 @selector(previewController:didScanCode:ofType:)]) {
               [_delegate previewController:self
                                didScanCode:obj.stringValue
                                     ofType:obj.type];
            }
         }

         [reportedCodes addObject:numberedCode];
      }
   }

   for (NSString *oneCode in _visibleCodes) {
      if (![reportedCodes containsObject:oneCode]) {
         NSLog(@"code disappeared: %@", oneCode);
      }
   }

   _visibleCodes = reportedCodes;
}
```

Creates a mutable set to take on codes that this pass of the method is reporting

Dictionary to count occurrences of a type + stringValue

Get the number of times this code was reported before in this loop

If it wasn't previously visible, has now appeared

Inform scan delegate about appearance of this code

Check which previously seen barcodes have disappeared

> **Barcode identifier overkill?**
>
> Assigning identities for all barcodes—even if you only ever plan to support scanning 1D barcodes—might feel like overkill. But Apple has been known to enhance existing APIs, and you shouldn't assume current limits to be set in stone.
>
> In the future, Apple might enhance its barcode detector to scan multiple 1D barcodes, or new barcode types might be printed next to GTINs (such as EAN-2 or EAN-5). Then you'll be glad that your code is smart enough to deal with multiple 1D barcodes being reported to you.

Figure 3.6 Bounds versus corners

3.2.5 *Marking detected barcodes on preview*

Enabling your scanner to detect and mark multiple barcodes on the video preview is a nice trick. As you tilt the device and the preview video changes, the detected barcodes should be marked with a shape that hugs the barcode outline.

All metadata objects report a bounds rectangle, which is perpendicular and has edges parallel to the preview view. Metadata objects for 2D barcodes also report the detected corners of the barcode (see figure 3.6). The detector for 1D barcodes works with multiple scan lines and is therefore only able to report the corners of the successful scan line.

It would have been nice if Apple provided the corners for 1D barcodes as well as for 2D barcodes. But since they don't, you can only show off the marker tracking with the currently supported 2D barcode types: PDF417, QR, Data Matrix, and Aztec.

Coordinates in metadata objects always use the video coordinate system, which has values between 0 and 1 (a percent value). Also, depending on the device, the origin might differ. To convert from video to view coordinates, you can employ the `rectForMetadataOutputRectOfInterest:` method found on the preview layer. This creates a copy of the barcode metadata object, but with bounds and corners in the coordinate system of the preview layer, which is ideally suited for creating shapes to display on top of the preview.

The following helper function gives you a Quartz `CGPath` that hugs the corners of the barcode. Put this into DTAVFoundationFunctions.m. Note that because `CGPath` is a Core Foundation object, this method will return a +1 reference that you'll have to release after use:

```
CGPathRef DTAVMetadataMachineReadableCodeObjectCreatePathForCorners(
                          AVCaptureVideoPreviewLayer *previewLayer,
              AVMetadataMachineReadableCodeObject *barcodeObject) {
   AVMetadataMachineReadableCodeObject *transformedObject =
   (AVMetadataMachineReadableCodeObject *)
   [previewLayer transformedMetadataObjectForMetadataObject:
    barcodeObject];                                            <-- Create copy of metadata object with preview layer coordinates

   CGMutablePathRef path = CGPathCreateMutable();  <-- Mutable CGPath to add corner points to

   CGPoint point;
   CGPointMakeWithDictionaryRepresentation((__bridge CFDictionaryRef)
                                    transformedObject.corners[0],
                                    &point);   <-- Property contains dictionary representation of point
   CGPathMoveToPoint(path, NULL, point.x, point.y);   <-- Add first point

   CGPointMakeWithDictionaryRepresentation((__bridge CFDictionaryRef)
                                    transformedObject.corners[1],
                                    &point);
   CGPathAddLineToPoint(path, NULL, point.x, point.y);  <-- Add second point

   CGPointMakeWithDictionaryRepresentation((__bridge CFDictionaryRef)
                                    transformedObject.corners[2],
                                    &point);
   CGPathAddLineToPoint(path, NULL, point.x, point.y);  <-- Add third point

   CGPointMakeWithDictionaryRepresentation((__bridge CFDictionaryRef)
                                    transformedObject.corners[3],
                                    &point);
   CGPathAddLineToPoint(path, NULL, point.x, point.y);  <-- Add fourth point

   CGPathCloseSubpath(path);            <-- Close path

   return path;         <-- Returns a +1 reference
}
```

To show these paths, you'll use one `CAShapeLayer` per barcode. To keep track of these shapes, you can add a mutable dictionary instance variable, `_visibleShapes`, to the list of private instance variables.

When a new barcode appears, you check this visible shapes lookup dictionary to see if you already have a shape layer for it. If you do, you just update the path shown by this layer. If not, you'll have to create one and configure the drawing parameters. When a barcode is no longer visible, you'll also need to remove the appropriate marking shape:

```
- (void)captureOutput:(AVCaptureOutput *)captureOutput
   didOutputMetadataObjects:(NSArray *)metadataObjects
        fromConnection:(AVCaptureConnection *)connection {
   NSMutableSet *reportedCodes = [NSMutableSet set];
   NSMutableDictionary *repCount = [NSMutableDictionary dictionary];
```

```
for (AVMetadataMachineReadableCodeObject *obj in metadataObjects) {
   if ([obj isKindOfClass:
        [AVMetadataMachineReadableCodeObject class]]
       && obj.stringValue) {                          <-- Barcode might contain empty stringValue

     NSString *code = [NSString stringWithFormat:@"%@:%@",
                       obj.type, obj.stringValue];

     NSUInteger occurencesOfCode = [repCount[code]
                                   unsignedIntegerValue] + 1;
     repCount[code] = @(occurencesOfCode);
     NSString *numberedCode = [code stringByAppendingFormat:@"-%lu",
                              (unsigned long)occurencesOfCode];

     if (![_visibleCodes containsObject:numberedCode]) {
        NSLog(@"code appeared: %@", numberedCode);

        if ([_delegate respondsToSelector:
             @selector(previewController:didScanCode:ofType:)]) {
           [_delegate previewController:self
                            didScanCode:obj.stringValue
                                 ofType:obj.type];
        }
     }

     [reportedCodes addObject:numberedCode];

     CGPathRef path =  2((ch02_26b1))                 <-- Get corner CGPath from helper function
     DTAVMetadataMachineReadableCodeObjectCreatePathForCorners(
                             _videoPreview.previewLayer, obj);

     CAShapeLayer *shapeLayer = _visibleShapes[numberedCode];   <-- Get previous shape layer for this code

     if (!shapeLayer) {                               <-- If no shapes are found, this is new shape
        shapeLayer = [CAShapeLayer layer];            <-- Create new shape layer and configure drawing parameters
        shapeLayer.strokeColor = [UIColor greenColor].CGColor;
        shapeLayer.fillColor = [UIColor colorWithRed:0
                                               green:1
                                                blue:0
                                               alpha:0.25].CGColor;
        shapeLayer.lineWidth = 2;

        [_videoPreview.layer addSublayer:shapeLayer];  <-- Add shape layer as sublayer of video preview
        _visibleShapes[numberedCode] = shapeLayer;     <-- Add shape layer to lookup dictionary
     }

     shapeLayer.frame = _videoPreview.bounds;          <-- Update frame to match video preview bounds
     shapeLayer.path = path;                           <-- Set barcode corner shape on the shape layer

     CGPathRelease(path);                              <-- Release +1 reference to CGPath
   } else if ([obj isKindOfClass:
              [AVMetadataFaceObject class]]) {
```

```
            NSLog(@"Face detection marking not implemented");
        }
    }

    for (NSString *oneCode in _visibleCodes) {
        if (![reportedCodes containsObject:oneCode]) {
            NSLog(@"code disappeared: %@", oneCode);

            CAShapeLayer *shape = _visibleShapes[oneCode];
            [shape removeFromSuperlayer];
            [_visibleShapes removeObjectForKey:oneCode];
        }
    }

    _visibleCodes = reportedCodes;
}
```

Remove shape layer for disappeared barcodes

This completes your code for the metadata object delegate.

Apple exposes the decoded barcode data as a `stringValue`; there's no access to the raw decoded data. So it might happen that you get a detected barcode, but the string value is `nil`. This might occur if somebody encoded arbitrary bytes into a QR Code, and on decoding it, iOS is unable to convert it into an `NSString`. Such metadata objects are quite useless as there's no way to retrieve the original data. You can safely ignore these as you loop through the detected barcodes.

3.2.6 *Building an optimal scanning UI*

At this point in the creation of your QR Scanner app, you have the scanning basics working. Now it's time to optimize the user interface. You should ask yourself four questions:

- Which types of barcodes do I want to detect?
- What situations will my users be in when they scan a barcode?
- Will there be many barcodes next to each other?
- What cues will inform the user that they should scan a barcode?

Asking these questions is necessary, because different answers will result in different optimal user interfaces for scanning.

QR Codes are most often encountered on large posters. Standard QR Codes are so ugly (in the eyes of creatives) that you'll rarely find more than one on an advertisement. A typical scanning situation would be a user scanning a code from across the subway tracks while waiting for a train.

In contrast, users will typically scan 1D barcodes off a product that's right in front of them. There might be multiple 1D codes in close proximity, like a GTIN, a product model code, and a serial number if it's a box for a consumer electronics device.

Your users should be getting UI cues to inform them that they're expected to point the active camera at a code for scanning.

For scenarios involving many codes next to each other, you'll want to reduce the active scanning area and show a box to inform the user that only inside this box will a code be recognized. There are also some capture device settings that are beneficial only for particular scenarios. We'll cover these in the next section.

Let's assume that your QR Scanner app is meant for scanning codes close by, like from the pages of this book, and you expect multiple codes in close proximity. This means that you don't want the entire preview to be active for scanning, but rather a much smaller part of it so that you can precisely target one code among several.

The UI in figure 3.7 consists of a custom `UIView` that draws four corners, and a `UILabel` that you place on top of the overlay and anchor in place with autolayout constraints.

To build this UI, create a new `UIView` subclass to represent the *interest box*—the marked area where barcodes will be scanned in. Name it `DTVideoPreviewInterestBox`. This code overwrites the `-drawRect:` method to draw the four corner marks:

Figure 3.7 Reduced scan area for better targeting

```
#define EDGE_LENGTH 10.0

@implementation DTVideoPreviewInterestBox

- (void)drawRect:(CGRect)rect {
   CGContextRef ctx = UIGraphicsGetCurrentContext();

   [[UIColor redColor] setStroke];

   CGFloat lineWidth=3;
   CGRect box = CGRectInset(self.bounds, lineWidth/2.0, lineWidth/2.0);

   CGContextSetLineWidth(ctx, lineWidth);

   CGFloat minX = CGRectGetMinX(box);
   CGFloat minY = CGRectGetMinY(box);

   CGFloat maxX = CGRectGetMaxX(box);
   CGFloat maxY = CGRectGetMaxY(box);

   CGContextMoveToPoint(ctx, minX, minY + EDGE_LENGTH);
   CGContextAddLineToPoint(ctx, minX, minY);
   CGContextAddLineToPoint(ctx, minX +  EDGE_LENGTH, minY);
```

Length of lines in corners

Drawing method for contents of view draws four marks for corners of the view

Bottom-left corner

```
    CGContextMoveToPoint(ctx, minX, maxY - EDGE_LENGTH);
    CGContextAddLineToPoint(ctx, minX, maxY);
    CGContextAddLineToPoint(ctx, minX + EDGE_LENGTH, maxY);

    CGContextMoveToPoint(ctx, maxX - EDGE_LENGTH, minY);
    CGContextAddLineToPoint(ctx, maxX, minY);
    CGContextAddLineToPoint(ctx, maxX, minY + EDGE_LENGTH);

    CGContextMoveToPoint(ctx, maxX - EDGE_LENGTH, maxY);
    CGContextAddLineToPoint(ctx, maxX, maxY);
    CGContextAddLineToPoint(ctx, maxX, maxY - EDGE_LENGTH);

    CGContextStrokePath(ctx);
}

@end
```

Top-left corner

Bottom-right corner

Top-right corner

In Interface Builder, you add a new view of this class on top of your preview view, as shown in figure 3.8. Add a label on top of that, and anchor everything in place with autolayout constraints so that when the device is rotated, all views are still centered. Limit the width and height of the interest box to 200 points. (You'll get the current size and location of this view in the next code snippet to configure the active scan area.)

The ideal place to retrieve the interest box view's coordinates in `DTCameraPreviewController` is in the `viewDidLayoutSubviews` method, which is called whenever the view hierarchy has been laid out: after the initial display and after each rotation. A helper method retrieves the current view coordinates of the interest box in relation to the

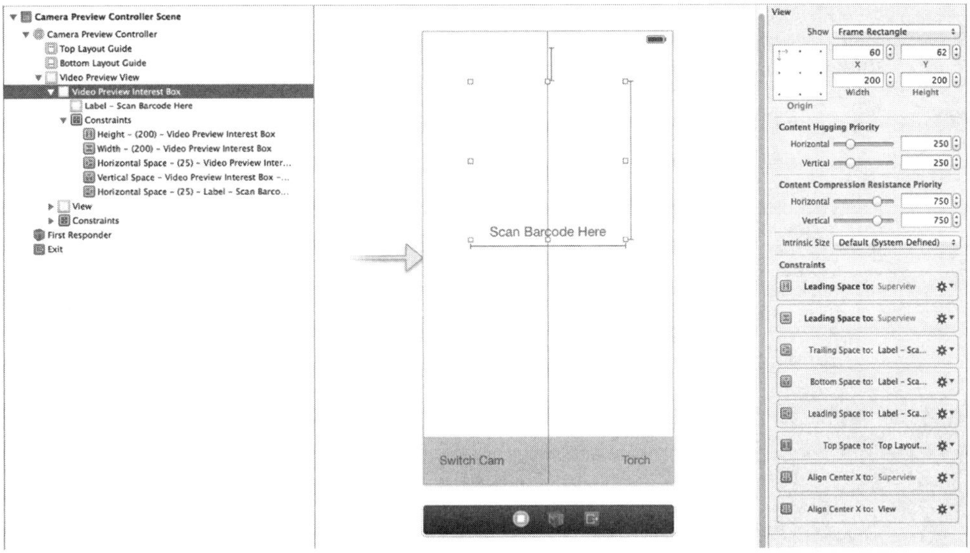

Figure 3.8 Adding a scan finder

preview, converts them to video coordinates, and sets these coordinates as the new `rectOfInterest` on the metadata output:

```
- (void)_updateMetadataRectOfInterest {
   if (!_captureSession.isRunning)  {            // Capture session must be running
      NSLog(@"Capture Session is not running yet, "\
            @"so we wouldn't get a useful rect of interest");
      return;
   }

   CGRect rectOfInterest = [_videoPreview.previewLayer
                            metadataOutputRectOfInterestForRect:
                            _iBox.frame];          // Get frame from interest box and convert to video coordinates
   _metaDataOutput.rectOfInterest = rectOfInterest;   // Set as new rectangle of interest for metadata output
}

- (void)viewDidLayoutSubviews
{
   [super viewDidLayoutSubviews];

   [self _updateMetadataRectOfInterest];
}
```

Scanning 1D barcodes

For detecting 1D barcodes, iOS employs scan lines. If one such scan line intersects with all the bars of a barcode, then it detects the code.

Depending on your device, there will be at least two scan lines in the horizontal and vertical centers of the rectangle of interest. Depending on the CPU power of the device your app is running on, there may be additional scan lines. On the iPhone 4—the oldest iPhone supported by iOS 7—only the center scan lines are used.

Apple's Technical Note TN2325 (https://developer.apple.com/library/ios/technotes/tn2325/) mentions that the additional scanning lines are also disabled if you enable 2D barcode scanning together with 1D barcodes. This is another reason why it might be better to optimize the UI for scanning either 1D or 2D barcodes.

If you don't reduce the rectangle of interest for detection, the user might be confused if a barcode isn't detected near the edges of the preview window. This could occur if a barcode is fully visible in the preview but is too far to the side to be crossed by one of the scan lines. On consumer electronics labels, you'll often find multiple 1D barcodes in close proximity to each other. If this is your usage scenario, you might want to adjust the shape of the rectangle of interest for scanning 1D barcodes to be as wide as the preview but not very tall, and then display a red line along the horizontal center. This informs the user that 1D barcodes are scanned with this "laser," and they're able to precisely target individual barcodes.

In any case, you should test the scanning user experience with an iPhone 4 (if you support iOS 7), because it's generally lacking the additional scan lines.

3.2.7 Tweaking capture device settings

There are several configuration options on iOS device cameras that help with barcode scanning performance and user experience. These are the most useful:

- *Capture session preset*—Determines the video quality and format delivered to the session by the capture device
- *Active video format*—Impacts the number of pixels in each video frame that the system has to work with
- *Video zoom factor*—Sends extra pixels to the detector that the CCD picks up but that are "zoomed out" by default
- *Smooth autofocus*—Prevents the nervous bobbing of the autofocus; focus is smoothly adjusted as you'd want it for recording video
- *Autofocus range restriction*—Restricts the range over which AF is adjusted, for scanning close up

Let's look at some of these in more detail.

The capture session preset determines the active video format flowing from the capture device, via the input, through the session's connection to the metadata output. The higher the quality preset, the more pixels are available for the barcode detector. If you don't set a session preset, the default is `AVCaptureSessionPresetHigh`, which is one level below `AVCaptureSessionPresetPhoto`. Using the photo preset instead of the default preset dramatically increases the number of pixels in the video stream, causing the detector to do much more work. The scanning results of using the photo preset are indistinguishable from using the default setting, but the drain on the battery is much greater due to higher CPU usage.

> **BARCODE GURU TIP** If you have a special use case in which you're displaying the scanner UI for a long continuous time, you should experiment with even lower-quality presets to reduce battery drain. For most scenarios, the default high setting is the sweet spot for barcode scanning.

The capture session preset and the capture device's active video format go hand in hand. If you set a preset, iOS knows which video format works best for the device. If you don't set a preset or format, the default preset of the capture session is used. The session then sets the active format when you add the capture device input. If you set the active format directly, this causes the session preset to change to `AVCaptureSessionPresetInputPriority`.

Fairly recent iOS devices have CCDs that can capture more pixels than are actually used by the media capture pipeline. Instead of passing on the original pixels, the video image is slightly shrunken, and this reduced-size version is sent to the capture device class. The scale factor used can be queried via the `videoZoomFactorUpscaleThreshold` property of the active video format.

For scanning barcodes close to the device, you can set the camera's video zoom factor to a value between 1 and the upscale threshold. This results in a zoomed-in part of the video being used, sort of like using a magnifying glass. But you don't want to overdo it—with video that's too zoomed-in, it becomes difficult to target an individual barcode on a page. If the upscale threshold is greater than 1, you can increase the zoom factor, but no further than 125%. For older devices that don't scale the video, this has no effect because the upscale threshold is 1.

The default mode for autofocus is to quickly change the focus several times until the picture is sharp. If the user is concentrating on targeting a barcode, this wild "bobbing" motion might cause discomfort. Newer iOS devices support *smooth autofocus*, where the focus is adjusted gradually. This was introduced by Apple as being beneficial for recording video, where the focus bobbing would be detrimental when moving from near focus to far focus or vice versa. For barcode scanning, smooth autofocus is a welcome feature because it removes an unnecessary form of visual noise.

Finally, if you know that your users are going to scan only nearby barcodes, you can restrict the autofocus range. This makes finding the focus much quicker, because iOS doesn't have to go through the entire focus range to determine the point where the image is in focus.

The following code snippet contains all the configuration optimizations for scanning nearby barcodes:

```
- (void)_configureCurrentCamera
{
   NSError *error;
   if (![_camera lockForConfiguration:&error]) {
      NSLog(@"Unable to lock current camera for config: %@",
            [error localizedDescription]);
      return;
   }

   _camera.subjectAreaChangeMonitoringEnabled = YES;

   if ([_camera isSmoothAutoFocusSupported]) {
      _camera.smoothAutoFocusEnabled = YES;
   }

   if ([_camera isAutoFocusRangeRestrictionSupported]) {
      _camera.autoFocusRangeRestriction =
      AVCaptureAutoFocusRangeRestrictionNear;
   }

   _camera.videoZoomFactor =
      MIN(_camera.activeFormat.videoZoomFactorUpscaleThreshold,
      1.25);

   if ([_camera isLowLightBoostSupported]) {
      _camera.automaticallyEnablesLowLightBoostWhenAvailable = YES;
   }

   [_camera unlockForConfiguration];
}
```

Always lock camera for configuration when making changes

Bail out in case of error

Get notified if subject area changes, for disabling focus lock

Prevent focus bobbing

Restrict autofocus range for scanning nearby barcodes

Send more pixels to image outputs

Activate low-light boost if necessary

Unlock configuration when done

3.2.8 Opening a scanned web address in Mobile Safari

Your scanning app so far marks 2D barcodes when they appear within the interest box. You've also optimized the scanning experience for nearby 2D barcodes. To wrap up this example, you need to do something with the decoded QR Codes.

In the app, the scanner view controller is the root of the storyboard. Storyboards unfortunately have no facility to connect an outlet defined in the app delegate, but the NIB loader will set the window's `rootViewController` property to the root view controller defined by the storyboard. Then you can grab a reference and set the scan delegate, as shown in the following code ❶.

To get the web address from the detected code's `stringValue`, you can employ an `NSDataDetector`. If you configure it for `NSTextCheckingTypeLink`, it will detect many kinds of URLs, including email addresses:

```
@interface AppDelegate () <DTCameraPreviewControllerDelegate>
@end

@implementation AppDelegate
{
   NSDataDetector *_urlDetector;
}

- (BOOL)application:(UIApplication *)application
        didFinishLaunchingWithOptions:(NSDictionary *)launchOptions {
    DTCameraPreviewController *previewController =
       (DTCameraPreviewController *)self.window.rootViewController;

    previewController.delegate = self;

    _urlDetector = [NSDataDetector dataDetectorWithTypes:
                    (NSTextCheckingTypes)NSTextCheckingTypeLink
                                                  error:NULL];

    return YES;
}
```

Private interface tagged with promise to implement protocol

Instance variable to hold detector for URLs in strings

❶ Scanner view controller is root view controller of window

Set delegate to self

Configure URL detector

Whenever the scanner controller detects a new barcode, you want to hear about it. You need to implement the `previewController:didScanCode:ofType:` method from your scanner delegate protocol:

```
- (void)previewController:(DTCameraPreviewController *)previewController
              didScanCode:(NSString *)code
                   ofType:(NSString *)type {
   NSRange entireString = NSMakeRange(0, [code length]);
   NSArray *matches = [_urlDetector matchesInString:code
                                            options:0
                                              range:entireString];

   for (NSTextCheckingResult *match in matches) {
```

❶ Contents of the scanned barcode

Type of the scanned barcode

❷ Find all URLs in string

```
            if ([[UIApplication sharedApplication] canOpenURL:match.URL]) {
                NSLog(@"Opening URL '%@' in external browser",
                   [match.URL absoluteString]);
                [[UIApplication sharedApplication] openURL:match.URL];

                break;
            }
            else {
                NSLog(@"Device cannot open URL '%@'",
                   [match.URL absoluteString]);
            }
        }
    }

@end
```

Ask iOS if there's an application that can handle this URL

Have system open the URL with the app registered for the URL scheme

Prevent additional URLs from opening

Log URLs that system doesn't know how to handle

In the code parameter ❶, you receive the entire string contents of a scanned barcode. The URL detector ❷ is tasked with finding contained URLs, and if one is found, you call `openURL:` to have iOS open it in Mobile Safari.

Congratulations! You've now built your own QR Scanner app. Any HTTP or HTTPS URLs will be opened by Mobile Safari, because it's the system-provided handler for these URL schemes.

Other QR Code contents

This example demonstrates only the most basic use case for scanning QR Codes: URLs. Any URL with a scheme supported by the iOS device will work. For example, http:// URLs are opened by Mobile Safari.

There are many different kinds of barcode content that can be represented with text-based QR Codes. Many kinds of content have become de facto standards because of their use by Japan's NTT DOCOMO and the open source Zebra Crossing project. All of these types use text tags followed by the field values:

- Calendar event
- Contact information
- Email address
- Geolocation
- Phone number
- Text message (SMS)
- URL bookmark with title
- WiFi network access setup

Documentation is scarce, but you can infer the structure of the tags by generating some codes with the Zebra Crossing QR Code generator (http://zxing.appspot.com/generator/).

3.3 Summary

Building a QR Code scanner taught you how to plug a metadata output into your AV Foundation video pipeline. All this knowledge is applicable to both 2D and 1D barcodes, with slight variations. Depending on your intended usage scenario, there are a few adjustment screws you'll want to turn to make the experience for your users delightful.

You've seen how the metadata objects' delegate works, how to filter the events, and how to mark the corners of 2D barcodes. (Because of the different ways that 1D barcode detection is implemented, you can't get nice corners for 1D barcodes.) You also restricted the rectangle of interest to facilitate easier targeting of one barcode among several. Finally, you optimized the camera settings for better scanning results.

These are the key takeaways of this chapter:

- `AVCaptureMetadataOutput` plugs into your `AVCaptureSession` for detecting faces and 1D and/or 2D barcodes.
- The delegate object implementing the `AVCaptureMetadataOutputObjectsDelegate`'s method receives an array of all detected barcodes multiple times per second.
- You can mark detected 2D barcodes via the reported `corners`. This won't work for 1D barcodes because 1D detection uses scan lines.
- You can specify a `rectOfInterest` to limit the area of the video frame where barcodes are detected.
- You can optimize the UI and camera settings for the scanning usage scenario so that the user will know what to do with the video preview. Some camera settings can enhance the scanning performance and user experience.

In the next chapter, you'll explore creating Passbook passes and reuse the barcode scanning code developed in chapters 2 and 3 to build a pass-verification app.

4 Passbook, Apple's digital wallet

This chapter covers

- Barcodes: the technology that makes Apple's Passbook system possible
- Micro-documents as a convenient digital alternative to paper tickets and plastic cards
- Creating Passbook tickets with Ruby
- A method for validating Passbook tickets without a server

We have all come into contact with small documents that provide some benefit if we present them to the right person at the right time in the right location. Such documents include *movie tickets* that allow you to enter the movie theater, *coupons* that entitle you to receive a promotional discount for certain products, *membership cards* that let you enter the gym, *loyalty cards* for collecting loyalty points at the supermarket chain where you faithfully shop, or *tickets* for planes, trains, ships, or other vehicles providing transportation. Long before the digital revolution, those micro-documents were usually printed on paper with varying measures to prevent somebody from creating illicit copies.

Consider, for example, tickets for a sold-out concert. The concert organizer might go as far as embedding holograms in the paper the tickets are printed on to make sure that there's no way for counterfeiters to produce their own tickets.

Apple, being constantly on the lookout for ways to enrich the lives of their customers, saw this plethora of micro-documents and developed *Passbook* as a digital alternative. The mobile phone has already replaced the wristwatch as a timekeeper. Passbook aims to make your wallet obsolete as well, or at least its function as a repository of paper tickets, membership cards, and other things you carry around besides cash.

> **NOMENCLATURE** The name *Passbook* is used by Apple as the umbrella term for all the pieces of this system. Passbook micro-documents are embodied by files with the extension .pkpass. Those files can represent different kinds of tickets, coupons, cards, and so on. For the sake of simplicity, these are all commonly referred to as *passes*. The iOS APIs for interacting with passes from within your apps are grouped in the `PassKit.framework`. The *Passbook.app* comes preinstalled on all iPhones since iOS 6 and provides access to all the passes users have on their device.

In the past, Apple had a reputation for developing technologies without considering the requirements of existing corporate systems. Passbook, first introduced in 2012 as part of iOS 6, was the first drastic departure from this methodology. Apple published everything companies needed to produce digital passes on their own systems—no Macs required. Because of this openness, most major companies have begun to offer Passbook passes as an option when delivering digital passes by email.

The goal of this chapter is to give you a basic understanding of how passes are created, and then to demonstrate in a sample app how you can validate passes you create without requiring an impressive server setup.

4.1 Barcodes in Passbook

Physical micro-documents—we'll call them "passes" for short—can contain human-readable information that a person can look at to determine the validity of the pass. But this activity becomes impractical at larger scales for several reasons:

- A ticket might look alright but could be counterfeit.
- It takes too long to manually type in a membership number printed on a member card.
- Such manual data transfer is prone to copying mistakes.
- Customers might prefer to not use their loyalty card if it means they're holding up the queue.

The creators of paper passes and plastic cards now often add a barcode to allow for automated scanning. These pieces of paper or plastic essentially now serve as a medium to transport the barcode.

When Apple designed Passbook, they evaluated which kinds of barcodes would be feasible. The core requirement was that scanners needed to be able to scan the barcode from the device's display. This is something that laser-based scanners can't do well because of reflection on iPhone glass displays. As a result, Apple decided to support only 2D symbologies for Passbook, as those are generally scanned with CCD-based scanners.

4.2 Producing digital passes for your users

After reading this chapter, you might get hired by a chain of movie theaters that needs your help in implementing a Passbook-based ticket flow. But for this example we'll scale down the scenario a bit. You are, more than likely, the owner of a state-of-the-art home movie theater (a.k.a. your TV). The size of your sofa puts a natural limit on the number of friends who can come over and attend a VIP movie night, so you do what every venue owner does: you create tickets with assigned seat numbers and the date and time of the movie night.

The point of this exercise is to demonstrate the workflow required to create valid tickets and distribute them. In all of its communication, Apple is promoting Passbook as something for large corporations with extensive server infrastructure to implement. Because of this, you might be harboring some fear that you need to have server-side skills. But this isn't the case. Once you've wrapped your head around the simple beauty of the pkpass format, you'll lose this worry and instead begin to see many other usage scenarios you'll want to explore.

The first two steps of the process are rather tedious, but you only need to do them once for the type of pass you want to create. You need to sign into your Apple developer account and create a digital certificate to sign your passes with. Once you have this setup step out of the way, you can begin to create valid passes. We'll explore pass validation afterward.

4.2.1 Requesting a certificate for signing passes

In the Passbook system, the role of the non-fakable hologram on paper tickets is taken on by a digital signature. A few initial setup steps are required to produce signatures that iOS and the Passbook app will accept as valid. These steps might seem like a lot of work, but you only need to execute them once per type of pass you want to sign.

Sign into the iOS Dev Center (https://developer.apple.com/devcenter/ios/) and go to the Certificates, Identifiers & Profiles section.

The *identifier* represents a certain type of pass that you're going to create. Use a different identifier for coupons than for movie tickets.

In the Identifiers section, shown in figure 4.1, you can create a new identifier for your passes. The description is only visible to you, and you should identify it so that you can tell it apart from the other pass types you might create in the future. For this example, use "VIP Movie Night" for the description. The identifier needs to start with *pass.* followed by reverse domain notation, as you would use for an app identifier.

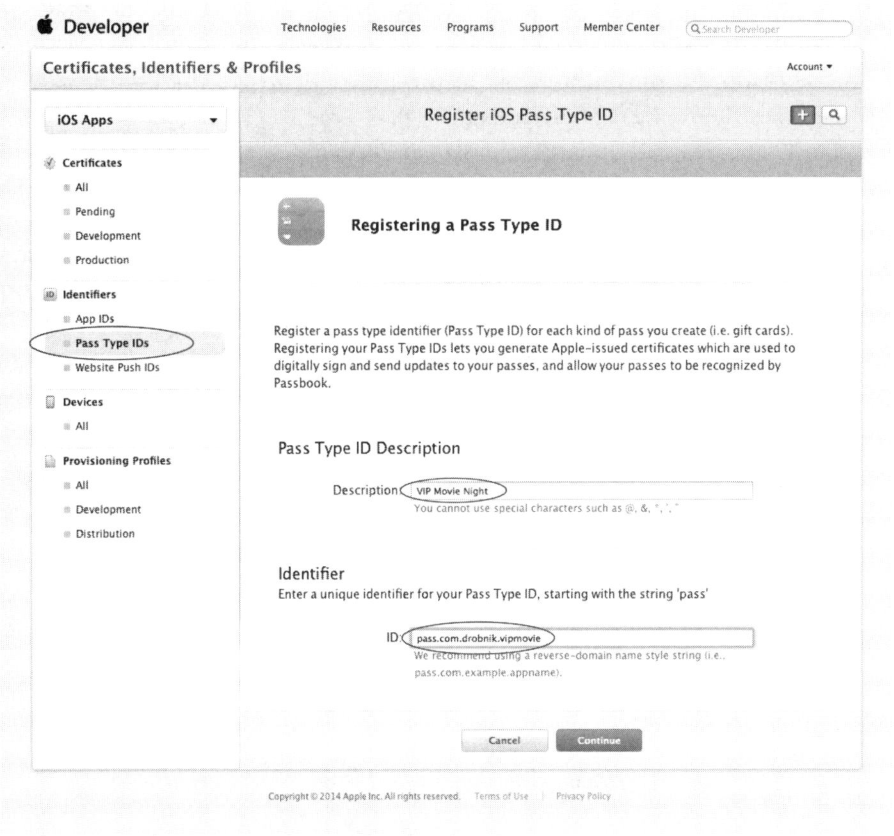

Figure 4.1 Creating a pass type identifier

Enter the ID `pass.com.`*`yourcompany`*`.vipmovie`, substituting your domain or company name for *yourcompany*.

On the confirmation screen that's displayed next, verify that both values are correct. I once made the mistake of entering a duplicate pass prefix, with the effect that the signing failed with weird error messages.

> **Different passes, different type identifiers**
>
> You can have as many pass types as you need. For example, you could issue loyalty cards to your clients and also one-off coupons with a promotional discount. Those would be two different types.
>
> For every different type of pass, you should configure a pass type identifier first and then request a signing certificate for it. When interacting with passes via the PassKit APIs, you can determine which type of pkpass you're looking at by checking its `passTypeIdentifier` property.

Next, you'll create a signing certificate that exactly matches the identifier. Still on the Certificates, Identifiers & Profiles page, enter the Certificates section. Under Production, click on the plus button (+) at the top right to get the certificate Select Type screen (see figure 4.2). There select the Pass Type ID Certificate option, which allows you to "Sign and send updates to passes in Passbook." While you're here, there's also a convenient link for downloading the Worldwide Developer Relations Certificate Authority. Download this before clicking Continue.

On the following screen (see figure 4.3), pick the pass type identifier that you want to configure the certificate for. Here you can see that Apple prefixes all your pass type IDs with your team ID to make them even more unique.

This screen is followed by an explanation of how to create a certificate request via the Keychain Access app. The subsequent screen contains an upload form for the certificate request file you'll create next.

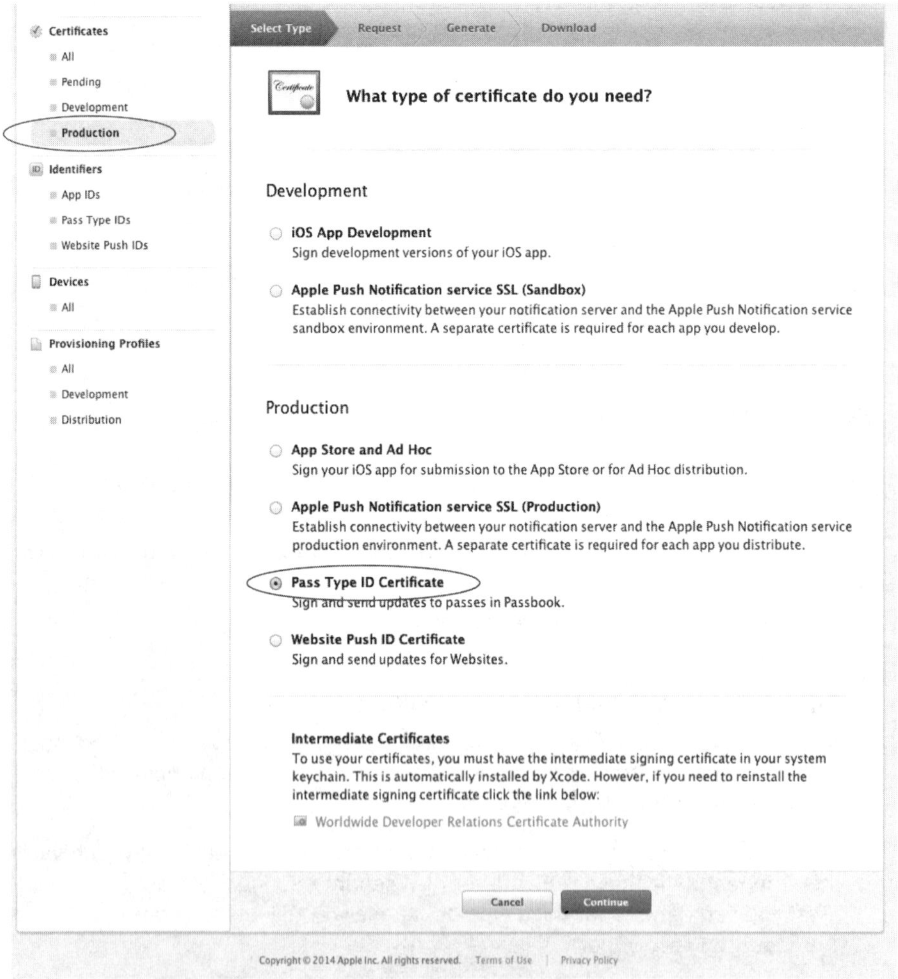

Figure 4.2 Creating a signing certificate

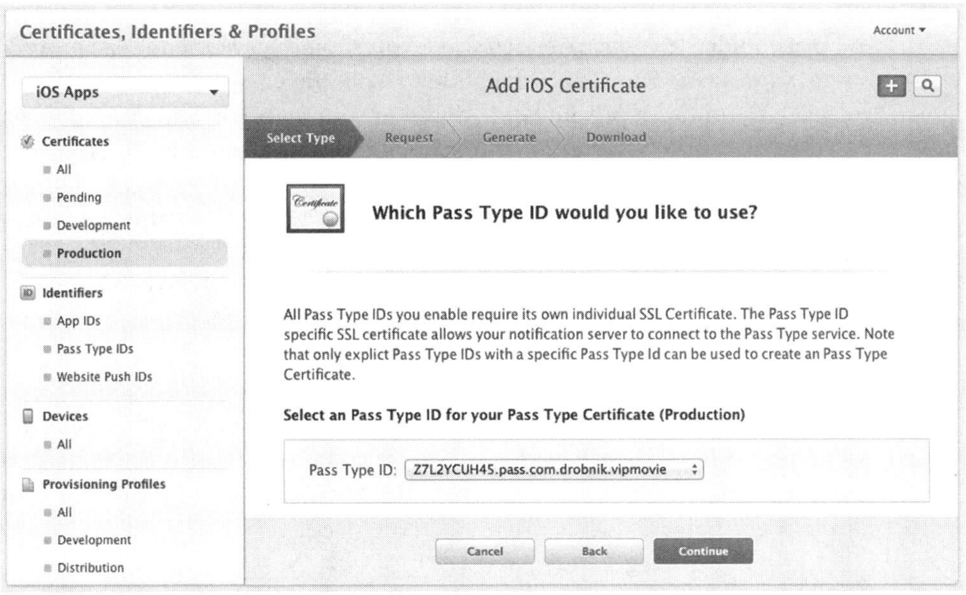

Figure 4.3 Creating a certificate for a pass type identifier

SSL certificates

SSL certificates employ an asymmetric scheme for encryption and digital signing. They consist of a pair of public and private keys. Data encrypted/signed with the private key can only be decrypted/verified with the public key.

You need to keep your private key secret but supply the public key with signed documents to allow verification of your signature.

The easiest method for creating SSL certificates on a Mac is via the Keychain Access app. In that app, select Keychain Access > Certificate Assistant > Request a Certificate From a Certificate Authority (see figure 4.4).

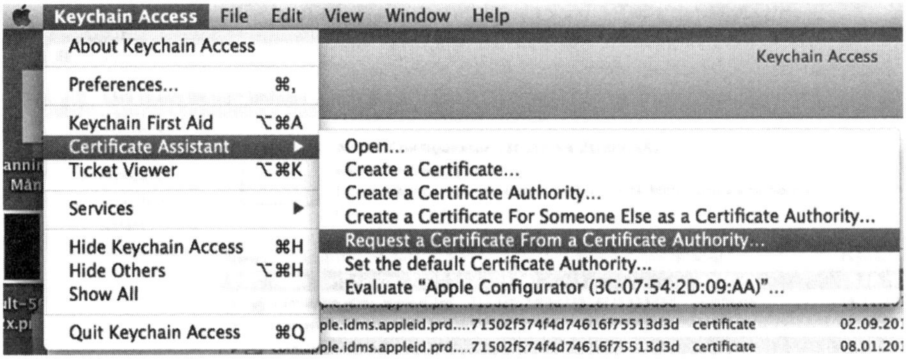

Figure 4.4 Use Certificate Assistant to create a private/public key pair

Fill in your Apple ID email address and your name as the common name. Even though the placeholder text states it's required, you should leave the CA Email Address field empty. Choose the Saved to Disk option to write the CA signing request to a file. When you click Continue, a private key is stored in your keychain and the public part is prepared to be sent to the Apple certificate authority for signing. The filename for this file doesn't matter.

Upload the signing request file via the upload form, and after a few seconds the signed request is ready (see figure 4.5).

Apple signed the public key part of your certificate, and back on your Mac the public key rejoins the private key in your keychain to form a complete key pair. Look in the My Certificates section in Keychain Assistant to see the private key listed below its certificate and the info showing that the certificate is valid and trusted (see figure 4.6).

The finished certificate is signed with Apple's Worldwide Developer Relations Intermediate Certificate, which depends on the Apple Inc. Root Certificate. Both can be downloaded from the Apple CA page (http://www.apple.com/certificateauthority/), although the latter is usually preinstalled on Macs.

4.2.2 Preparing signing certificates

You'll sign your passes with the `openssl` command-line tool. This tool doesn't have the ability to get the certificate from the OS X keychain where you stored it in the previous

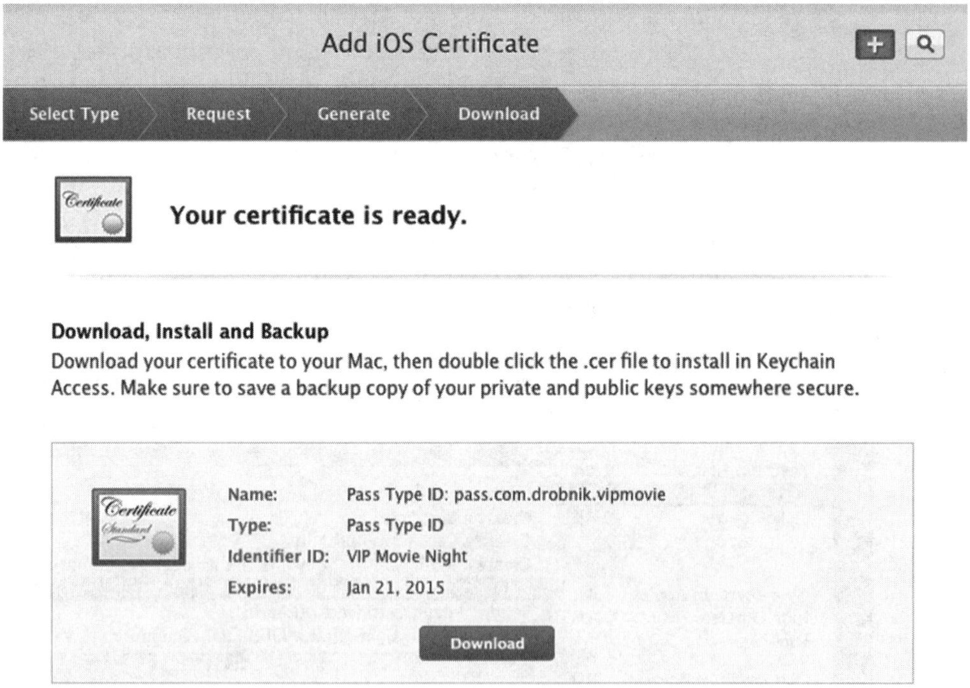
Add iOS Certificate
Select Type
Request
Generate
Download
Your certificate is ready.
Download, Install and Backup
Download your certificate to your Mac, then double click the .cer file to install in Keychain Access. Make sure to save a backup copy of your private and public keys somewhere secure.
Name: Pass Type ID: pass.com.drobnik.vipmovie
Type: Pass Type ID
Identifier ID: VIP Movie Night
Expires: Jan 21, 2015
Download

Figure 4.5 Your certificate is ready.

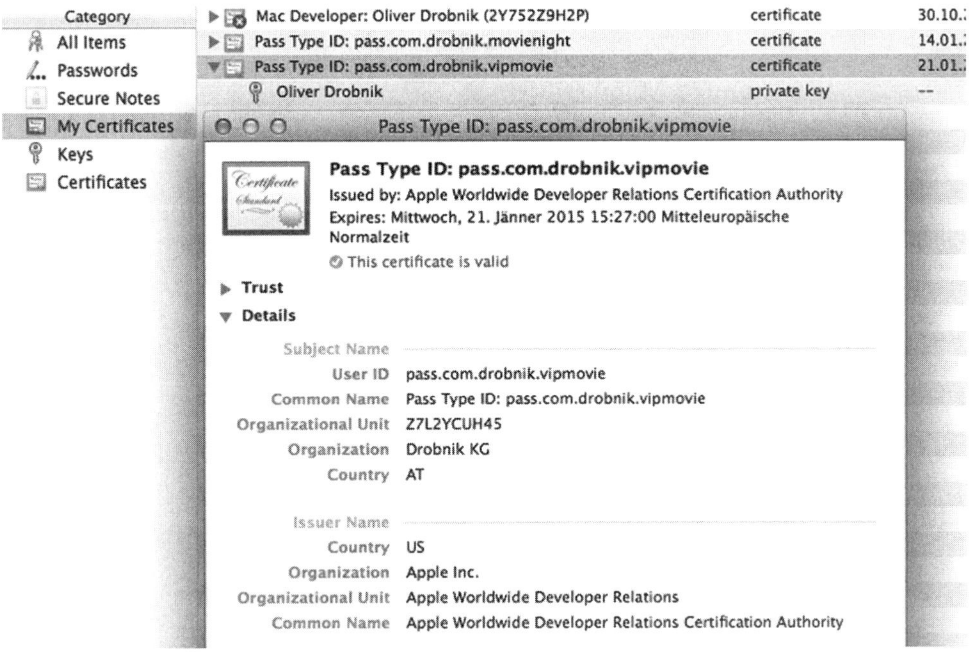

Figure 4.6 Finished certificate in keychain

section, so you first need to export the certificate into a file and convert it into a format that the utility can work with.

> **OpenSSL**
>
> OpenSSL is a collaborative project developing a robust, commercial-grade, full-featured and open source toolkit. It provides a plethora of functions for working with SSL certificates, decoding and encoding data, creating and validating cryptographic hashes, and much more.
>
> You can access the `openssl` utility from the Terminal command line, and it's also available from many modern programming languages, such as Ruby and Python.
>
> Apple doesn't provide OpenSSL to developers. Instead, a comprehensive set of cryptography functions is packaged in the `CommonCrypto.framework` available on both Apple platforms.

OpenSSL needs three pieces for the signing process, which you'll save in a working folder with specific names for simplicity:

- The WWDR (Worldwide Developer Relations) intermediate certificate, downloaded from Apple and saved as AppleWWDRCA.cer
- The pass type certificate, saved as passtypecert.pem
- The signing key matching the pass type certificate, saved as passtypecertkey.pem

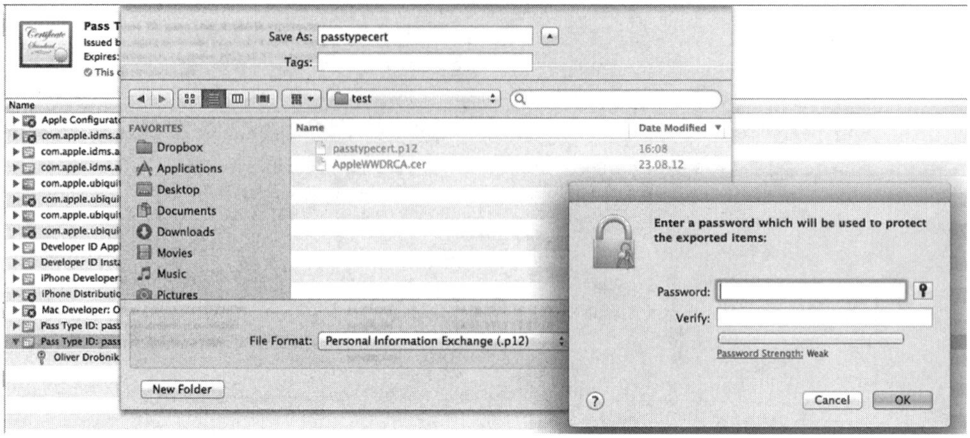

Figure 4.7 Export pass type certificate as p12 file

Keychain Access doesn't allow you to directly export separate private and public keys for the pass type certificate, so you must first export the pair into a p12 file and then use OpenSSL to create the distinct files.

In Keychain Access, select the certificate, right-click on it, and select the export option. Choose the p12 format, and leave the password for the exported file blank (see figure 4.7).

In Terminal, change into the directory where you placed the p12 file and run the following commands:

```
openssl pkcs12 -in passtypecert.p12 -clcerts -nokeys \
   -out passtypecert.pem -passin pass:
openssl pkcs12 -in passtypecert.p12 -nocerts -out passtypecertkey.pem \
   -passin pass: -passout pass:12345
```

Copy public key into PEM file, blank password

Copy private key into pem file, with password

For a public key, security is irrelevant, but for the private key file you might want to specify a strong password, especially if you're going to be creating passes on a web server. The WWDR intermediate certificate in CER format is already in a format that you can use.

4.2.3 Constructing passes

Passes are usually created on a web server. In the case of a movie theater chain, it would be the ticketing system that creates paper tickets or allows customers to print their own paper tickets at home.

Figure 4.8 shows the steps involved in creating a Passbook pass.

For our example VIP Movie Night scenario, you'll create the tickets with a Ruby script. Ruby on Rails is one of the predominant modern frameworks for developing web applications, and Ruby is also the scripting language of choice for most iOS developers. Passbook is not in any way dependent on Apple hardware or software.

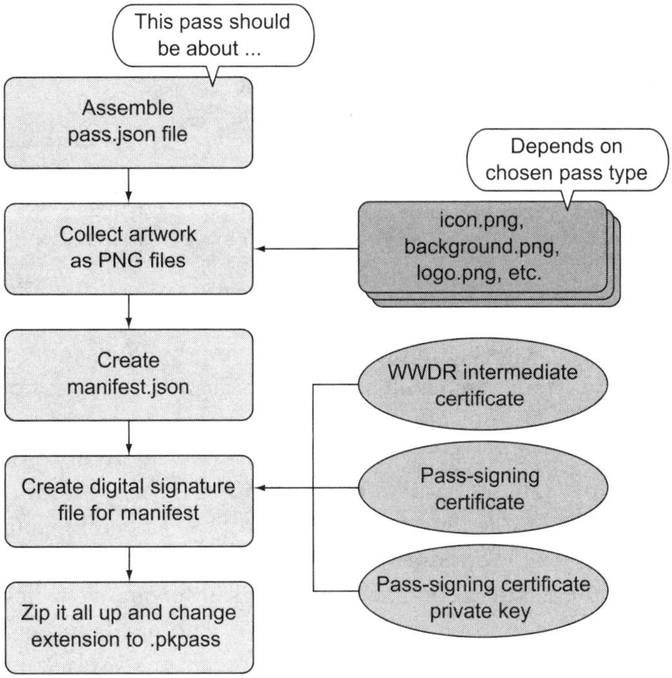

Figure 4.8 Pass creation flow

Ruby comes preinstalled on your Mac with OS X, so no setup is required. Ruby provides OpenSSL out of the box and also has great support for JSON, which is the format used for making passes.

CONFIGURING THE PASS BUILD SCRIPT

The following Ruby code snippets are all part of the makepass.rb script, which you'll find in the source code for this book.[1] Put the script file in the directory where you prepared the certificates. This script is intentionally simplistic to demonstrate the bare essentials for building a pass. It has no command-line parameters—you'll have to edit the script to change the contents of any pass fields.

You can configure all details for the pass by modifying the variable assignments at the top of the Ruby script:

```
passTypeIdentifier = "pass.com.drobnik.vipmovie"
teamIdentifier = "Z7L2YCUH45"
organizationName = "Cocoanetics Cinema"
logoText = "Cocoanetics"
description = "VIP Movie Night Sofa Seat"
eventDate = Time.new(2014, 8, 13, 16, 0, 0, "+02:00")
```

Pass type identifier configured on portal (passTypeIdentifier)

Team identifier from member center (teamIdentifier)

Name of organization (doubles as a fallback relevancy message) (organizationName)

Text to display next to the logo image (logoText)

Description of the pass, used for VoiceOver (description)

Event date construction with time zone offset (eventDate)

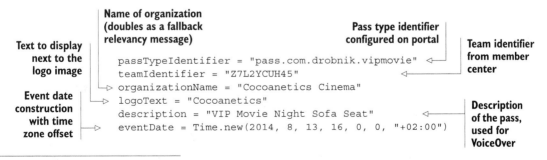

[1] For source code, see www.manning.com/BarcodeswithiOS.

```
seat = "1A"                                          # On your sofa, all seats are front row
event_latitude = 14.5877                             # Geographic location of the event
event_longitude = 48.0528

serialNumber = Time.now.to_i.to_s                    # Use current Unix timestamp as pass serial number
passFileName = serialNumber + ".pkpass"              # Serial number is used for filename with extension
eventDateString = eventDate.utc.strftime("%Y-%m-%dT%H:%M:%SZ")   # Dates represented in W3C format
```

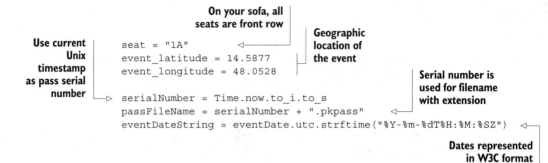

The most important things to check and possibly adjust are the *team identifier* and the *pass type identifier*. Those need to match your signing certificate or you can't produce a valid signature. You can look up your team identifier in the Apple developer member center (https://developer.apple.com/membercenter). You might also remember from figure 4.3 that Apple combines both of these identifiers for an even more unique pass type identity; this is the signing identity that the certificates need to match.

The `eventDateString`—the event time from the general pass info formatted as a W3C string—doubles as the `relevantDate`, which is logical for an event ticket that's relevant at the time of the beginning of the event. This date needs to be complete with hours and minutes—seconds are optional. The `locations` array contains the geocoordinates of the event location—you should replace them with the location where the pass will be relevant. For testing, the GPS coordinates of your sofa would work well.

Beginning with iOS 7, you can also add an array of `beacons` to specify iBeacon identifiers. iBeacons are small, battery-powered devices that emit an identifier via Bluetooth. For example, a bus could have an iBeacon next to the driver, and this would cause bus tickets to be shown on the device's lockscreen.

Let's take the Ruby script for a spin now that all certificates and keys are present and you've adapted the pass details to your liking. In Terminal, change into the working directory where you put the certificate files and the edited Ruby script:

```
cd ~/Desktop/MyPass        # Change directory to working folder
chmod +x makepass.rb       # Make script executable
./makepass.rb              # Run it
```

Running the script will dynamically create the pass.json file containing the pass details, the manifest.json file that contains the checksums of the pass files, and a signature file with the cryptographic signature of the manifest. The pieces will be zipped up into a .pkpass file in the same directory.

If you double-click on the .pkpass file, OS X will show a preview. You can also inspect the pass.json file to see the beautiful JSON reflecting the details you set up in the Ruby script. Figure 4.9 shows the pass.json file compared to the front and back of the pass as displayed by QuickLook preview on OS X.

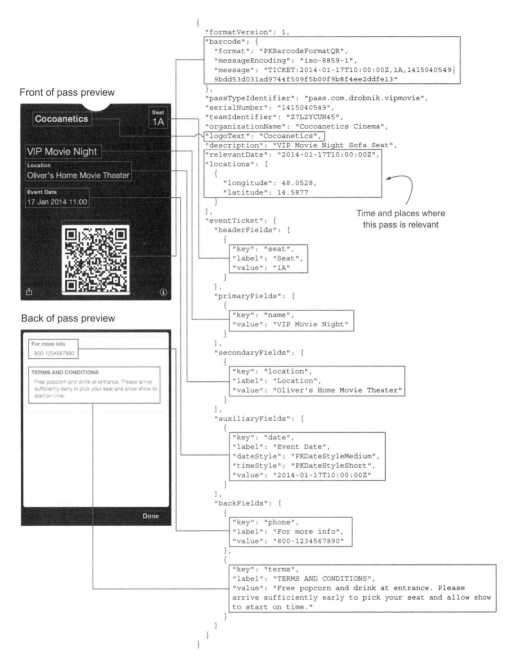

```
{
  "formatVersion": 1,
  "barcode": {
    "format": "PKBarcodeFormatQR",
    "messageEncoding": "iso-8859-1",
    "message": "TICKET:2014-01-17T10:00:00Z,1A,1415040549|
    9bdd53d031ad9744f509f5b00f9b8f4ee2ddfe13"
  },
  "passTypeIdentifier": "pass.com.drobnik.vipmovie",
  "serialNumber": "1415040549",
  "teamIdentifier": "Z7L2YCUH45",
  "organizationName": "Cocoanetics Cinema",
  "logoText": "Cocoanetics",
  "description": "VIP Movie Night Sofa Seat",
  "relevantDate": "2014-01-17T10:00:00Z",
  "locations": [
    {
      "longitude": 48.0528,
      "latitude": 14.5877
    }
  ],
  "eventTicket": {
    "headerFields": [
      {
        "key": "seat",
        "label": "Seat",
        "value": "1A"
      }
    ],
    "primaryFields": [
      {
        "key": "name",
        "value": "VIP Movie Night"
      }
    ],
    "secondaryFields": [
      {
        "key": "location",
        "label": "Location",
        "value": "Oliver's Home Movie Theater"
      }
    ],
    "auxiliaryFields": [
      {
        "key": "date",
        "label": "Event Date",
        "dateStyle": "PKDateStyleMedium",
        "timeStyle": "PKDateStyleShort",
        "value": "2014-01-17T10:00:00Z"
      }
    ],
    "backFields": [
      {
        "key": "phone",
        "label": "For more info",
        "value": "800-1234567890"
      },
      {
        "key": "terms",
        "label": "TERMS AND CONDITIONS",
        "value": "Free popcorn and drink at entrance. Please
        arrive sufficiently early to pick your seat and allow show
        to start on time."
      }
    ]
  }
}
```

Time and places where this pass is relevant

Figure 4.9 Pass preview compared to pass.json

This pass has several generally applicable elements at the top, and the `eventTicket` key groups fields that are specific to this pass being an event ticket. The relevancy information in `relevantDate` and `locations` specifies conditions that make this pass relevant for display on the iPhone lock screen. Apple doesn't publish the exact algorithm for determining when a pass should be shown on the lock screen, so you'll have to trust them to do so in a manner useful to the user.

The following sections walk you through the Ruby script so that you can understand the process of assembling passes.

CHECKING AND LOADING SIGNING CERTIFICATES

Once the pass details have been set up, the Ruby script loads and checks the three certificates needed to perform the signing of the manifest. They're in `begin/rescue/end` blocks so they'll gracefully fail should one of the certificates be missing or faulty. To keep things simple, the names of the three files are hardcoded:

```
begin
  rootCertFile = File.read('AppleWWDRCA.cer')
  rootCert = OpenSSL::X509::Certificate.new rootCertFile
rescue => err
  puts "Cannot load root certificate: #{err}"
  exit 1
end
```

Check/load WWDR certificate

```
begin
  certificate = OpenSSL::X509::Certificate.new

  File.read('passtypecert.pem')
rescue => err
  puts "Cannot load signing certificate: #{err}"
  exit 1
end
```

Check/load signing certificate

```
begin

  privateKeyFile = File.read('passtypecertkey.pem')
  privateKey = OpenSSL::PKey::RSA.new privateKeyFile, '12345'
rescue => err
  puts "Cannot load private signing key: #{err}"
  exit 1
end
```

Check/load private signing key

ADDING A BARCODE

The barcode is generated for you based on the contents of the `barcodeMessage` key. We want to be able to validate tickets without having to ping a server, so we'll add some extra secret "salt" to the message and create an SHA1 hash as a signature. Because we're the only ones who know the value of the salt, nobody else can create tickets with a correct barcode message signature. The following code snippet is a continuation of makepass.rb:

```
barcodeMessage = "TICKET:#{eventDateString},#{seat},#{serialNumber}"
salt = "EXTRA SECRET SAUCE"
barcodeMessageSignature = Digest::SHA1.hexdigest barcodeMessage + salt
```

String with the ticket info

A secret string to "salt" the hash

Create SHA1 hash of message and salt

Combine message with SHA1 signature

```
barcodeMessage = barcodeMessage + "|#{barcodeMessageSignature}"

barcode = {
  "format" => "PKBarcodeFormatQR",
  "messageEncoding" => "iso-8859-1"
}
barcode["message"] = barcodeMessage
```

Specify contents, type to use, and character encoding for the barcode

Passbook supports the three most-used 2D barcode symbologies: QR, Aztec, and PDF417 (see section 1.2.2 for details about their differences). Generally speaking, all three types can encode arbitrary strings. If you can spare the space and are free to choose, I recommend QR or Aztec Codes, as these have built-in error correction and are recognized faster and more reliably. PDF417 is more compact and thus better suited for passes with lots of info on the front.

Barcode character encoding

The ISO-8859-1 message-encoding format (also known as *Latin 1*) is the de facto standard for most barcode readers. This is why Apple suggests you use this as the character encoding for the contents of the pass barcode.

You can specify any character encoding scheme supported by `NSString` in the `messageEncoding` value of the barcode dictionary in pass.json.

The data content of the barcode is completely independent of the other content of the pass. It's up to you whether you want to encode all the pass details in the barcode or whether you only encode a serial number there and then look up the information needed for validation from your server.

As you can see in the previous code snippet, you specify the contents, barcode type to use, and character encoding when creating the JSON file for the pass. When iOS or OS X displays the pass, it renders a barcode symbol according to this information.

ASSEMBLING THE PASS DETAILS

You configured the pass details at the top of the Ruby script (near the beginning of section 4.2.3).

The contents of the pass are assembled in a Ruby hash, the equivalent of a dictionary in Objective-C. This can easily be transformed into a JSON file. The first few entries are taken from variables you set up earlier; a few of the fields change less frequently and have hardcoded values. You may also customize these to your needs with your text editor:

```
headerFields = [{
      "key" => "seat",
      "label" => "Seat",
      "value" => seat
}]
```

Header fields at top right of pass

```
primaryFields = [{
      "key" => "name",
      "value" => "VIP Movie Night"
}]
```

Primary fields below header fields

```
secondaryFields = [{
      "key" => "location",
      "label" => "Location",
      "value" => "Oliver's Home Movie Theater"
}]
```

Secondary fields below primary fields

```
auxiliaryFields = [{
      "key" => "date",
      "label" => "Event Date",
      "dateStyle" => "PKDateStyleMedium",
      "timeStyle" => "PKDateStyleShort",
      "value" => eventDateString
}]
```

Auxiliary fields below secondary fields

```
backFields = [{
      "key" => "phone",
      "label" => "For more info",
      "value" => "800-1234567890"
},
{
      "key" => "terms",
      "label" => "TERMS AND CONDITIONS",
      "value" => "Free popcorn and drink at entrance. " +
         "Please arrive sufficiently early to pick your seat " +
         "and allow show to start on time."
}]
```

Fields on back of pass

```
pass = {
  "formatVersion" => 1
}
```

Create a hash to contain pass info

```
pass["barcode"] = barcode
```

Add barcode info to hash

```
pass["passTypeIdentifier"] = passTypeIdentifier
pass["serialNumber"] = serialNumber
pass["teamIdentifier"] = teamIdentifier
pass["organizationName"] = organizationName
pass["logoText"] = logoText
pass["description"] = description
```

Add meta info from earlier defined variables

```
pass["relevantDate"] = eventDateString
pass["locations"] = [{
      "longitude" => event_longitude,
      "latitude" => event_latitude
}]
```

Add relevancy info to hash

```
pass["eventTicket"] = {
  "headerFields" => headerFields,
  "primaryFields" => primaryFields,
  "secondaryFields" => secondaryFields,
  "auxiliaryFields" => auxiliaryFields,
  "backFields" => backFields
}

passJSON = JSON.pretty_generate(pass)
passSHA1 = Digest::SHA1.hexdigest passJSON
```

Assemble the pass fields in event ticket hash

Create pass JSON string for output to file

Get SHA1 of pass JSON for manifest

ADDING ARTWORK TO THE PASS

At this point, the JSON string for the pass is complete, but it yields rather boring visuals, as you can see on the left side of figure 4.10. To spice it up and brand it, you can add a number of images to the pass. Their exact use on the pass depends on its type, and some experimentation might be required. For each image, you'll also need to include the Retina version, denoted by the @2x filename:

- icon.png and icon@2x.png are the icons to display in the Mail app. Without this, iOS rejects the pass.
- thumbnail.png and thumbnail@2x.png are small images to add beside the pass details.
- strip.png and strip@2x.png are background images to place behind the thumbnail. These can't be combined with the background.
- background.png and background@2x.png are background images that get blurred and placed over the entire area of the pass. These can't be combined with the strip image.

Figure 4.10 shows the dramatic difference you get from adding artwork files. Because the background image is blurred anyway, you can get away with a smaller-resolution image.

Figure 4.10 What a difference a few PNGs make ...

LOOKING FOR DESIGN LOVE The artwork to produce these results is included in the Passbook folder in the book's example code. Please forgive my unprofessional choice of art—I'm a developer and not a designer. Passes you plan to distribute to actual users should receive the loving care of a design professional.

To prevent somebody from tampering with a pass by replacing artwork files, they're also featured in the pass manifest. This is likely a gesture by Apple to give pass issuers a greater feeling of security and thus inspire trust in the platform. At validation time, if the signature is valid, then neither the JSON nor the resources could have been altered.

The following Ruby code from makepass.rb scans the current directory for suitable resources and determines the SHA1 checksum for each:

```
possibleResources = ['icon.png', 'icon@2x.png',
                     'thumbnail.png', 'thumbnail@2x.png',
                     'strip.png', 'strip@2x.png',
                     'logo.png', 'logo@2x.png',
                     'background.png', 'background@2x.png']

resources = possibleResources & Dir['*']

manifest = {"pass.json" => passSHA1}

zipCommand = ["zip", "-
   q", passFileName, "pass.json", "signature",

          "manifest.json"]

resources.each do |resource_file|
  file = File.open(resource_file, "rb")
  contents = file.read

  contents_SHA1 = Digest::SHA1.hexdigest contents

  manifest[resource_file] = contents_SHA1
  zipCommand << resource_file
end

manifestJSON = JSON.pretty_generate(manifest)

manifestFile = open("manifest.json", "w")
manifestFile.write(manifestJSON)
manifestFile.close

passFile = open("pass.json", "w")
passFile.write(passJSON)
passFile.close
```

Files that are possible in pkpass

Filter possible resources with actual files in folder

First file is the JSON

Keep track of files to put in zip

Iterate over resources

Load file contents into variable

Get resource SHA1

Add resource file and SHA1 to manifest hash

Create manifest JSON string

Write manifest to disk

Write pass file to disk

After this, both the manifest and pass JSON files have been written to disk. The manifest.json file has the SHA1 checksums for all files to prevent tampering.

SIGNED, SEALED, DELIVERED

In the last step in makepass.rb, the manifest JSON gets digitally signed and the result is output to a standalone signature file. Then all the files belonging to the pass get zipped up into a .pkpass file:

```
signature = OpenSSL::PKCS7.sign(certificate, privateKey,
                                manifestJSON,
                                [rootCert],
                                OpenSSL::PKCS7::BINARY |
                                OpenSSL::PKCS7::DETACHED).to_der

signatureFile = open("signature", "wb")
signatureFile.write signature
signatureFile.close

system(*zipCommand)
```

Create signature (annotation on the `OpenSSL::PKCS7.sign` call)

Write signature to disk (annotation on the `signatureFile` lines)

Execute zip command (annotation on `system(*zipCommand)`)

The signature is output in binary DER format into a detached file. Note that the `rootCert` is also included. iPhones usually don't have the WWDR intermediate certificate installed, so it needs to be present inside the signature file so that the chain of trust (see figure 4.11) can be validated on the user's device.

Instead of using the convenient Ruby script provided, you can also perform all the steps manually. For sake of completeness, here are the Terminal command equivalents for signing and zipping the pkpass file:

```
openssl smime -binary -sign -certfile AppleWWDRCA.cer \
        -signer passtypecert.pem \
        -inkey passtypecertkey.pem -in manifest.json -out signature \
        -outform DER -passin pass:12345
zip -q ticket.pkpass manifest.json pass.json signature *.png
```

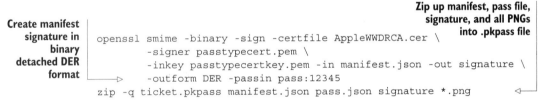

Create manifest signature in binary detached DER format (annotation on the `openssl smime` command)

Zip up manifest, pass file, signature, and all PNGs into .pkpass file (annotation on the `zip` command)

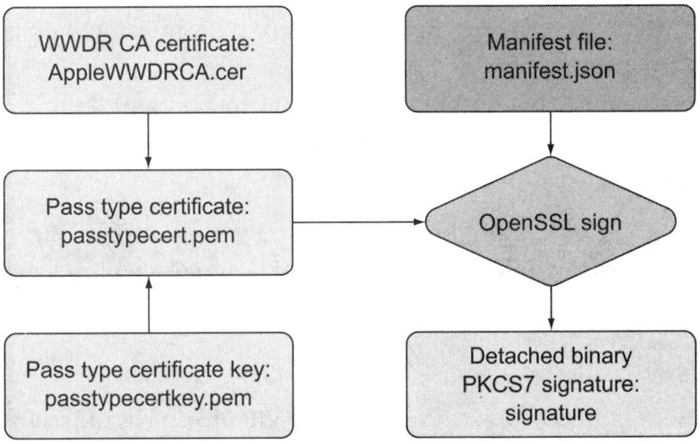

Figure 4.11 Passbook chain of trust

This manual approach requires you to create the pass and manifest JSON files by hand, which is as tedious as it is error prone. I think you'll agree that editing a few values in the makepass.rb script is much more convenient.

> **Debugging passes**
>
> The OS X preview app will happily show you passes even if they have errors. Besides the signature being valid, there are a number of other conditions that need to be met for iOS to accept a pass. For example, passes require an icon image when sending them via email or else iOS will reject them.
>
> To ensure that your pass creation is OK, mail yourself a pass file. Connect your iPhone to your Mac via USB and open the Xcode Organizer's console view. When you open the email with the pass, you'll see in the log if there are any problems with the pass. If iOS lets you add the pass to Passbook, you know it's OK.

4.2.4 Pass creation takeaways

At this point, you're able to produce a batch of passes with different seat numbers for your VIP Movie Night event. By modifying the Ruby script, you can set the event date, specify the correct latitude and longitude of your sofa, and adjust the seat assignments. Adding images makes your passes much prettier. You should also make sure your iPhone will accept one such pass as valid to check that the creation was successful.

Some key takeaways:

- Passbook aims to make carrying tickets, passes, coupons, and vouchers on your iPhone quite convenient.
- Apple made the technology totally independent of any Apple hardware or software to facilitate it becoming the de facto standard.
- The certificate used for signing passes needs to be created in your Apple iOS developer account.
- For devices to be able to verify the signature, the WWDR intermediate certificate needs to be included.
- A manifest contains the SHA1 hashes of all artwork images and the pass.json file.
- This manifest is cryptographically signed to prevent tampering with the pass details or any artwork.

The procedure for creating a pass might seem a bit daunting at first. But once you work through this complexity, you'll start seeing possible usage scenarios everywhere you look.

4.3 Validating passes

You counted the seats on your sofa as seating for your VIP Movie Night. You set a location, date, and time for the event. You produced valid digital Passbook tickets for the event. You emailed these tickets to your guinea pigs ... um, friends. Now you need to be able to verify tickets at the door to the venue (a.k.a. your living room). This section will teach you how to use the barcode scanning code you built in chapters 2 and 3 and build an app for doing that.

Several validation checks occur when a user adds the pass to their pass library. iOS will silently refuse to add any invalid passes, so if the pass is inside the Passbook library, it hasn't been modified or otherwise tampered with. Additional validation levels (see figure 4.12) depend on your usage scenario. A big chain of movie theaters might want to check the ticket info against their ticket server.

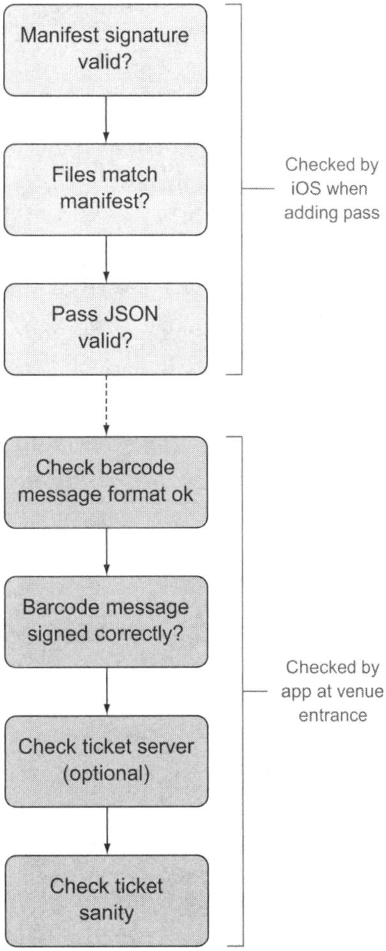

Figure 4.12 Validating passes on multiple levels

If you had a big chain of movie theaters, you'd have your development department build an app that you could install on a number of iOS devices. Those ticket-checking devices would be used by the employees checking tickets at the door. They'd check paper tickets visually as they have always done, and they'd scan Passbook tickets with the app. This app would check the ticket and indicate whether they should let the ticket holder enter.

You probably don't have a department doing the developing for you, so you'll do this yourself. You also won't have an army of ushers, but you might be able to delegate that job to your children. Another key difference between this scenario and real life is that you don't have a ticketing server with a web API that you could check scanned tickets against.

For this reason, a *cryptographic signature* was included in the barcode message in the previous section. This signature ensures that only you can create valid passes for your event—no server required! Another benefit of this serverless approach is that it's extremely fast. Imagine the long queue of people holding popcorn and cola, all of them wanting to get to their seats. The faster you can determine the eligibility of each visitor, the better. In an ideal implementation, the checking of a ticket would be as fast as glancing at a paper ticket.

The last of the validation steps depends on your usage scenario. For a small venue—like your living room—you can easily see if somebody has a duplicate seat assignment. Other scenarios might keep track of which seats have already been scanned and flag duplicates this way. Movie theaters in the United States usually won't have assigned seating because of the hassle and cost of enforcing it.

In the following section you'll create a serverless app for checking tickets and have it output the event details and assigned seats for valid tickets.

4.3.1 Building a ticket-verifier app

You're now back on iOS terra firma and have finished your excursion into the world of cross-platform scripting with Ruby. This section demonstrates the serverless validation approach on iOS. You'll see that the Ruby cryptographic functions—which use OpenSSL—have equivalents in iOS in the `CommonCrypto.framework`.

Your ticket-verifier app will have these features:

- It will have a single-screen UI for hassle-free scanning at the venue entrance.
- It will scan QR, Aztec, and PDF417 codes.
- It will only accept tickets with a properly formatted barcode message.
- It will verify cryptographic signatures in barcode messages.
- It will reject tickets if their encoded event time differs by more than one hour from the current time.
- It will show the event details and seat number in case of success, or an alert detailing the reason for failure.

The finished ticket-verifier app scanning a valid ticket is shown in figure 4.13.

4.3.2 Reusing barcode scanner code

The QR Code scanning app you developed in chapter 3 has all the pieces you need for the ticket-verifier app. It's already set up for scanning the three 2D barcode symbologies supported by iOS and Passbook. It was developed in a reusable manner (nice interfaces, delegation, proper prefixes), so it provides a great starting point. Let's get started.

Figure 4.13 Passbook ticket-verifier app

Create a new Xcode project, and from the QR Scanner project copy these files to the new project:

- DTAVFoundationFunctions.h and .m
- DTCameraPreviewController.h and .m
- DTVideoPreviewInterestBox.h and .m
- DTVideoPreviewView.h and .m

You'll also reuse the Main.storyboard file, which has a full-screen video preview with a focus box. Make the focus box a bit wider in Interface Builder (see figure 4.14), so that it's more convenient for targeting those rather wide PDF417 barcodes.

As is usual when using the iPhone camera, you'll need to add `AVFoundation.framework` in the Link Binary with Libraries build phase.

For the sake of simplicity, the UI will be generated from the storyboard. The scanning logic for this app will be in the app delegate. The following addition to AppDelegate.m grabs a reference to the scan preview view controller and sets itself as a delegate. This causes the delegate callback for when a new barcode has been detected to call into the app delegate for processing:

```
- (BOOL)application:(UIApplication *)application
      didFinishLaunchingWithOptions:(NSDictionary *)launchOptions {
DTCameraPreviewController *previewController =
(DTCameraPreviewController *)self.window.rootViewController;
previewController.delegate = self;

   return YES;
}
```

Scanner view controller is root view controller of window

Set scan delegate to self (app delegate)

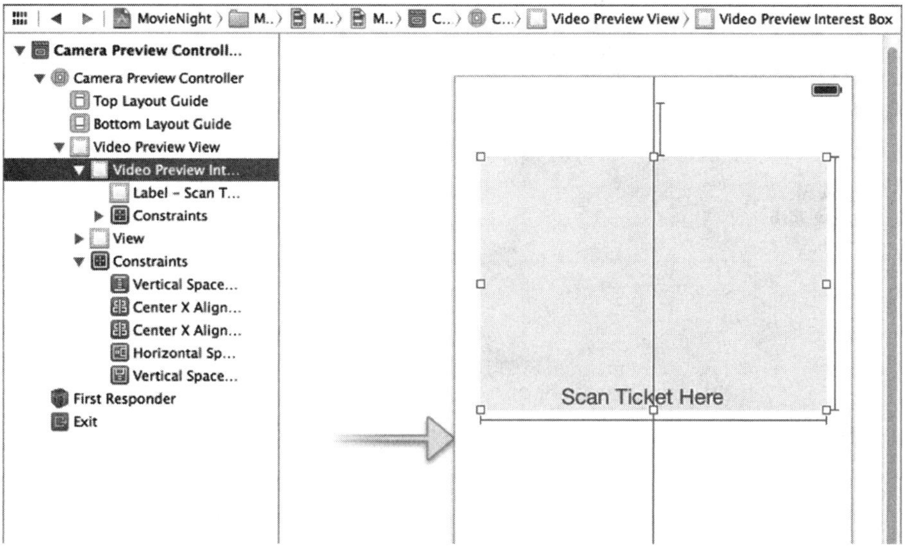

Figure 4.14 Making the scan box wider

4.3.3 Serverless pass validation

To validate the barcode message signature, you need a way to get a hex representation of a string's SHA1 hash. Here's such a helper method, which uses `CommonCrypto.framework`. This framework is automatically linked with all apps via the `System` dynamic library, so you don't need to add it to the linking build phase but only import the header for using it:

```
#import <CommonCrypto/CommonCrypto.h>                    // Add this to imports at the top

- (NSString *)_SHA1ForString:(NSString *)string {
  NSData *data = [string dataUsingEncoding:NSUTF8StringEncoding];   // Convert NSString to NSData
  uint8_t digest[CC_SHA1_DIGEST_LENGTH];                  // A byte array to receive the output SHAI hash

  CC_SHA1(data.bytes, (CC_LONG)data.length, digest);      // Calling the C function for creating the SHAI hash

  NSMutableString *output = [NSMutableString stringWithCapacity:
                                     CC_SHA1_DIGEST_LENGTH * 2];
  for (int i = 0; i < CC_SHA1_DIGEST_LENGTH; i++) {
     [output appendFormat:@"%02x", digest[i]];
  }                                                       // Make a hex representation of output hash

  return output;
}
```

The following code snippet shows two helper methods for reporting to the user either a valid pass or what went wrong validating one. The latter's basic functionality is achieved with a `UIAlertView`:

```
- (void)_reportValidTicketDate:(NSDate *)date seat:(NSString *)seat {
   NSDateFormatter *formatter = [[NSDateFormatter alloc] init];
   [formatter setDateStyle:NSDateFormatterShortStyle];
   [formatter setTimeStyle:NSDateFormatterShortStyle];
   NSString *msgDate = [formatter stringFromDate:date];   // Format ticket date to suit the device locale
   NSString *msg = [NSString stringWithFormat:@"Seat %@\n%@", seat,
                    msgDate];                             // Alert states the formatted date and seat number from ticket

   alert = [[UIAlertView alloc] initWithTitle:@"Ticket Ok"
                                      message:msg
                                     delegate:self
                            cancelButtonTitle:@"Ok"
                            otherButtonTitles:nil];
   [alert show];                                          // Show alert view with message
}

- (void)_reportInvalidTicket:(NSString *)msg {
   alert = [[UIAlertView alloc] initWithTitle:@"Invalid Ticket"
                                      message:msg
                                     delegate:self
                            cancelButtonTitle:@"Ok"
                            otherButtonTitles:nil];
   [alert show];
}
```

Now for the scan delegate method. This method checks the validity of the pass on several levels, and if it reaches the bottom, it reports a valid pass. You want to ignore new barcodes while an alert is still showing to prevent multiple alerts from stacking on top of each other:

```
- (void)previewController:(DTCameraPreviewController *)previewController
             didScanCode:(NSString *)code
                  ofType:(NSString *)type {
   if ([alert isVisible]) {
      return;
   }

   if (![code hasPrefix:@"TICKET:"]) {
      return;
   }

   NSArray *components = [code componentsSeparatedByString:@"|"];

   if ([components count] != 2) {
      NSLog(@"Ticket without Signature ignored");
      return;
    }

    // server-less verification
    NSString *salt = @"EXTRA SECRET SAUCE";
    NSString *details = components[0];
    NSString *saltedDetails = [details stringByAppendingString:salt];
    NSString *signature = components[1];
    NSString *verify = [self _SHA1ForString:saltedDetails];

    if (![signature isEqualToString:verify]) {
        [self _reportInvalidTicket:@"Ticket has invalid signature"];
        return;
    }

   NSString *ticket = [details substringFromIndex:7];
   NSArray *comps = [ticket componentsSeparatedByString:@","];
   NSString *dateStr = comps[0];
   NSString *seat = comps[1];
   NSString *serial = comps[2];

   NSDateFormatter *parser = [[NSDateFormatter alloc] init];
   parser.dateFormat = @"yyyy-MM-dd'T'HH:mm:ssZZZZ";
   NSDate *date = [parser dateFromString:dateStr];

   NSTimeInterval intervalToNow = [date timeIntervalSinceNow];

   if (intervalToNow < 3600) {
   [self _reportInvalidTicket:@"Event on this ticket is more than "
                              "60 mins in the past"];
      return;
   }
```

Don't handle if alert showing

Barcode message must have this prefix to be considered

Divide message and signature at pipe character

Ignore ticket without signature

Use the same salt string as in Ruby script

String for check hash consists of details and salt

Create verification hash via helper method

Check if verification hash matches

Separate ticket details

Parse UTC date with date formatter

Determine time interval between ticket date and current time

Ticket date is too far in the past

```
    if (intervalToNow > 3600) {
        [self _reportInvalidTicket:@"Event on this ticket is more than "
                                    "60 mins in the future"];
        return;
    }

    [self _reportValidTicketDate:date seat:seat];
}
```

Ticket date is too far in the future

Report valid ticket details

These checks—if statements with a return—weed out tickets that aren't valid for the current event. These checks are performed on top of the checks that iOS already made when the user added this pass to the device. You could say that Apple's checks pertain to the pass's *syntax*, whereas you're responsible for verifying the pass's *semantics*. This is natural, because only you know under which circumstances you would want to consider a pass to be valid.

And you're done!

Now, with the Ruby script, generate a pass with an event time that's no more than 60 minutes away. Send this to your iPhone by email and add it to Passbook. Open up the pass so that the barcode is visible. Then scan this pass with the verifier app, and it should be reported as valid. Change the event's time to be further away, and the pass should be reported as being too far in the future.

Here are some suggestions as to how you could further improve this ticket-verification solution:

- Detect duplicate seat assignments by tracking which seat numbers have been filled.
- Configure specific events and validate tickets against these instead of using the current time.
- Improve the user interface by replacing the alert views with something nicer.
- Communicate scanned tickets to a server-based API.

4.3.4 Pass validation takeaways

The sample app you built in this chapter demonstrates a simple way of validating Passbook passes without a server. You'll usually want to be able to verify passes as quickly as possible while the user is holding out the iPhone for you to scan. There is little room for delay or for not being able to scan a pass because you lack an internet connection.

Even nowadays with ubiquitous 3G/LTE internet, there are places where connectivity is limited or utterly demolished by the sheer number of iPhones around. At large conferences promising free WiFi, people often bring their own wireless hotspots (a.k.a. MiFis) and multiple iOS devices, and these often overwhelm the limited WiFi frequencies and destroy the organizer's WiFi network. Time slots on 3G antennas are even more likely to get overloaded by too many devices being in close proximity to each other, such as in a sports stadium.

You should evaluate your real-world scenario and determine whether you absolutely need server connectivity or if you can validate tickets first and then upload the scan info to your server later on. The serverless verification technique discussed in this chapter might save your life (as an iOS developer).

These are the key verification takeaways:

- Being able to quickly verify tickets as they are being presented is important for avoiding "traffic jams" at the venue entrance.
- If your usage scenario involves many iOS developers in close proximity, then plan for times without connectivity.
- Using a secret "salt" phrase together with a cryptographic hash at both creation and verification time is a powerful technique for validating passes without a server.
- Providing an enterprise-level pass-verification app can be fun as well as lucrative.

Creating passes for other companies

Many people have ideas for Passbook-based solutions that involve creating passes for clients or users. I asked Apple about an app where one user would create an IOU for a friend. This would be a coupon stating that user A owes a sum of money to user B. User B could redeem this coupon at a later stage in exchange for user A returning the money. Apple stated categorically that they would not approve such an app.

Apple's review guidelines state thus:

> *23.3 Passes must be signed by the entity that will be distributing the pass under its own name, trademark, or brand or the App will be rejected and Passbook credentials may be revoked*

Apple's rule would require user A to have a developer account and signing certificate so that he can distribute the IOU pass in his own name.

As this chapter has demonstrated, it would be easy to create valid passes for—say—Coca Cola. Logos and suitable artwork can be come by with ease. If Apple allowed everybody to create passes for anyone, this would quickly erode trust in Passbook. The suggested workaround is that if a company wants to implement Passbook, they should register a developer account. If you're contracting for them, they can add you as a team member. This way you could take care of their Passbook type identifier and certificate on their behalf.

4.4 Summary

In this chapter we focused on two major aspects of Passbook, both of which related to barcodes. You've learned how to create signed Passbook passes on any platform that has Ruby, and you built a verification app that checks those passes at the entrance to your venue.

iOS also includes view controllers and methods you can use to access the passes in the user's pass library that match your developer prefix. These APIs are grouped within the `PassKit.framework`. With this framework's methods, users can add passes to their pass library without leaving your app. Imagine a boarding pass app that lets the user add passes for flights. Or that allows the user to pick a seat during online check-in. This app could communicate with the airline's server and update the pass with the new seat number. Apple refers to this kind of app as a *companion app*.

Another feature that we didn't cover is the ability of passes to contain a web API URL where apps can register for push notifications. This allows you to push any updates to passes to the individual users. This goes hand in hand with Apple's Push Notification service for updating passes. Read the documentation on Apple's website for all the features of Passbook and PassKit.

I hope that you're beginning to see the promise of Passbook, and that it doesn't have to be only for big corporate uses. With the information in this chapter, you can come up with your own usage patterns. Your knowledge of Passbook and barcode scanning will allow you to innovate at both ends.

But Apple's Passbook system couldn't exist without system-level support for displaying barcodes. In the next chapter we'll look at how iOS generates 2D barcodes.

5 Generating barcodes

This chapter covers

- Producing 2D barcodes for display and print with Core Image
- Printing sheets of barcodes with AirPrint
- Saving paper with the AirPrint Printer Simulator
- Generating 1D barcodes with BarCodeKit
- Printing to AirPrint roll-feed printers

Half of your world already has barcodes on it. The other half has only been waiting for you to finish this chapter, so that you can remedy the barcode vacuum wherever you might encounter it. This chapter will teach you how to generate barcodes for display and print. With this knowledge under your belt, you'll be able to extend your scannable barcode universe virtually without limit.

The ability to print barcode stickers was long the domain of large corporations or supermarkets who could afford to buy special printers for this purpose. Nowadays companies like Brother offer label printers that print to inexpensive thermal-paper rolls for less than $100. Those make the physical printing of barcodes attainable for everybody. In turn, Apple added AirPrint support for such label printers in iOS 7. Wireless printing of single stickers from any iOS device is a huge convenience.

For example, users could catalog their personal library and keep track of their books by adding stickers stating, "This book is the property of ..." and a serial number barcode. Another app might let you keep track of the contents of moving boxes—you could keep track of what you put into which box, and then the app would create a manifest listing the boxes and their contents. A barcode sticker affixed to each box would link the box back to the matching manifest.

A whole new world of creative and productive label apps is waiting to be created by iOS developers.

5.1 Producing barcodes for display or print

In chapter 4 you created digital passes that included one of three different kinds of 2D barcodes. In that chapter it was sufficient to include a pass's content and type in the pkpass JSON file. The barcode shown when presenting the pass was generated on the fly by Passbook via the Core Image framework.

Passbook passes are meant to be scanned off device screens by CCD-based scanners or cameras. The reflectivity of the glass display plays tricks on laser-based scanners, which are still widely used for scanning 1D barcodes. This is the official reason for the lack of 1D barcode support in iOS.

> **Requesting enhancements**
>
> Apple is an engineering-driven company with limited engineering resources. If you wish for native support of 1D barcode generation in a future iOS version, please pause right now and file an enhancement request on Apple's bug reporter website (https://bugreport.apple.com).
>
> If you do file such an enhancement request, mention rdar://14767897 as the original request for 1D barcodes, which will allow the Apple engineer dealing with your request to count it as a *vote* on the earlier request.
>
> The bug reports and enhancement requests that gather the most votes—a.k.a. *dupes*—have higher priority when Apple is putting together the feature set for the next major iOS version.

To be able to generate 1D barcodes despite the lack of official support, I developed *BarCodeKit*, a commercial framework that you can use to generate the most common types of 1D barcodes. Readers of this book—as a thank you—receive a free license to use BarCodeKit for their projects.

Printing on iOS happens via *AirPrint*, which may initially seem somewhat difficult to grasp because of the many options for simplified printing of objects such as images and attributed strings. You'll learn how to customize the rendering of content for print. Besides traditional sheet-based printers, there are now roll printers that are particularly well suited for printing barcode stickers. We'll look at printing sheets of QR Code stickers in the first half of this chapter, and individual serial number stickers in the second half.

5.1.1 Thoughts on barcode size

When printing barcodes, you should consider the distance from which people will typically scan them. A 1D serial number sticker would typically be scanned from a short distance. The minimum bar width a printer is able to output sets a lower limit on how small you can print 1D barcodes.

People scanning a QR Code on a poster might be much further away; for example, the poster might be on the other side of the subway tracks. If the QR Code on such a poster is too small, you'll be putting people's lives in danger if they have to lean over the tracks to scan the code.

As a rule of thumb for QR Codes, the width of the printed code should be no less than a tenth of the scanning distance for low-complexity codes. The size of the code needs to increase as complexity and error correction increase. For the highest-complexity codes, you want the width to be at least a quarter of the scanning distance. If you put a QR Code with a diameter of 30 centimeters (about 12 inches) into your office window, the maximum distance from which people could scan it is about 3 meters (about 10 feet).

5.1.2 QR Code error correction

QR Codes can have one of four error-correction levels, which determines the level of redundancy spread over the area of the code:

- *L*—7%
- *M*—15% (iOS default)
- *Q*—25%
- *H*—30%

The higher the redundancy level, the more a code can be covered or damaged while retaining its scannability.

In figure 5.1 the content on the left was encoded four times with identical scaling factors—only the redundancy level was modified. You can see that the size needed increases with redundancy, and thus complexity.

Figure 5.1 QR Code error-correction levels

> **BARCODE GURU TIP** The error-correction level used is indicated in the QR Code by the two squares (referred to as *modules*) next to the lower-left centering mark, as shown in figure 5.1. Two black modules in this space indicate the lowest level of error correction; if this space is void of modules, that indicates the highest level of error correction. If you commit this to memory, you can impress your friends by being able to tell them which error-correction level was used just by glancing at a code on a poster.

Error-correction levels L and M are recommended for general marketing use. Levels Q and H should be preferred in industrial scenarios, where keeping the code clean or undamaged might be a challenge.

For engineers, the error-correction level is a means to increase reliability. For designers, it's an opportunity for branding. Often you'll see parts of QR Codes replaced with a company logo or graphics, as in figure 5.2. For this example, which is based on an H-level complexity QR code, I counted off 10 modules from each side toward the center, and placed my photo within that boundary.

Figure 5.2 Adding a personal touch to a marketing QR Code

Other possible customizations include rounding off edges between modules, changing colors, and sprinkling in tiny graphical accessories. As long as there's sufficient contrast between modules and enough information visible, the code can still be scanned. QR Codes are an astonishingly robust technology to be able to withstand such an onslaught of design.

5.2 Generating 2D barcodes

iOS 7 introduced generators for the three 2D barcode types supported in Passbook. Of these, only the generator for QR Codes is a public API that you can use in App Store apps. The other two—Aztec and PDF417—work just as well, but they're undocumented and thus considered private. I know this because I emailed the responsible frameworks evangelist at Apple.

But let's not hang our heads in sadness over this. Of the bunch, QR Codes are by far the most widely used and most versatile. QR Codes can be used to represent any kind of data, but their most prevalent use is for containing a website address.

You probably have a stack of printed business cards that—unfortunately—lack a scannable QR Code with your website address. How much more convenient would it be if recipients of your cards could open your home page by simply scanning your card?

Manually copying a URL from a business card into your browser's address bar is *so* last century.

5.2.1 Building a QR Code Builder app

Let's build an app to fix your business cards. You'll configure and preview a QR Code for your home page on the iOS device screen. You probably have many business cards that need to be QR-enhanced, so we'll focus on printing an entire sheet of identical QR Code stickers that you can stick on the blank backs of your cards.

The QR Code Builder app will have the following features:

- The user can enter a website URL into a text field.
- The app will generate a QR Code as the characters are input and display a live preview.
- The user can adjust the error-correction level with a slider.
- The user can copy the image to the pasteboard with a long-press gesture.
- The app will print the configured QR Code to a sheet of stickers.

The finished QR Code Builder app will look like figure 5.3.

5.2.2 Introducing Core Image

At their core, images consist of colored pixels. Depending on the color space, they might have different numbers of "channels," most commonly red, green, blue, and alpha. Usually one byte is used per channel. The size in bytes for such a bitmapped image is calculated as `width x height x bytes_per_channel x number_of_channels`.

Core Graphics—a.k.a. Quartz—represents such bitmapped images as `CGImage` instances. The Core Graphics framework is written in pure C, meaning that it's impossible to use `CGImage` instances directly with UIKit. Apple created `UIImage` as an Objective-C wrapper class around `CGImage` to bridge the gap. `UIImage` instances usually carry a `CGImage` in their belly that contains the actual image data.

Figure 5.3 Finished QR Code Builder app with printed output

When manipulating images in UIKit or Quartz, you never get the benefit of the GPU. That's why Apple created *Core Image* as a framework for manipulating images in real time with the full benefit of hardware acceleration by the graphics processor.

In Core Image you don't deal with individual pixels but rather with *manipulation steps*. Each such step, represented by a `CIFilter`, is a recipe for manipulating images represented by `CIImage` instances. If you chain multiple manipulation steps, Core Image compiles those down to a single GPU program, called a *shader*. When you request the final output of such a filter chain, the initial input is loaded on the GPU, the compiled shader is run, and you receive the resulting output. Figure 5.4 shows a `CGImage` being turned into a `CIImage`, the chained filters doing their work on that, and a new `CGImage` being created via a `CIContext`.

`CIImage` instances can be created from a wide variety of sources. Static images will usually come from `CGImage` instances. You can also pass `CVPixelBuffer` instances if you want to handle live video coming from an `AVCaptureDevice` (see chapter 2).

Most Core Image filters have an `inputImage` parameter for supplying the source image. One category of Core Image filters—the so-called *generators*—don't, because they themselves are able to generate images. Generators can serve as input for other filters,

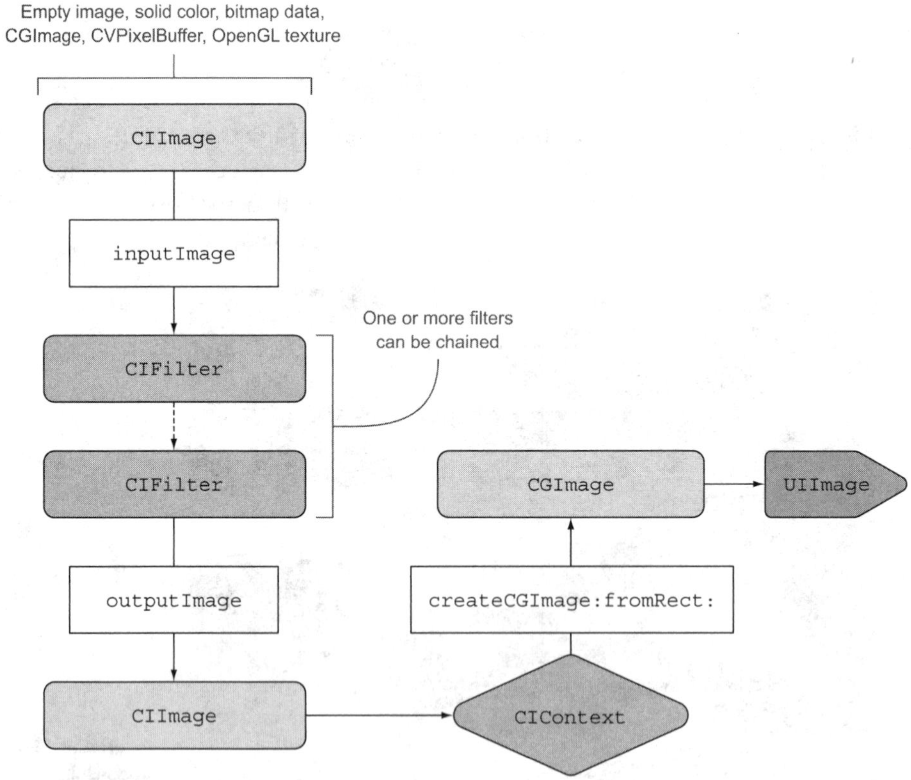

Figure 5.4 Core Image filter chain

or you can simply poll their output. For example, you can use `CIConstantColorGenerator` for creating images consisting of a single solid color or `CICheckerboardGenerator` for creating an image with a checkerboard pattern.

Let's try out a simple Core Image generator by creating an 8 x 8 checkerboard suitable for display with a `UIImageView`. Note the use of `CIColor` for specifying colors and `CIVector` for specifying an x-y offset. Those are the typical immutable parameter objects used by Core Image. Values are specified as `NSNumber` objects:

```
CGFloat scale = [UIScreen mainScreen].scale;

CGRect bounds = self.imageView.bounds;
bounds.size.width *= scale;
bounds.size.height *= scale;

CGFloat oneSquareWidth = bounds.size.width/8.0;
CIColor *darkColor = [CIColor colorWithRed:0 green:0 blue:0];
CIColor *lightColor = [CIColor colorWithRed:0.9 green:0.9 blue:0.9];
CIVector *originOffset = [CIVector vectorWithCGPoint:CGPointZero];

CIFilter *filter = [CIFilter filterWithName:@"CICheckerboardGenerator"];
[filter setValue:@(oneSquareWidth) forKey:kCIInputWidthKey];
[filter setValue:originOffset forKey:kCIInputCenterKey];
[filter setValue:darkColor forKey:@"inputColor0"];
[filter setValue:lightColor forKey:@"inputColor1"];

CIContext *context = [CIContext contextWithOptions:nil];
CGImageRef cgImage = [context createCGImage:filter.outputImage
                                   fromRect:bounds];
UIImage *image = [UIImage imageWithCGImage:cgImage
                                     scale:scale
                               orientation:UIImageOrientationUp];
CGImageRelease(cgImage);

self.imageView.image = image;
```

Get content scale from main device screen

Scale checkerboard bounds accordingly (Core Image works with actual pixels)

Prepare filter parameters

Create generator and set parameters

Plain Core Image context is sufficient

Render Quartz image via the context

Wrap Quartz image into a UIKit image object, setting the scale

Creation method returns a +1 reference, so you need to release the Quartz image

Generators output `CIImage` instances via their `outputImage` method. To use one with UIKit, you need to render it into a `CGImage` by means of a `CIContext`. As you can see in the preceding example, Core Image doesn't have any knowledge of the device's content scale, which would be 2 for Retina displays. Because of this, you need to double the size of the generated image and then specify this scale in the method that makes a `UIImage` out of the `CGImage`.

This should give you enough information about the general workings of Core Image generators. You'll be using the specialized Core Image filters that generate 2D barcodes next.

Barcode scanning in Core Image

In iOS 8, Core Image's `CIDetector` gained the ability to scan rectangles and QR Codes. Up until iOS 7, it could only be used to detect faces. Core Image is designed to work with static images, so this is more of a novelty than of practical use for barcode scanning. It would be frustrating for users to have to retake pictures until they finally detect a barcode.

5.2.3 Project setup for Core Image

Now that you understand the basics of Core Image, let's take advantage of this knowledge and implement the QR Code Builder app for producing QR Codes.

Start a new Xcode project from the Single View Application template. As you can see in figure 5.5, I named the sample app *QRBuilder*. Add the `CoreImage.framework` to the app target's Link Binary With Libraries build phase, as shown in figure 5.5.

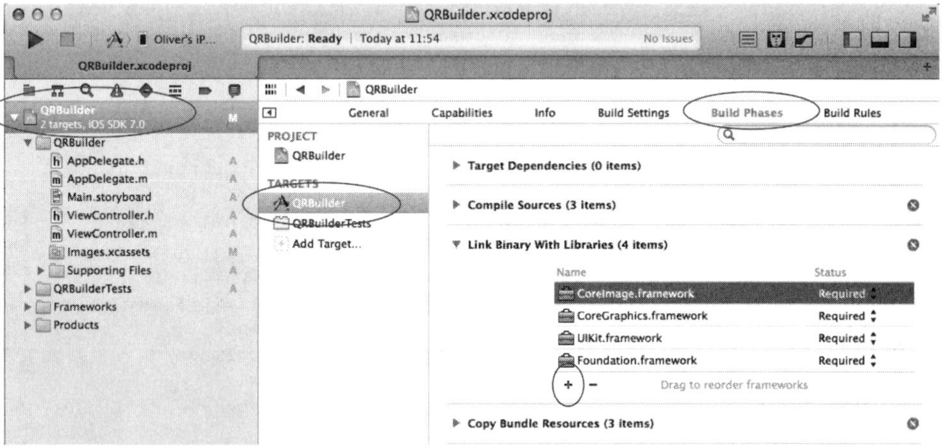

Figure 5.5 Link app with Core Image

To add the corresponding import to the prefix header file and make Core Image available throughout the app, put the following into your QRBuilder-Prefix.pch file:

```
#ifdef __OBJC__
   #import <UIKit/UIKit.h>
   #import <Foundation/Foundation.h>
   #import <CoreImage/CoreImage.h>
#endif
```

Framework autolinking

The LLVM compiler is able to automatically link most common system frameworks without you having to link or import anything. The Link Frameworks Automatically build setting is enabled by default for new projects.

(continued)
Any iOS app includes UIKit, and its UIImage.h header references Core Image, so you don't need to manually import the header. This is also why the autolinking feature can add Core Image for you. Nevertheless, it's good to know what's going on behind the scenes and how to include frameworks manually if necessary.

For the basic UI of the QR Code Builder app, you'll need to add the following items to the storyboard, with the standard spacing suggested by Interface Builder:

- Add a `UIImageView` sized 160 x 160 points to the top left of the view, and set the view mode to Center. This will display the QR Code preview.
- Add a `UISlider` below it. Use the inspector to configure the minimum value as `0`, the maximum value as `3`, and the current value as `0`. This will allow users to set the error-correction level.
- Add a `UITextField` below that, and add placeholder text to show that users will enter a URL here. Set the URL keyboard type and disable autocorrection. This is where users will enter the QR Code contents.

Figure 5.6 shows these three UI controls making up the user interface. You can also configure the autolayout constraints so that elements stretch together with the view. All elements are positioned such that, if the keyboard shows, they remain visible.

Create three outlets in ViewController.h to connect to the three UI elements you just added to the storyboard by Ctrl-dragging them from Interface builder onto the

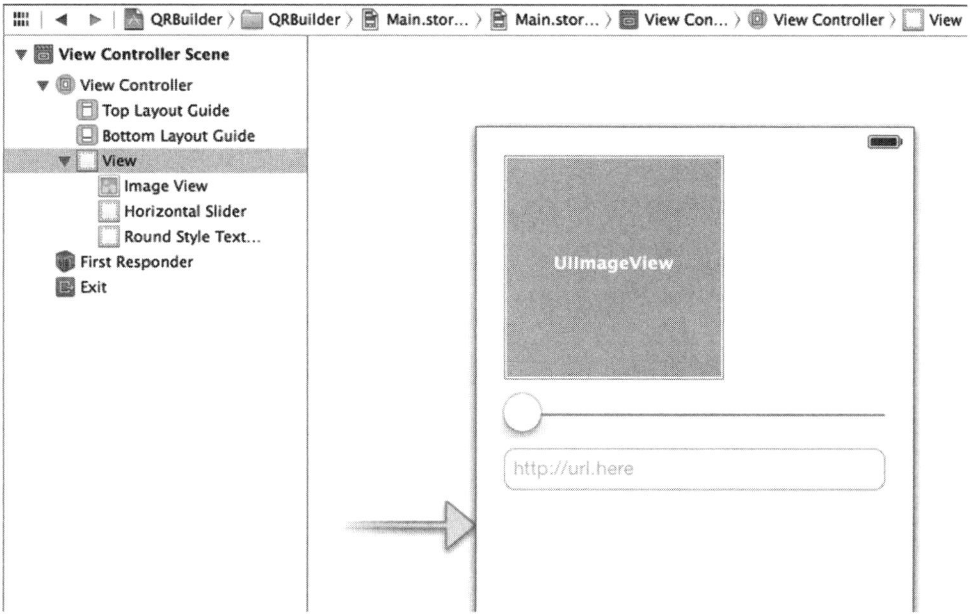

Figure 5.6 Set up the basic user interface.

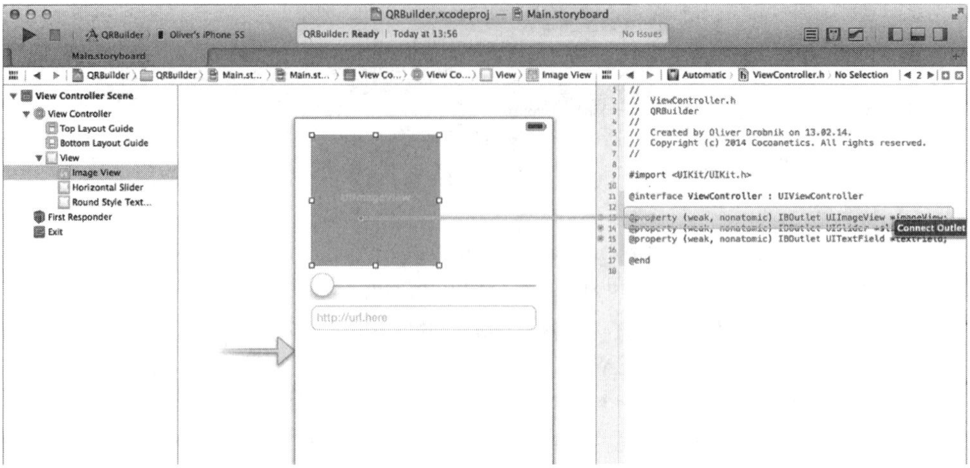

Figure 5.7 Ctrl-drag to create and connect outlets.

Assistant Editor view showing the view controller's header file (see figure 5.7). These new outlet properties will allow you to interact with these elements from inside the view controller's implementation.

With the same Ctrl-drag technique, add and connect an `IBAction` for the slider's Value Changed action and another `IBAction` for the text field's Editing Change action in ViewController.m (see figure 5.8). Those fire every time there's a change in the slider's position or text is entered into the text field.

This concludes the basic app setup. These controls will give you the input values for generating your QR Code.

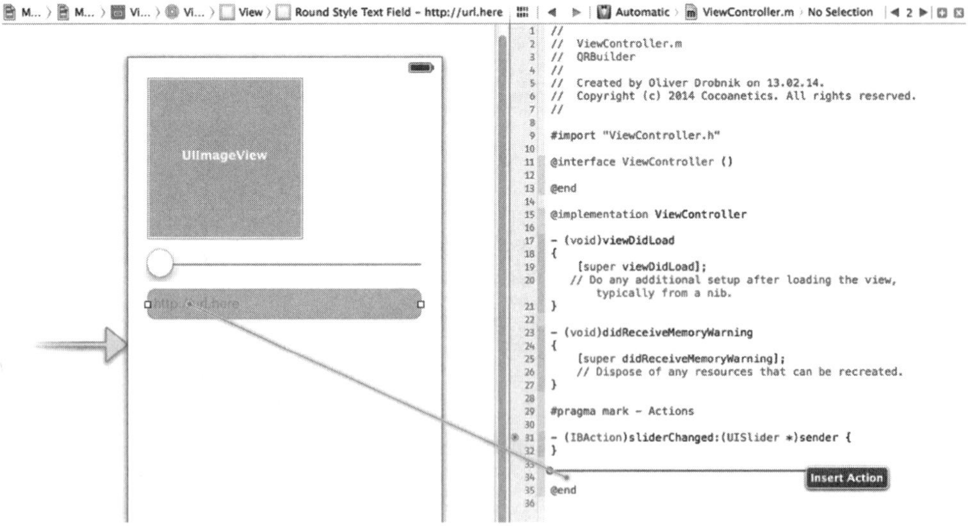

Figure 5.8 Ctrl-drag to create and connect actions.

5.2.4 Generating QR Codes with Core Image

The Core Image generator for producing QR Codes is CIQRCodeGenerator. You create the generator object, set the contents in the inputMessage parameter, and retrieve the CIImage from the outputImage property:

```
NSString *text = @"A message";
NSData *data = [text dataUsingEncoding:NSUTF8StringEncoding];
CIFilter *code = [CIFilter filterWithName:@"CIQRCodeGenerator"];
[code setValue:data forKey:@"inputMessage"];
[code setValue:@"H" forKey:@"inputCorrectionLevel"];
CIImage *output = code.outputImage;
```

Convert the barcode message to UTF-8 data.

Create the QR Code generator.

Set the data as a parameter.

Set the error-correction level; defaults to "M" if omitted.

Retrieve the generated output image.

The inputCorrectionLevel parameter specifies the error-correction level for output QR Codes. If you omit this parameter, the generator defaults to the 15% level (*M*). All the error-correction levels mentioned in section 5.1.2 are available for this parameter.

The CIImage that comes out of the generator is not yet usable with UIKit. It first needs to be rendered and scaled.

SCALING QR CODES

The generator creates an image with a module size of 1 pixel. There's no parameter to increase the module size coming out of CIQRCodeGenerator, so you need to scale those tiny QR Codes to a more useful size.

A CIImage isn't a finished image but rather a recipe that's executed when you render the image into some context. There's a method to make a UIImage from a CIImage, but if you set this on a UIImageView, you'll find that it gets blurry as it's scaled up. iOS gives you no control over the interpolation that happens in the Core Image filter chain.

The best way around this limitation is to render the CIImage into a CGImage of same size first. Then you can scale the resulting CGImage and disable interpolation on the CGContext. The following convenience method does that for you:

```
- (UIImage *)_scaledImageFromCIImage:(CIImage *)image
                           withScale:(CGFloat)scale {
   CIContext *ciContext = [CIContext contextWithOptions:nil];
   CGImageRef cgImage = [ciContext createCGImage:image
                                         fromRect:image.extent];
   CGSize size = CGSizeMake(image.extent.size.width * scale,
                            image.extent.size.height * scale);
   UIGraphicsBeginImageContextWithOptions(size, YES, 0);
   CGContextRef context = UIGraphicsGetCurrentContext();
```

Create Core Image context

Create CGImage by rendering the CIImage into the CIContext

Calculate scaled-up size

Begin new image context, opaque and with automatic content scale

Retrieve CGContext for drawing with Quartz

```
   CGContextSetInterpolationQuality(context, kCGInterpolationNone);   <-- Disable interpolation
   CGAffineTransform flip = CGAffineTransformMake(1, 0, 0, -1, 0,      <-- Flip coordinates so that upper
                                                  size.height);            side of QR Code has two boxes
   CGContextConcatCTM(context, flip);
   CGRect bounds = CGContextGetClipBoundingBox(context);   <-- Get current drawing bounds
   CGContextDrawImage(context, bounds, cgImage);   <-- Draw temporary CGImage into the new context
   UIImage *scaledImage = UIGraphicsGetImageFromCurrentImageContext();   <-- Retrieve UIImage from image context
   UIGraphicsEndImageContext();   <-- Release image context
   CGImageRelease(cgImage);   <-- Release temporary CGImage
   return scaledImage;
}
```

HOOKING UP THE INTERACTIVE CONTROLS

The preceding method goes into ViewController.m, together with the code shown next, which updates the QR Code preview on several occasions—when the view is first shown and whenever the slider is moved or the text field contents are changed:

```
@implementation ViewController

- (void)viewDidLoad {
   [super viewDidLoad];
   [self _updateBarcodePreview];   <-- Update QR Code with initial content
}

- (void)_updateBarcodePreview {
   NSString *text = self.textField.text;
   NSData *data = [text dataUsingEncoding:NSUTF8StringEncoding];
   CIFilter *code = [CIFilter filterWithName:@"CIQRCodeGenerator"];
   [code setValue:data forKey:@"inputMessage"];

   NSUInteger errorCorrLevel = roundf(self.slider.value);
   switch (errorCorrLevel) {   <-- Set error-correction level based on slider position
      case 0:
         [code setValue:@"L"
                 forKey:@"inputCorrectionLevel"];
         break;
      default:
         [code setValue:@"M"
                 forKey:@"inputCorrectionLevel"];
         break;
      case 2:
         [code setValue:@"Q"
                 forKey:@"inputCorrectionLevel"];
         break;
      case 3:
         [code setValue:@"H"
                 forKey:@"inputCorrectionLevel"];
         break;
   }
```

```
    CGSize originalSize = code.outputImage.extent.size;
    CGSize maxSize = self.imageView.bounds.size;
    NSInteger scale = truncf(MIN(maxSize.width/originalSize.width,
                            maxSize.height/originalSize.height));
    UIImage *scaledImage = [self _scaledImageFromCIImage:code.outputImage
                                               withScale:scale];
    self.imageView.image = scaledImage;
}

- (IBAction)sliderChanged:(UISlider *)sender {
   [self _updateBarcodePreview];
}

- (IBAction)textFieldChanged:(UITextField *)sender {
   [self _updateBarcodePreview];
}

@end
```

Find a scale factor that fits in image view bounds

Update QR Code when slider is moved

Update QR Code for changes to text field

Launch the app now and enter a web address in the text field. If you move the slider from left to right, you'll see the generator adding additional complexity to the preview image. This is the additional redundancy for the higher error correction.

5.2.5 Copying the QR Code to the pasteboard

Generating and previewing the QR Code is nice, but if you can't get the code out of the app, it gets old quickly. We'll add the ability to long-press the preview image to copy it to the device pasteboard. This way the user can configure a QR Code and then copy/paste it into another app.

Create a subclass of `UIImageView` named `DTBarcodeImageView` with the following implementation:

```
@implementation DTBarcodeImageView

- (instancetype)initWithFrame:(CGRect)frame {
   self = [super initWithFrame:frame];
   if (self) {
      [self _commonSetup];
   }
   return self;
}

- (void)awakeFromNib {
   [self _commonSetup];
}
```

```
- (void)_commonSetup {
  UILongPressGestureRecognizer *longPress =
  [[UILongPressGestureRecognizer alloc] initWithTarget:self
                                  action:@selector(handleLongPress:)];
  [self addGestureRecognizer:longPress];
  self.userInteractionEnabled = YES;
}

- (BOOL)_hasBarcodeSet {
  if (self.image) {
     return YES;
  }
  return NO;
}

- (BOOL)canBecomeFirstResponder {
  return [self _hasBarcodeSet];
}

- (BOOL)canPerformAction:(SEL)action withSender:(id)sender {
  if (action == @selector(copy:)) {
     return [self _hasBarcodeSet];
  }
  return [super canPerformAction:action withSender:sender];
}

- (void)copy:(id)sender {
  [[UIPasteboard generalPasteboard] setImage:self.image];
}

- (void)handleLongPress:(UILongPressGestureRecognizer *)gesture {
  if (gesture.state == UIGestureRecognizerStateBegan) {
     if (![self _hasBarcodeSet]) {
        return;
     }
     [self becomeFirstResponder];
     UIMenuController *menu =
         [UIMenuController sharedMenuController];
     [menu setTargetRect:self.bounds inView:self];
     [menu setArrowDirection:UIMenuControllerArrowLeft];
     [menu setMenuVisible:YES animated:YES];
  }
}

@end
```

Install long-press gesture recognizer

Enable user interaction; image views have this disabled by default

Convenience method to determine if an image is set

Can only become first responder if there is image content

Determine if Copy context menu action should be possible

Put current image contents into the global pasteboard

Ignore long-press if there's no image set

Becoming first responder makes iOS show context menu on next run loop

Configure context menu

In Interface Builder (see figure 5.8), change the class name for the image view to DTBarcodeImageView. No other changes are necessary.

If you push down on the image view (see figure 5.9), the context menu appears, offering a friendly Copy option. Click on it to copy the barcode image to the pasteboard. To verify that this worked, switch to any other app that lets you paste images, such as the Mail app when you begin a new email. Pasting there from the pasteboard should reveal the same barcode you configured in your QR Code Builder app.

Figure 5.9 QR Code Builder app showing Copy menu

At this point, the image copied to the pasteboard is the same as the one displayed in the image view. For some use cases you might find it desirable to put a larger-scale barcode image on the pasteboard. To do this you'd have to hold onto the `CIImage` coming out of the Core Image generator and then produce a larger-scale image for this purpose. You shouldn't have any trouble implementing this on your own.

5.2.6 *Private APIs for Aztec and PDF417 codes*

If you want to be bold and experiment with creating the two private types shown in figure 5.10, you can. You only have to replace `CIQRCodeGenerator` with `CIAztecCodeGenerator` or `CIPDF417BarcodeGenerator` in the ViewController.m QRCode view preview update. Remove the `inputCorrection` parameter, because this isn't supported for these codes.

For apps that you plan to put on the App Store, you have to stick to the public `CIQRCodeGenerator`. Enterprise apps, on the other hand, can make use of these private barcode types because they don't have to be approved by the app review team.

I have a strong feeling that Apple will make these public as soon as it's convenient for them. You can help them along with their decision by sending them an enhancement

`CIQRCodeGenerator` `CIPDF417BarcodeGenerator` `CIAztecCodeGenerator`

Figure 5.10 One public and two private 2D barcode generators

request. If you find a strong use case in an enterprise scenario, be sure to mention this to Apple.

NOTE In iOS 8, Apple added a Core Image generator for Code 128, `CICode128BarcodeGenerator`. Until Apple adds documentation for it, you should also consider it a private API.

5.2.7 *Printing barcodes with AirPrint*

Displaying your QR Code on the device's screen is a nice first step, but printing it on something physical can make it much more useful. This section will show you how to print a grid of QR Codes on a sheet of paper or stickers.

> **No more printer drivers**
>
> The big idea behind AirPrint is that it eliminates the need for printer drivers altogether. Any iOS device and any modern Mac are able to print to any AirPrint-enabled printer. Even though the prefix "Air" suggests something wireless, the AirPrint protocol works just as well over an Ethernet connection.
>
> Printer companies are able to license AirPrint for zero cost. There's no better deal than *free*, and this is why most printer vendors are adding it to their new models. Often AirPrint can also be added by means of a free firmware update.
>
> Apple maintains a list of all certified printer models in their knowledge base (http://support.apple.com/kb/HT4356). Those models have gone through a testing procedure to ensure that the AirPrint protocol has been implemented correctly.

There are two main ways that allow the user to pick a printer and options: `UIPrintInteractionController` and `UIActivityViewController`. The former takes the user straight to the print options. The latter displays the Print button next to other activities like copying or sharing the item over social networks.

If you choose the Print button on an activity view controller, iOS will also present the print options from the print interaction controller. Think of the activity view as an extra option allowing the user to perform other activities besides printing on a selected item.

Of these, `UIPrintInteractionController` is the simpler view controller—you always use the shared instance you get from the `+sharedPrintController` method. When you use this controller, you need to specify what to print. There are four ways to do that, as shown in figure 5.11.

iOS is able to do a good job of representing most common file types on paper. You can simply pass one `printItem` or an array of `printItems` to iOS and have the operating system take care of the layout and drawing. Let's try this first.

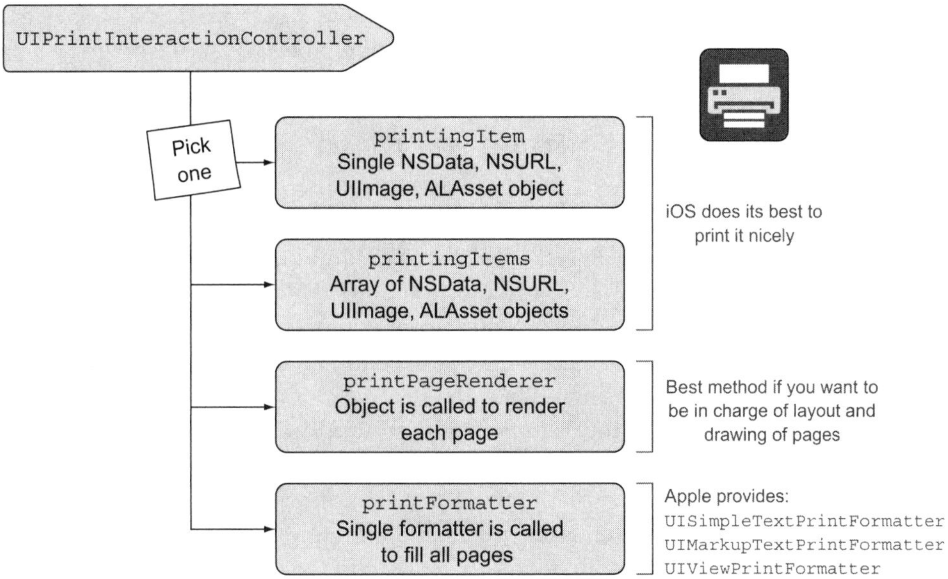

Figure 5.11 Four ways to specify what to print

With Interface Builder, add a new Print button to the right of the QR Code preview. Connect that to a new `print:` action in ViewController.m:

```
- (IBAction)print:(id)sender {
    UIPrintInfo *printInfo = [UIPrintInfo printInfo];
    printInfo.outputType = UIPrintInfoOutputGrayscale;
    printInfo.jobName = @"QR Codes";
    printInfo.duplex = UIPrintInfoDuplexNone;

    UIPrintInteractionController *printController =
       [UIPrintInteractionController sharedPrintController];
    printController.printInfo = printInfo;
    printController.showsPageRange = NO;
    printController.printingItem = self.imageView.image;

    void (^completionHandler)(UIPrintInteractionController *,
                              BOOL, NSError *) =
      ^(UIPrintInteractionController *printController,
        BOOL completed, NSError *error) {
      if (!completed && error) {
        NSLog(@"FAILED! Error in domain %@ with code %ld",
              error.domain, (long)error.code);
      }
    };

    [printController presentAnimated:YES
                   completionHandler:completionHandler];
}
```

Create printInfo object to take on hints for AirPrint

Grayscale is good enough for QR Code

Set a job name for user's benefit (the default is the app name)

No duplex printing necessary for a single item

Get shared print interaction controller

No range selection necessary for a single item

Set current preview image as the print item

Completion handler logs an error if there was a problem

Show print interaction controller

You should give AirPrint some hints about what you're trying to do by specifying properties in a `UIPrintInfo` object as needed. This enables iOS to select the best paper and optimal color settings for your print job.

5.2.8 *Saving trees with the iOS Printer Simulator*

Apple provides a Printer Simulator app that prints to PDF, allowing you to test how your code will print without wasting any trees. It's included in the Hardware IO Tools for Xcode package available on the Apple developer downloads portal (https://developer.apple.com/downloads/index.action). You can launch it via the Xcode > Open Developer Tool > Printer Simulator menu option. As long as the Printer Simulator is running on any Mac in your WiFi network, all the simulated printers will be visible to any simulated or physical iOS device.

Figure 5.12 shows the Printer Simulator app in use. The yellow border you see around printed pages marks the nonprintable area that printers typically have. This example came out somewhat blurry because of the small preview image being scaled up to the page size. In real life you'd send a higher-resolution image or create a custom page renderer, as we'll do in the next section.

Figure 5.12 Simulated sample app printing to simulated inkjet printer

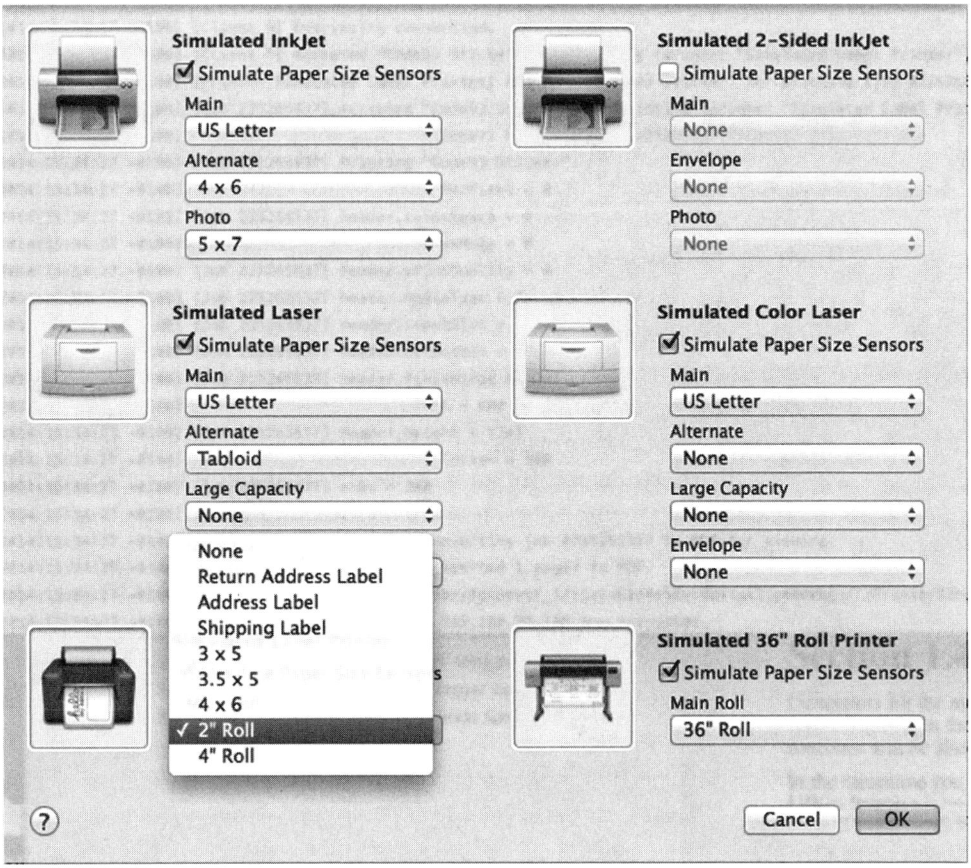

Figure 5.13 Simulated media options in iOS Printer Simulator

Various kinds of printers are available for testing printing, as you can see in figure 5.13. You can also "load" different kinds of simulated printing media into the simulated printers by clicking on the Load Paper toolbar button.

The simulated label printer in the bottom left of figure 5.13 will be important in the second half of this chapter, where you'll be printing individual labels. For label printers, the 2" Roll and 4" Roll options simulate endless rolls where the cut length is relevant. The other options simulate precut stickers.

The iOS Printer Simulator is a great tool that lets you try out many different combinations of printers and output media. Nevertheless, I advise you to try printing on a physical printer before you ship an AirPrint-enabled app to the App Store.

5.2.9 *Custom drawing with UIPrintPageRenderer*

Apple provides several specialized subclasses of `UIPrintFormatter` for laying out simple text, attributed strings, and views. We won't be looking at those because our ultimate goal is to print a grid of QR Codes.

To render a sheet of QR Codes, we'll create a specialized page renderer that determines how many pages there are and how to render each page for a given index. Although `UIPrintFormatter` is a public API, Apple discourages developers from subclassing `UIPrintFormatter` themselves. Instead, you should customize a `UIPrintPageRenderer` for custom printing. Pages can either be completely custom-drawn or you can specify print formatters to be used if you want to mix custom-drawing with pages containing only text.

There are four relevant rectangles on each page:

- `paperRect` always has a (0,0) origin and specifies the media size for the sheet of paper being printed on.
- `printableRect` specifies the actual area on the page that the printer is physically able to print on.
- `headerHeight` and `footerHeight` specify the heights of the header and footer respectively. By default, these heights are set to zero, but if you set them to a greater value, their custom drawing methods are called.

Figure 5.14 shows where these rectangles are located on a piece of print media.

All previously mentioned rectangles are measured in *points*, and 1 point equals 1/72 of an inch. You can calculate the number of points in a print of a given size by multiplying

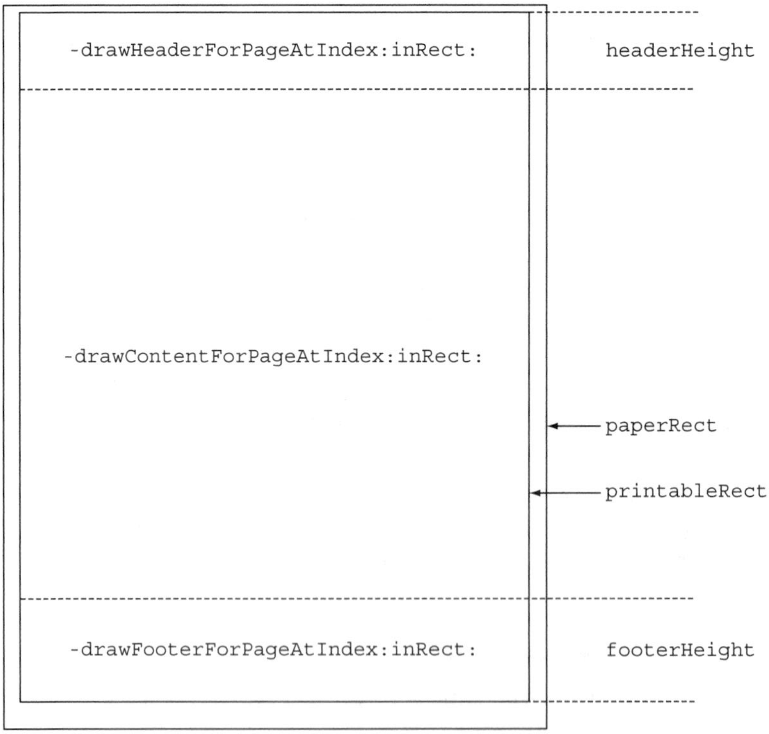

Figure 5.14 `UIPrintPageRenderer` methods and properties

the print size in inches by 72. If you're using centimeters, multiply the size in centimeters by 72 and then divide the result by 2.54. Here are two preprocessor macros to simplify the math for you:

```
#define IN_TO_POINTS(in) in*72.0
#define CM_TO_POINTS(cm) cm*72.0/2.54
```

For this example, we don't care about the header or footer so we won't set a height for either. To further simplify the example, we'll assume fixed label sizes. You'll position the labels relative to the `paperRect`'s origin (top left). You'll likely need to adjust the following measurements to fit your own sticker sheets:

```
#define MARGIN_TOP_CM 1.0
#define MARGIN_LEFT_CM 1.0
#define LABEL_WIDTH_CM 1.5
#define LABEL_HEIGHT_CM 1.5
#define MARGIN_AROUND_IMAGE_CM 0.125
```

With these measurements defined, you can implement the method for drawing the page content in `QRCodeSheetRenderer` as follows:

```
- (void)drawContentForPageAtIndex:(NSInteger)pageIndex
                           inRect:(CGRect)contentRect {
  CGRect labelRect = CGRectMake(CM_TO_POINTS(MARGIN_LEFT_CM),
                                CM_TO_POINTS(MARGIN_TOP_CM),
                                CM_TO_POINTS(LABEL_WIDTH_CM),
                                CM_TO_POINTS(LABEL_HEIGHT_CM));
  while (1) {
    [self drawLabelInRect:labelRect];
    labelRect.origin.x += CM_TO_POINTS(LABEL_WIDTH_CM);
    if (CGRectGetMaxX(labelRect)>=CGRectGetMaxX(contentRect)) {
      labelRect.origin.x = CM_TO_POINTS(MARGIN_LEFT_CM);
      labelRect.origin.y += CM_TO_POINTS(LABEL_HEIGHT_CM);
      if (CGRectGetMaxY(labelRect)>=CGRectGetMaxY(contentRect)) {
        break;
      }
    }
  }
}
```

First label is at top left of sheet

Go to label to the right of the current one

Draw label in the calculated rectangle

At end of row, go back to first column and next row

Once printable rect has been filled, you're done

You need something to draw, so let's add an `image` property to the `QRCodeSheet-Renderer` header. You can set this image to be repeated on all stickers:

```
@interface QRCodeSheetRenderer : UIPrintPageRenderer
@property (nonatomic, strong) UIImage *image;
@end
```

Now you can implement the method for drawing individual labels:

```
- (void)drawLabelInRect:(CGRect)labelRect {
  CGContextRef ctx = UIGraphicsGetCurrentContext();
  CGContextSaveGState(ctx);
  CGContextSetInterpolationQuality(ctx, kCGInterpolationNone);
  CGFloat imageMargin = CM_TO_POINTS(MARGIN_AROUND_IMAGE_CM);
  CGRect imageRect = CGRectInset(labelRect, imageMargin, imageMargin);
```

Disable interpolation to get crisp, scaled code modules

Calculate inset rectangle for QR Code image

```
        [self.image drawInRect:imageRect];
        CGContextRestoreGState(ctx);
    }
```

Draw QR Code into the calculated rectangle

As you can see, there's nothing out of the ordinary in the drawing code. You're using the same functions and methods you've always used for drawing the contents of custom views. `UIPrintPageRenderer` takes care of setting up the graphics context to fit the points-based coordinate system on each sheet of print media. You don't have to learn any new functions for drawing on paper.

Compared to a view's `drawRect:`, you can think of the inset printable region as the clipping rectangle. Only what you draw inside of that area will appear on paper. Some printers are able to print photos with no borders, but your code still needs to assume that there will be a margin that can't be reached by your drawing operations.

5.2.10 AirPrint paper selection

By default, AirPrint selects the paper to be used based on the specified `outputType` and device locale. If you specified that you'll be printing photos, the output size defaults to an appropriate small photo size like 4 x 6 inches or A6. The general and grayscale output types default to US-letter or A4 format.

The print interaction controller can have a delegate with a method for inquiring about paper size. Print interaction delegate objects can implement one or more methods of the `UIPrintInteractionControllerDelegate` protocol. The simplest implementation uses a `UIPrintPaper` class method to select an optimal paper from the list of papers the printer provides. The following code snippet informs the print interaction controller that the app would prefer US-letter-sized paper for output. As before, the size is specified in points:

```
- (UIPrintPaper *)printInteractionController:
        (UIPrintInteractionController *)printInteractionController
                              choosePaper:(NSArray *)papers {
   CGSize requiredSize = CGSizeMake(8.5 * 72, 11 * 72);
   return [UIPrintPaper bestPaperForPageSize:requiredSize
                         withPapersFromArray:papers];
}
```

Paper and tray selection through AirPrint is opaque to developers. Newly certified printers are required to have paper sensors so that they can accurately report what kind of media they have loaded. Apple's philosophy with AirPrint is to unburden the user from having to wade through many screens of printer settings. Instead, you—on behalf of the user—make a few assertions about ideal paper size and output type, and AirPrint does the rest.

5.2.11 QR Code Builder app summary

Your QR Code Builder app is now feature-complete, as far as this chapter is concerned. You can configure a QR Code for a web address and then print a sheet of copies.

There are many enhancements you could make to the app, such as encoding a vCard for your business as the code data. You could also implement a view for configuring the positions and sizes of stickers on specific sticker sheets. Such a view would have to be called before showing the print interaction controller, because the print interaction controller triggers the actual printing.

5.3 Generating 1D barcodes

With iOS 7 and 8, Apple only supports the generation of 2D barcodes via Core Image, so I created BarCodeKit to fill this niche until Apple adds 1D barcode generators to the operating system. There's no shortage of application scenarios where you might want to display or print 1D barcodes. One example I've encountered is an app for beer connoisseurs that lets users scan the GTIN barcode on a bottle of beer to track which bottles they have in their collection or have tasted. The app displays the GTIN barcode on the details page for each beer—a crisply rendered barcode looks much nicer than a photo.

Previous sections in this chapter introduced you to AirPrint for getting user-generated content into the physical world. Whereas you'll generally want to print a larger number of identical QR Codes on a sheet of stickers, 1D barcodes are typically serial numbers or product codes that you'll want to print one at a time. This makes their production an ideal use case for the new breed of roll-feed printers. They allow you to output a single sticker from the roll without having to waste an entire sheet of stickers.

Label printers have dropped in price to below $100, which makes them an inexpensive convenience to keep around. Some AirPrint-enabled models, like the Brother QL-710W (see figure 5.15), feature built-in WiFi, which makes it easy to hook them into your wireless network for printing from your iOS devices. In this section you'll learn how to generate 1D barcodes and how to support roll-feed printers over AirPrint.

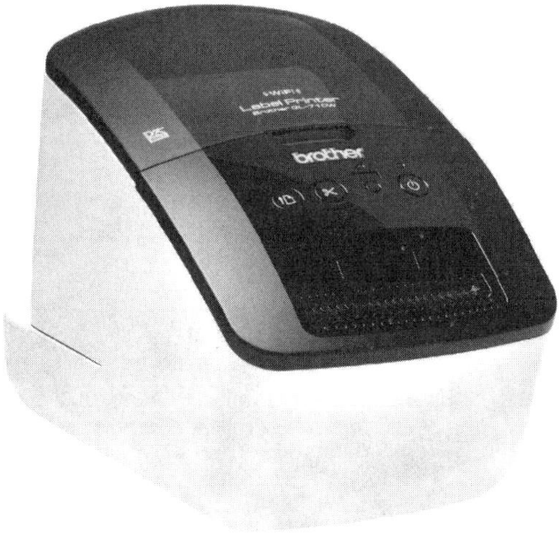

Figure 5.15 Brother QL-710W WiFi label printer

5.3.1 Building a Serial Number Tag app

Imagine that you have an inventory system—like one you'd find in a corporation's IT department—where each computer gets a unique serial number. Those inventory numbers let the system keep track of hardware assigned to individual employees and also keep track of issues afflicting particular machines in the corporation's help-desk software.

The app you'll build next will produce a single serial number barcode sticker to affix to one machine. You want to implement the following features:

- Allow the user to enter a numeric serial number into a text field
- Encode the serial number as a Code 93 barcode
- Show a preview of the serial number sticker on the screen as you type
- Print a single sticker on a roll-feed printer over AirPrint

The finished Serial Number Tag app is shown in figure 5.16.

5.3.2 Introducing BarCodeKit

When I began to research material for this book, I looked for open source projects that would produce 1D barcodes on iOS. Jeff LaMarche created CocoaBarCodes for OS X, which was last updated in May 2009. Chris Zelenak forked the project and implemented basic support for iOS, mostly by commenting out Mac-specific code. This project was abandoned in January 2013.

This prompted me to start a fresh project. My design goals for BarCodeKit were to build it using modern object-oriented methodologies, use ARC, and make sure it was simple to extend. Three volunteers and I gradually enhanced BarCodeKit to support the most commonly used 1D barcode symbologies. Besides all the 1D barcode types that iOS (italic in this list) can scan, many more are supported:

- Codabar
- Code 11
- *Code 39* (plain, modulo 43, full ASCII)
- *Code 93*
- *Code 128*
- Facing Identification Mark (FIM)
- GTIN family: EAN-8, EAN-13, UPC-A, UPC-E, EAN-2, EAN-5
- *Interleaved 2 of 5, ITF-14*
- MSI
- Pharmacode One Track
- Standard 2 of 5

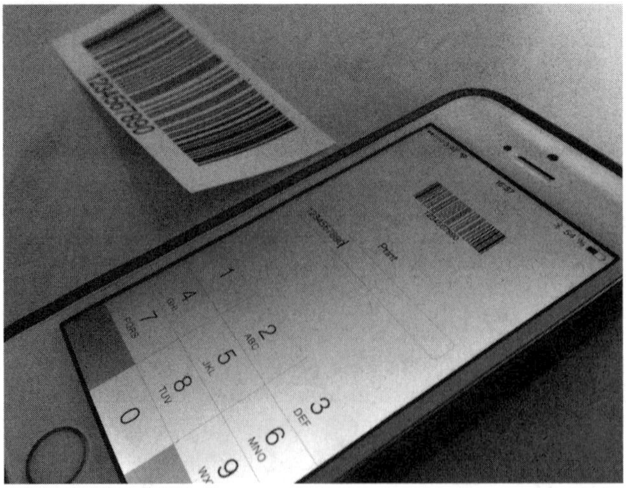

Figure 5.16 Finished Serial Number Tag app with one printed label

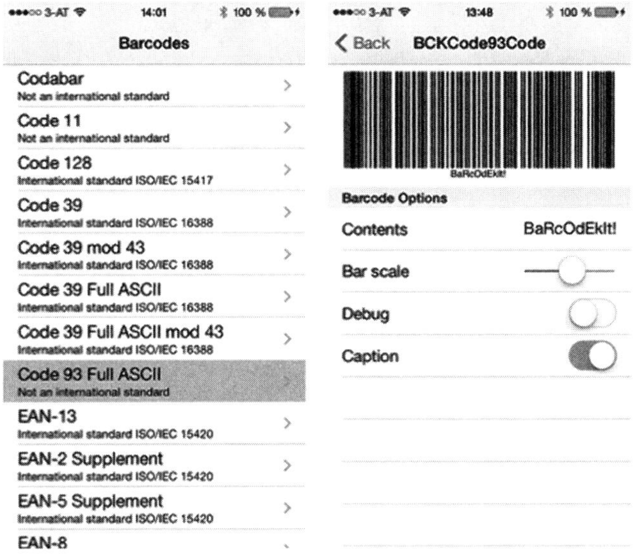

Figure 5.17 BarCodeKit iOS demo app

The BarCodeKit source is included with the other source code for this book (www.manning.com/BarcodeswithiOS). Open the Xcode project and run the iOS demo (shown in figure 5.17) to try out the various barcode types and settings.

To the outside world, BarCodeKit is a *commercial library* that costs €150 to license per developer. But because I want to thank you for reading this book, you get a *free license.* As long as you own a copy of this book, you may use BarCodeKit in all your apps at no charge.

5.3.3 Adding BarCodeKit to your project

To start on the Serial Number Tag app, create a new iOS app project based on the Single View Application, and name it SerialSticker.

The next step is to add BarCodeKit as a dependency to your project and link in its static library target to make its functionality available to your app. Create a new group to take on external references via File > New Group, and name it *Externals.* Drag BarCodeKit.xcodeproj from the BarCodeKit folder in the sample code into this group (see figure 5.18).

When you add a file to a project like this, it won't ask if you want to add a copy of the file or add a reference to it. The default for project files is to add a reference. Project files often have relative references to other resources and source files, so it wouldn't make much sense to add a copy of the xcodeproj to your project, because that would break those relative paths. Dropping the project file reference into your project makes it a *subproject.*

Click on the SerialSticker root in the Xcode project navigator to reveal the targets and build settings in the right pane. In the SerialSticker target, under Build Phases,

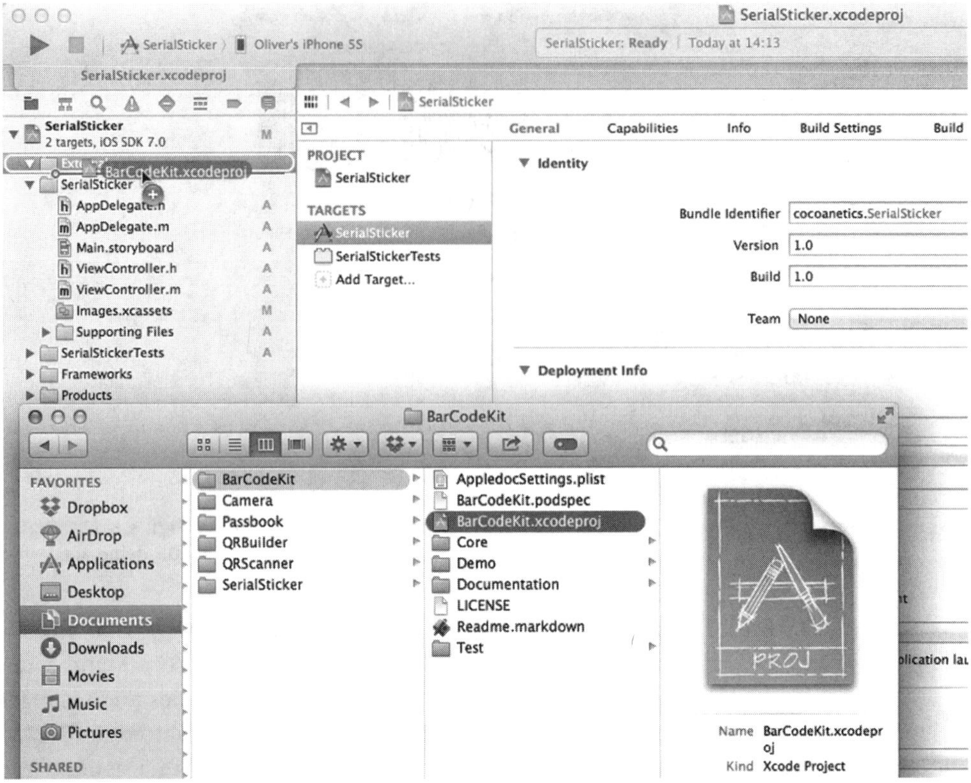

Figure 5.18 Making BarCodeKit a subproject

click on the plus button to reveal possible frameworks and libraries you can link to your app (see figure 5.19). Add the libBarCodeKit.a static library for iOS.

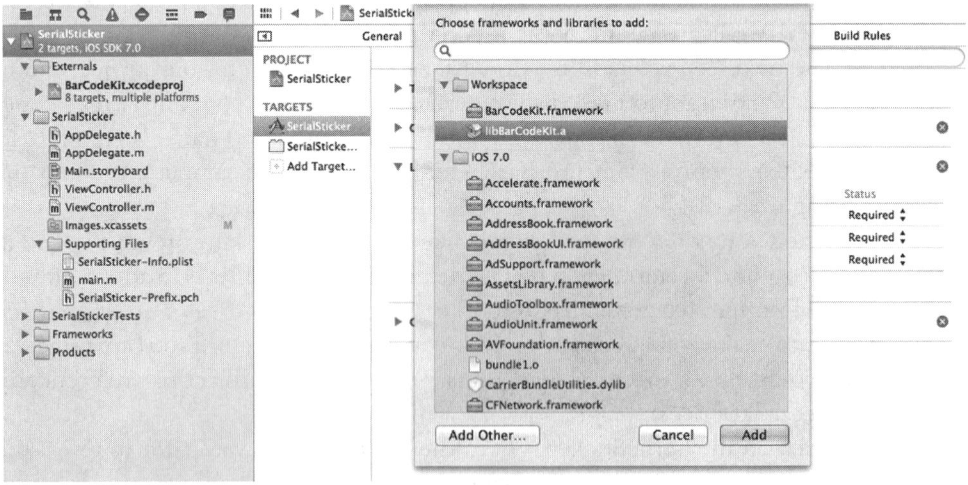

Figure 5.19 Linking with the BarCodeKit library for iOS

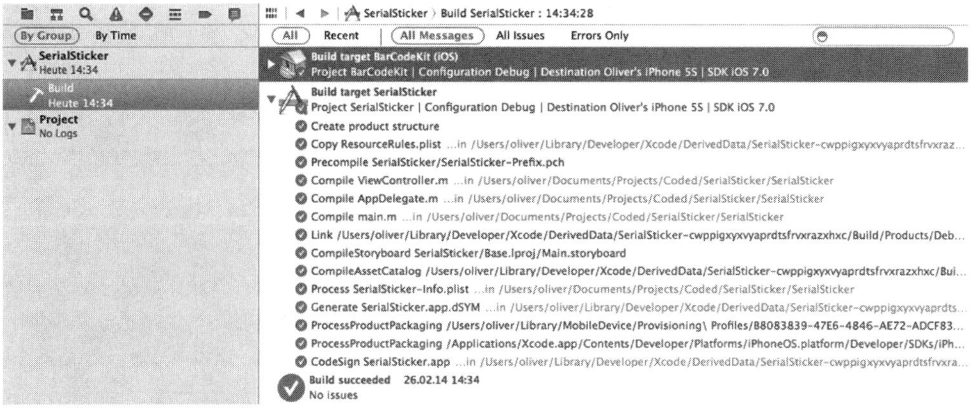

Figure 5.20 Implicit dependency built before app itself

When building your app, Xcode checks to see if all dependencies have been built before building the app itself. From this reference to the iOS static library, the build system knows that it needs to build the product of the subproject first. You can easily verify this by building the app now (Cmd-B). In the build log you'll see that *BarCodeKit (iOS)* gets built first and the SerialSticker target follows suit (see figure 5.20).

Even though you never explicitly specified that the static library would be needed at link time, it still gets built in time. This is why it's called an *implicit dependency*. Xcode infers it. If you wanted to be explicit about this necessity, you could add an *explicit dependency* in the Target Dependencies build phase, but modern Xcode has made this obsolete.

When linking in static libraries containing Objective-C code, you need to give the linker a hint indicating that. The `-ObjC` linker flag does that. Most importantly, this flag enables the linker to also load categories from the static library. Without this setting, the linking build phase would fail because in BarCodeKit there's a category on `UIImage`. The `-ObjC` linker flag is added in the app target's Build Settings tab in the Other Linker Flags line (see figure 5.21).

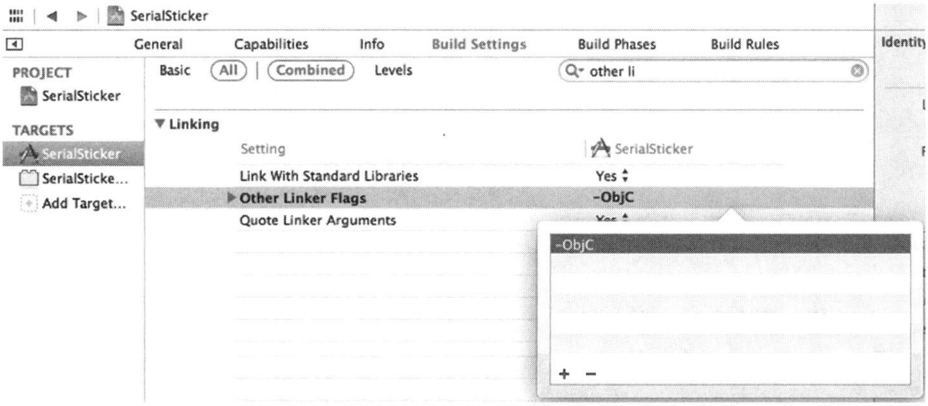

Figure 5.21 Adding the `-ObjC` linker flag

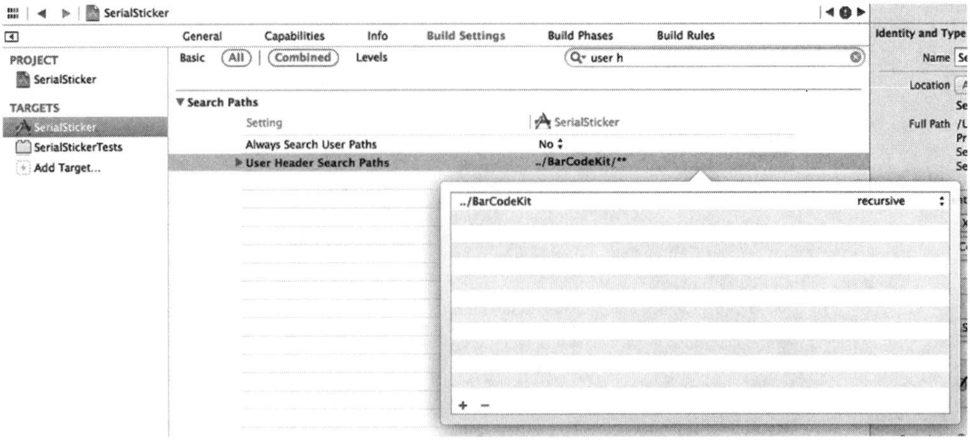

Figure 5.22 Specifying the header search path

You tell Xcode where it can find the BarCodeKit header files by specifying this location in the target's build settings, on the User Header Search Paths line (see figure 5.22). Select the recursive option so that Xcode will look for headers in this folder and all its subfolders.

> **SETTING THE USER HEADER SEARCH PATHS** The User Header Search Paths setting is relative to the location of the app's project file. In the book's sample code, you get to it by going up one folder to the samples root and back down one folder into BarCodeKit. Depending on your project setup, the BarCodeKit sources might be in a different location. Adjust the path accordingly.

I recommend adding imports for larger framework or library headers to the prefix header file because this speeds up compilation and saves you from having to repeat the import in every class you're using it from. Put the following in your SerialSticker-Prefix.pch file:

```
#ifdef __OBJC__
   #import <UIKit/UIKit.h>
   #import <Foundation/Foundation.h>
   #import "BarCodeKit.h"
#endif
```

After these setup steps are complete, you're ready to use BarCodeKit functionality to generate 1D barcodes.

5.3.4 *Setting up the Serial Number Tag app's UI*

Your Serial Number Tag app needs a UI so that you can enter the serial number in a `UITextField`, view a preview in a `UIImageView`, and have a `UIButton` to push for printing the sticker.

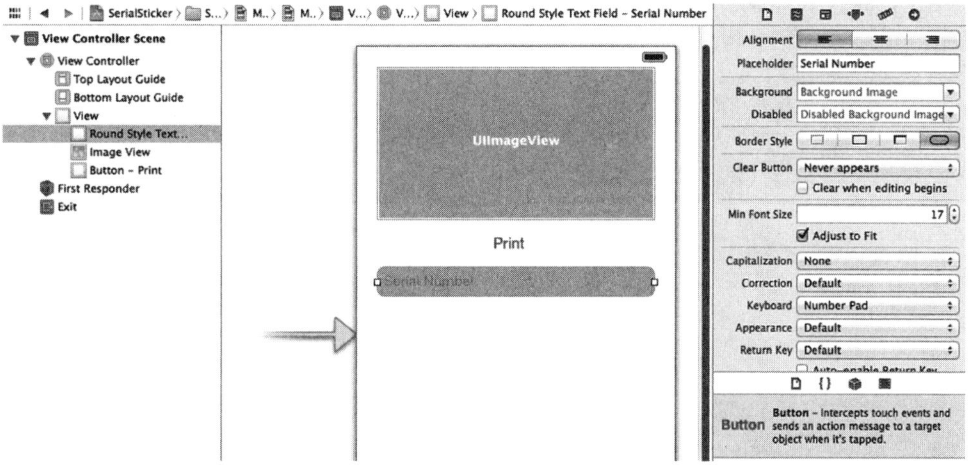

Figure 5.23 Basic UI for the Serial Number Tag app

Position those three UI elements in Interface Builder as shown in figure 5.23. Set the image view's content mode to Center. Set the text field's placeholder, and change the keyboard to the Number Pad option.

You need `IBOutlets` in the ViewController.h header for the field and image views so that you can manipulate them from code. Open the header in Assistant Editor and Ctrl-drag them to the header to make them outlets (see figure 5.24).

Similarly, Ctrl-drag from the button and text fields (see figure 5.25) into the View-Controller.m implementation file to create `IBActions`. The control event type for the button should be *Touch Up Inside*. You want to get all changes for the text field, so pick *Value Changed*.

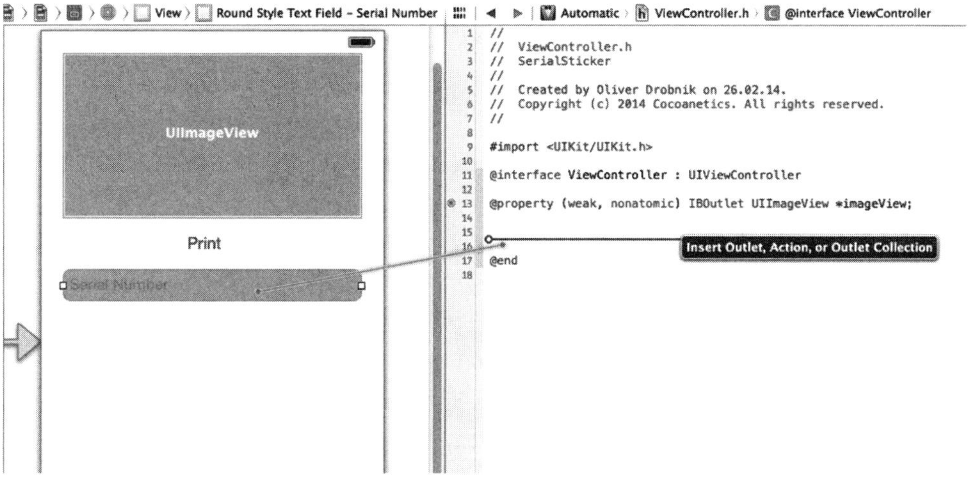

Figure 5.24 Connecting Serial Number Tag app outlets

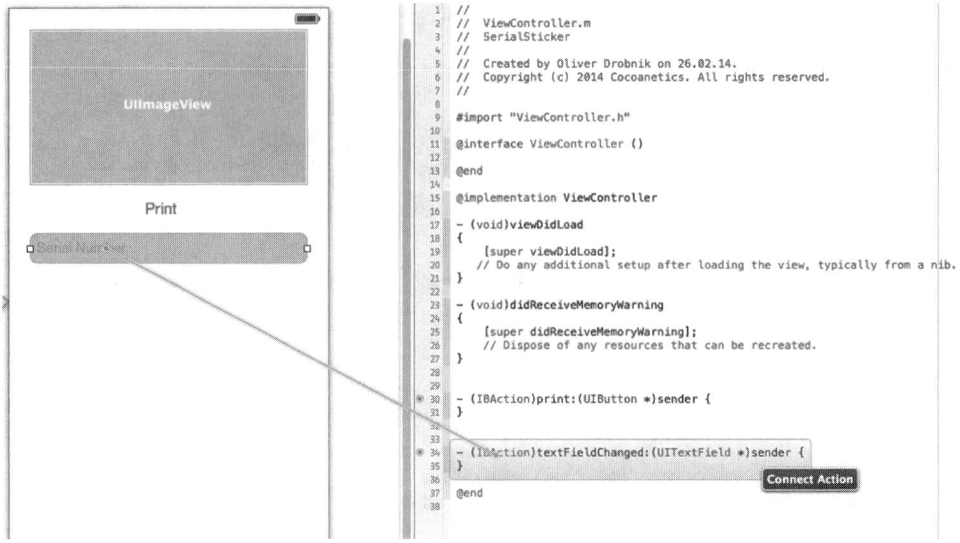

Figure 5.25 Connecting Serial Number Tag app actions

Do a quick test to see if everything is connected correctly by adding two quick NSLog statements, as follows. The editor will show filled bullets to the left of the method prototypes to indicate the connection:

```
- (IBAction)print:(UIButton *)sender {
   NSLog(@"Print pushed");
}

- (IBAction)textFieldChanged:(UITextField *)sender {
   NSLog(@"New value: %@", sender.text);
}
```

If you type in the text field, you should get output after each typed number and a single log entry if you click on the Print button. Now you're ready to start converting the serial number into a barcode.

5.3.5 Generating 1D barcodes with BarCodeKit

Barcodes in BarCodeKit are all concrete subclasses of `BCKCode`. With the previous setup out of the way, you can create a Code 93 from the text field's contents. The following snippets all go into ViewController.m.

Let's start with a convenience method that gets you the current barcode:

```
- (BCKCode *)_currentBarcodeFromTextField {
   NSError *error;
   BCKCode93Code *code = [[BCKCode93Code alloc]
                    initWithContent:self.textField.text
                              error:&error];
```

Create new Code 93 object

```
    if (!code) {
       NSLog(@"%@", [error localizedDescription]);
    }

    return code;
}
```

Log error if the text field contents are invalid for producing a code object

BCKCode doesn't have a built-in graphical representation because it's essentially only a string of bars and spaces. To get an image representation, you use a category method on UIImage that takes an optional dictionary of rendering options. The single most important rendering option is BCKCodeDrawingBarScaleOption, which defaults to 1. This is the number of points representing each barcode module.

Now you can add some code to refresh the barcode preview when the view controller loads the first time and whenever something is typed into the text field:

```
- (void)viewDidLoad {
    [super viewDidLoad];

   self.textField.text = @"1234567890";
   [self _updatePreviewImage];
}

- (void)_updatePreviewImage {
   BCKCode *barcode = [self _currentBarcodeFromTextField];

   if (!barcode) {
      self.imageView.image = nil;
      return;
   }

   NSInteger barScale = BCKCodeMaxBarScaleThatFitsCodeInSize(barcode,
                                          self.imageView.frame.size,
                                                               nil);
   NSDictionary *options = @{BCKCodeDrawingBarScaleOption: @(barScale)};
   UIImage *image = [UIImage imageWithBarCode:barcode options:options];
   self.imageView.image = image;
}

- (IBAction)textFieldChanged:(UITextField *)sender {
   [self _updatePreviewImage];
}
```

Set initial value for text field

Call preview refresh method after view is loaded

Determine maximum bar scale at which the preview image still fits the image view

Remove previous preview image if there was a problem

Create rendering options dictionary

Create image from the barcode using the rendering options

Set generated image on the preview image view

Call preview refresh method after text field is modified

The BCKCodeMaxBarScaleThatFitsCodeInSize convenience function determines the maximum bar scale at which the resulting image will still fit in the specified space. By only using integer values for the bar scale, you ensure that entire pixels are always painted with the bars. Otherwise you'd get anti-aliasing effects, causing the bars to be blurry and possibly even unscannable. This is the same reason you disabled scaling for the preview imageView when setting up the UI in Interface Builder.

At this point you can build and run the sample app. Type in various serial numbers and observe how the preview barcode is updated constantly. You'll also find that you can enter a limited range of nondigit characters. As explained in chapter 1, Code 93 can represent these characters as well.

5.3.6 AirPrint and roll-feed printers

A single serial number barcode should identify a single machine in our imagined inventory system, and it makes no sense to fill an entire sheet of stickers with copies of a single code, as you did for the QR Code Builder app. Rather, this is the perfect use case for specialized sticker printers.

AirPrint has been supporting roll-feed printers since iOS 7. Two kinds of stickers are supported: endless rolls and die cut. The former needs to get info from you as to where to cut between stickers; the latter usually has paper sensors telling you the correct size of the individual precut labels.

In contrast to the QR Code Builder app, which rendered a whole page of stickers, you'll implement a page renderer for the Serial Number Tag app that knows how to render a single sticker. Create a new `BarCodeStickerRenderer` class as a subclass of `UIPrintPageRenderer`. You'll need a property to set the barcode instance and a convenience method that will tell you the cut length if it's an endless label roll:

```
@interface BarCodeStickerRenderer : UIPrintPageRenderer

@property (nonatomic, strong) BCKCode *barcode;

- (CGFloat)cutLengthForRollWidth:(CGFloat)width;

@end
```

Barcode object to be printed is set on this property

Convenience method to determine cut length for the barcode

To determine the cut length, you can use an approach similar to the way you determined the optimal bar scale for the preview:

```
- (NSInteger)numberOfPages {
   return 1;
}

- (CGFloat)cutLengthForRollWidth:(CGFloat)width {
   CGSize fitSize = CGSizeMake(CGFLOAT_MAX, width);
   NSUInteger barScale =
      BCKCodeMaxBarScaleThatFitsCodeInSize(self.barcode,
                                           fitSize,
                                           nil);
   NSDictionary *options = @{BCKCodeDrawingBarScaleOption: @(barScale)};
   CGSize neededSize = [self.barcode sizeWithRenderOptions:options];

   return neededSize.width;
}
```

One sticker on one page

Don't care about width; the roll width becomes the height to fit

Determine maximum bar scale that fits

Determine output size with this scale

Width of the output size is the cut length

You'll call `cutLengthForRollWidth:` later from the view controller.

Now let's add the print rendering of the label to complete the `BarCodeStickerRenderer` class implementation. This print-rendering method will again determine the output size of the barcode because the `cutLengthForRollWidth:` function will only be called if the printer actually requires it.

Even though you might be returning an integer cut length from `cutLengthForRollWidth:`, the stepper motor of the label printer might not be able to reach all values for the cutting operation, so the `paperRect` might have a smaller non-integer value for the width or height. AirPrint reduces the cut-length value to the next smaller reachable value, so you have to round up the value to ensure that you arrive at the same bar scale in the methods shown in the previous and following code snippets:

```
- (void)drawContentForPageAtIndex:(NSInteger)pageIndex
                          inRect:(CGRect)contentRect {
   CGSize fitSize = self.paperRect.size;
   fitSize.width = ceilf(fitSize.width);
   fitSize.height = ceilf(fitSize.height);
   NSUInteger barScale =
      BCKCodeMaxBarScaleThatFitsCodeInSize(self.barcode,
                                           fitSize,
                                           nil);
   NSDictionary *options = @{BCKCodeDrawingBarScaleOption: @(barScale),
                        BCKCodeDrawingReduceBleedOption: @(YES)};

   CGSize barcodeSize = [self.barcode sizeWithRenderOptions:options];
   CGPoint origin = CGPointMake((self.paperRect.size.width -
                                barcodeSize.width)/2.0,
                               (self.paperRect.size.height -
                                barcodeSize.height)/2.0);

   CGContextRef ctx = UIGraphicsGetCurrentContext();
   CGContextTranslateCTM(ctx, origin.x, origin.y);
   [self.barcode renderInContext:ctx options:options];
}
```

Page size might be less than cut length, so round up

Option for reducing bleed improves fidelity of output on thermal printers

Calculate origin to center barcode on paper

Position context translation matrix to center barcode

Render barcode directly into the graphics context

Here you're not producing a `UIImage` first, but are rendering straight to the current context. Barcodes created with BarCodeKit can display caption text below the bars, so you can't simply disable interpolation. If you did, you'd get ugly artifacts around the caption text when scaling the image instead of it looking crisp.

Internally, AirPrint uses vector-based graphics contexts. By rendering into such a context directly—without a detour via an image—the barcode bars become vector rectangles and the caption text is added as vector glyphs. This produces crisp output regardless of the actual resolution.

You can now wire up everything in ViewController.m:

```
- (CGFloat)printInteractionController:
      (UIPrintInteractionController *)printInteractionController
            cutLengthForPaper:(UIPrintPaper *)paper
{
   BarCodeStickerRenderer *renderer = (BarCodeStickerRenderer *)
```

```
                        printInteractionController.printPageRenderer;

    return [renderer cutLengthForRollWidth:paper.paperSize.width];
}

- (IBAction)print:(UIButton *)sender {
    UIPrintInfo *printInfo = [UIPrintInfo printInfo];
    printInfo.outputType = UIPrintInfoOutputGrayscale;
    printInfo.jobName = @"Code93 Sticker";
    printInfo.duplex = UIPrintInfoDuplexNone;
    printInfo.orientation = UIPrintInfoOrientationLandscape;

    BarCodeStickerRenderer *renderer = [[BarCodeStickerRenderer alloc]
                                          init];
    renderer.barcode = [self _currentBarcodeFromTextField];

    UIPrintInteractionController *printController =
       [UIPrintInteractionController sharedPrintController];
    printController.printInfo = printInfo;
    printController.showsPageRange = NO;
    printController.printPageRenderer = renderer;
    printController.delegate = self;

    void (^completionHandler)(UIPrintInteractionController *,
                              BOOL, NSError *) =
    ^(UIPrintInteractionController *printController,
      BOOL completed, NSError *error) {
       if (!completed && error) {
          NSLog(@"FAILED! due to error in domain %@ with error code %ld",
                error.domain, (long)error.code);
       }
    };

    [printController presentAnimated:YES
                   completionHandler:completionHandler];
}
```

Call cut-length method implemented in the sticker renderer

Rotate printing to landscape

Set up sticker renderer

The -print: method—called when the user taps on the Print button—is virtually identical to the one for producing the QR Code sheets. The only differences are a different job name, the orientation is rotated to landscape, and the BarCodeSticker-Renderer is used instead of QRCodeSheetRenderer (compare to section 5.2.9).

Thermal bleeding

Thermal-label printers employ heat for printing. The heat radiates outward from the area where it's applied, and as a result, a one-point line will always be slightly wider than one point of white space. This effect is called *bleeding*.

If you don't compensate for this effect, small barcodes will become unscannable because the ratio between bars and spaces would be too irregular. BarCodeKit has an option to reduce the width of printed bars: BCKCodeDrawingReduceBleedOption.

5.3.7 Serial Number Tag app summary

This completes our second sample app for this chapter, focusing on printing a single 1D barcode to a roll-feed printer. Many usage scenarios become possible when you can output a single label or sticker. The serial-number-barcode scenario happens to fit with the theme of this book, but you can probably imagine several other uses for such barcodes.

BarCodeKit fills the niche of 1D barcode generation until Apple adds such functionality to the iOS SDK, which I hope they'll do eventually. To learn more about the various kinds of barcodes you can produce with BarCodeKit, please look at the online documentation (https://docs.cocoanetics.com/BarCodeKit/), which also lists the class names of the various barcode symbologies supported.

5.4 Summary

Core Image has fallen behind AV Foundation—covered in chapters 2 and 3—in regard to the number of supported barcode symbologies. This makes the interaction between physical items and mobile users somewhat lopsided. This chapter tried to remedy this situation by emphasizing the ease of barcode generation—in particular, on iOS devices—for display or print.

As more mobile users get used to scanning barcodes, it will increasingly make sense in various scenarios to help users interact with the physical world by attaching barcodes to different items. This chapter helps you fuel this fortuitous circle. What situations can you think of where you could simplify a workflow by adding barcodes?

These are the key barcode-generation takeaways:

- You can generate a great variety of one-dimensional barcodes with the free BarCodeKit library.
- Two-dimensional barcode generation is covered by Core Image, particularly QR Codes.
- Check the Core Image documentation to determine which barcode symbologies are documented. Those are the ones that are App Store–legal. Others might technically exist, but you use them at your own risk or outside of App Store distribution.
- All printing under iOS, whether to sheets or rolls, is done via AirPrint.
- Inexpensive roll-feed printers allow you to print individual barcode stickers with a minimum of waste.
- You can't specify a specific output medium with AirPrint. Instead, you specify the purpose and target output size, and AirPrint selects the best print medium for you.
- Custom print layouts let you make the best use of the medium and help you avoid empty borders, such as if your layout is for US-letter size, but your user prints to European A4 paper.

This chapter and the one before it dealt directly with barcodes in iOS to give you an understanding of barcodes in general, how to scan them, and how to produce them.

The remaining two chapters of this book will dive into technologies that don't directly relate to barcodes but that—as you'll see—are highly relevant to barcode apps: retrieving metadata for scanned barcodes and leveraging information about the situational context of the app user.

6 Getting metadata for barcodes

This chapter covers

- Modern networking with NSURLSession
- Updating Core Data databases asynchronously
- Presenting a barcode scanner modally, and using unwind segues
- Calling RESTful web services
- Unit testing web service wrappers

When you scan a barcode on a product, you end up with a GTIN (Global Trade Item Number). As an engineer, you might be marveling at the beauty of those digits, but your users will want more interesting benefits from having scanned the bars.

A traditional point-of-sale (POS) system has a local database mapping GTINs to products and their prices. But having a mobile barcode scanner in your pocket and the ability to retrieve product metadata over the internet gives you a leg up on POS.

Having barcode scanning and internet connectivity together in a mobile device enables a new breed of apps that can be as niche-specific as they are product-centric.

When Apple introduced iOS 7, they gave networking a major overhaul by introducing `NSURLSession`. Prior to that, you had to create and configure requests individually, and you only had a global cache to work with. URL sessions take on most of the configuring work and have their own session-local caching. As an added bonus, you can perform downloads outside of your app (a.k.a. "out-of-process") with an iOS background downloading daemon.

If you support barcode scanning in your app, you have to require at least iOS 7. And having iOS 7 as a minimum deployment target for your app means that you can also make full use of the goodness found in Apple's new networking APIs.

Whether you're a seasoned iOS developer or you only started developing apps after iOS 7 was introduced, you're on the same footing as everybody else when it comes to modern networking APIs. The only difference might be that the seasoned pro has an appreciation of why the new APIs are so much more comfortable, comparing how difficult networking was in the past with how much simpler it is now.

6.1 Modern networking with NSURLSession

Strictly speaking, there's more to the umbrella term "networking" than we'll cover in this chapter. Here we'll focus on performing HTTP-based downloads and uploads as opposed to communicating with other devices or dealing with iCloud. Those are also interesting topics, but they're quite tangential to the purpose of this book, which is to enable you to build exciting niche-specific, product-centric apps that use barcodes to identify physical items.

The centerpiece of the new style of networking, introduced in iOS 7, is `NSURLSession`. This class is usually created based on one of multiple predefined `NSURLSessionConfiguration` instances. Those determine the setting presets for the session. Think of the URL session object as the manager of multiple network tasks. It provides factory methods that create three kinds of tasks:

- *`NSURLSessionDownloadTask`*—Downloads a file from a web server
- *`NSURLSessionUploadTask`*—Uploads a file to a web server
- *`NSURLSessionDataTask`*—Implement a custom HTTP communication, such as for raw data transfers

You can mix and match those to your heart's content (see figure 6.1). As long as the session lives, every task you create from its factory methods will get its settings from the session and be managed by the session. These settings determine whether requests should be performed over cellular radios, which HTTP cookie policy to use, timeout values, and whether or not responses should be cached. You configure those settings once on the URL session, and each task you create for it inherits them.

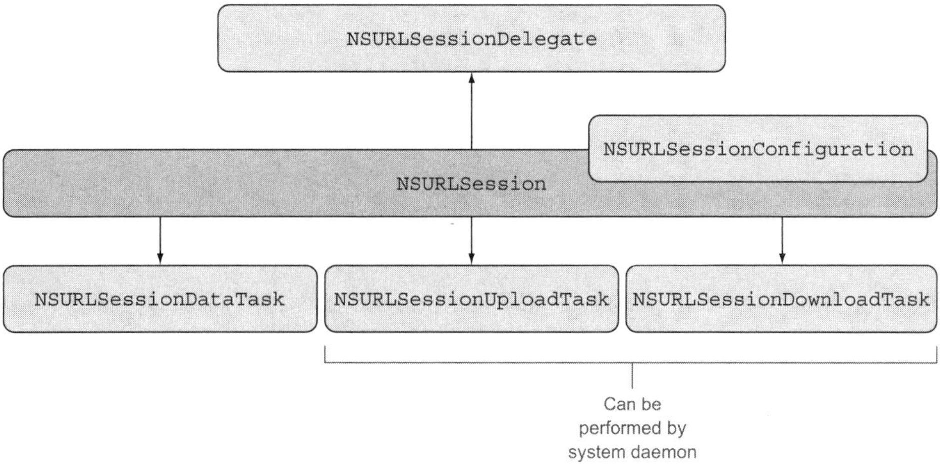

Figure 6.1 `NSURLSession` **components**

> **When we were young ...**
>
> Before iOS 7, you had to work with `NSURLConnection` objects for everything. You had to implement a class to be the delegate and then assemble multiple `NSData` objects into the total file. There were some synchronous and asynchronous convenience methods, but if you wanted to get the download progress or needed to deal with authentication, those tasks were far from convenient.
>
> Many smart software engineers built networking wrappers to work around those shortcomings, such as ASIHTTPRequest by Ben Copsey, MKNetworkKit by Mugunth Kumar, AFNetworking by Matt Thompson, and DTDownload by yours truly.
>
> `NSURLSession` and its related session tasks promise to make those libraries all but obsolete, much as barcode functionality since iOS 7 is making third-party scanning libraries obsolete.

6.1.1 File downloads with NSURLSessionDownloadTask

Let's look at how simple it is to download a file from a web address with `NSURLSession`.

The following code snippet is part of the SimpleDownload sample app that you can find in the book's source code. This app has a text field for a URL and a button to start the download. This is the action method linked to the button:

```
- (IBAction)download:(id)sender {
   NSURLSessionConfiguration *conf = [NSURLSessionConfiguration
                                       defaultSessionConfiguration];
   NSURLSession *session = [NSURLSession
                             sessionWithConfiguration:conf];
   NSURL *URL = [NSURL URLWithString:self.urlField.text];
   NSURLRequest *request = [NSURLRequest requestWithURL:URL];
```

Get default configuration and create a session with it.

Create a request from the URL in the text field.

```
        NSURLSessionDownloadTask *task =
           [session downloadTaskWithRequest:request
              completionHandler:^(NSURL *location,
                                  NSURLResponse *response,
                                  NSError *error) {

           if (error) {
              NSLog(@"download error: %@", [error localizedDescription]);
              return;
           }

           NSHTTPURLResponse *httpResponse = (NSHTTPURLResponse *)response;
           if (![httpResponse isKindOfClass:[NSHTTPURLResponse class]]) {
              NSLog(@"Not a HTTP response!");
              return;
           }

           NSDictionary *headers = [httpResponse allHeaderFields];
           NSString *contentType = headers[@"Content-Type"];
           if (![contentType hasPrefix:@"image"]) {
              NSLog(@"Not an image!");
              return;
           }

           NSData *data = [NSData dataWithContentsOfURL:location];
           dispatch_async(dispatch_get_main_queue(), ^{
              UIImage *image = [UIImage imageWithData:data];
              self.imageView.image = image;
           });
        }];

        [task resume];
     }
```

Create a download task with a completion handler

Log error and bail if something went wrong

Make sure it's an HTTP response (only NSHTTPURLResponse has a property to access HTTP headers).

Proceed only if you received an image file.

Load data right away because the file will be deleted at end of block.

Create image from data and set it on the image view (on main thread).

All tasks are created in suspended state. This starts the newly created data task.

The basic process illustrated in this example is to create an `NSURLRequest` for the `NSURL` you want to download. Then you create an `NSURLSession` with one of the three predefined configurations:

- *defaultSessionConfiguration*—Uses default settings, for most common tasks allowing caching
- *ephemeralSessionConfiguration*—Specifies settings for tasks not needing caching or cookies
- *backgroundSessionConfiguration*—Specifies settings to allow out-of-process downloading

The biggest portion of the preceding code does various kinds of error checking. First, if there's a transmission error due to an invalid URL or a timeout, you bail out of the completion handler. Next you check that you received an HTTP response. Conceivably—if you used a different protocol than HTTP—you might not be getting an `NSHTTPURLResponse` instance here, and trying to access the `allHeaderFields` property would cause an exception. By coding defensively you can verify that you have the correct class. Then, from the header fields, you get the content type (MIME type) of the response, and you check to make sure that you indeed received an image.

If the download occurred without issues, the downloaded file will be available at the `location` URL parameter, but only until the completion block returns. Because of this, you'll want to either load the data into memory—as done here—or move the file to a more permanent location.

The last step inside the completion handler block is to switch to the main thread and set the image as the content of the image view. If there's no valid image data, the `imageWithData:` would return `nil` and nothing would happen.

All tasks are created in a suspended state, so the last line of the method resumes the task to get the download rolling.

This is about all you need to know about basic networking as it should be done from iOS 7 onward. Next we'll query a REST-based JSON web API using `NSURLSessionDataTask`.

6.1.2 Building a Music Collection app

Most people have some sort of music collection at home. If they started collecting before the advent of iTunes, there's usually a sizable number of CDs sitting on a shelf. Hard-core audiophile enthusiasts (including my development editor) swear by the audio quality of their vinyl LP collections.

Let's build an app for those "niche users" to help them catalog and organize their collections. Adding items to a collection by scanning them is much more convenient than having to enter all those details by hand. Our data will be provided by Discogs (www.discogs.com), a massive database of information about music, artists, and media collected by music enthusiasts. This app will teach you the best practices for creating a reusable wrapper around a RESTful web service.

Our Music Collection app will have the following features:

- The user can tap on a plus button to show the barcode scanner.
- When a barcode is detected, the barcode scanner is hidden and a new row appears in the app's list of music media, initially showing the GTIN.
- Discogs is queried asynchronously, and if a result is found, the row is updated with the retrieved information.
- An Edit button toggles the table view into deletion mode to remove items.
- Music media is sorted into sections by genre. Inside the genre, they're sorted by title.
- Tapping on an item will open the related Discogs page.

The finished app will look like figure 6.2 (CDs not included).

Because of the size of the sample app, I won't reproduce all source code in this chapter. Rather, I'll highlight specific portions of interest. Please look at the book's sample code to see it all working together.

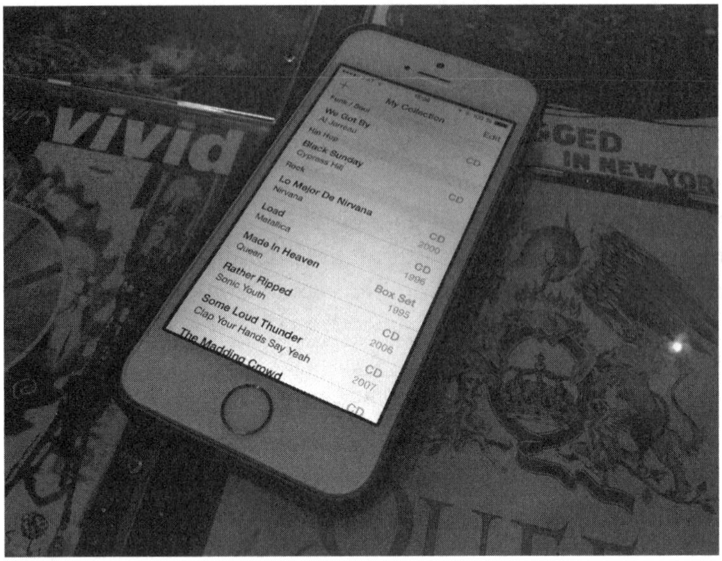

Figure 6.2 Music Collection app

> **Discogs**
>
> The main reason why I chose Discogs as the data source for this example is that all Discogs data is licensed under the Creative Commons CC0 license. This license places no restrictions on what you can do with the data, making it ideal for use in mobile applications even if you plan to make money with them.
>
> Discogs is getting its crowd-sourced data from audiophile enthusiasts. When building and testing the sample app, you'll inevitably encounter barcodes that can't be found through a simple Discogs search.
>
> The main reason for this is that some barcodes have been entered with spaces where the elongated marker bars are, and the Discogs API isn't smart enough to ignore these spaces. For a professional app, you might want to also query for the GTIN variant including spaces, if the first query doesn't yield a result.
>
> Another reason—albeit much rarer—can be that the "release" embodied by the CD in your hand has not been added to Discogs yet. In this case, you have a chance to return the favor and give back to Discogs by adding the missing info.

6.1.3 Asynchronous Core Data updates

The main view of the Music Collection app consists of a table populated by a fetched results controller. This is powered by a Core Data stack consisting of these ingredients:

- `DiscogsModel.xcdatamodeld`—Core Data data model defining a `Release` entity
- `Release` *class*—Represents `Release` instances
- `MediaListViewController`—Contains the setup for the Core Data stack and fetched results controller

Please refer to the sample code's MediaListViewController.m file to see the lazy instantiation of the objects involved in `-fetchedResultController` and `-managedObjectContext`. These lazy initialization methods store their results in two private instance variables, and on subsequent calls those are returned. The `NSFetchedResultsController` watches the `Release` entity and keeps the table view in sync with it. It's configured to sort the entities by genre, title, and artist, with the genres also being the section titles.

The managed object context (MOC) uses the `NSMainQueueConcurrencyType` so that it's usable from UIKit methods, which are usually only to be used on the main thread. For this example, you probably could get by using the MOC for all purposes, including updates. But if you had an API call resulting in a sizable number of updates, then doing this work on the main thread would be a performance bottleneck—the user would experience pauses and jerkiness while scrolling the table view if the updates were taking place at the time.

Being performance-conscious, you want to avoid doing work on the main MOC wherever possible. The following helper method creates a temporary child MOC, and once the updates are done, it lets them bubble up to the main MOC. This offloads the work to a background thread, leaving more CPU time on the main thread for UIKit:

```
- (void)_performDatabaseUpdatesAndSave:
                (void (^)(NSManagedObjectContext *context))block {
  NSParameterAssert(block);
  NSManagedObjectContext *tmpContext = [[NSManagedObjectContext alloc]
          initWithConcurrencyType:NSPrivateQueueConcurrencyType];
  tmpContext.parentContext = _managedObjectContext;

  [tmpContext performBlock:^{
    block(tmpContext);

    if ([tmpContext hasChanges]) {
      NSError *error;
      if ([tmpContext save:&error]) {
        dispatch_async(dispatch_get_main_queue(), ^{
          NSError *error;
          if (![_managedObjectContext save:&error]) {
            NSLog(@"Error saving main context: %@",
                  [error localizedDescription]);
          };
        });
      } else {
        NSLog(@"Error saving tmp context: %@",
              [error localizedDescription]);
      }
    }
  }];
}
```

Code annotations:

- Assert that this method is only called with non-nil block
- Create child MOC with the main MOC as the parent context
- Work on temporary context needs to happen on its private queue
- Call the block doing updates and pass temporary context
- Saving the temporary context pushes changes up to main MOC
- Saving the main MOC writes changes to persistent store

With the preceding method in place, you can perform asynchronous updates with ease. The method returns right away, because the update occurs on the private background queue of the temporary worker context. When it's done, the changes bubble up to the main queue MOC and are saved there asynchronously as well. Using this helper method is straightforward, as shown in the following code snippet:

```
[self _performDatabaseUpdatesAndSave: ^(NSManagedObjectContext *context) {
   // do asynchronous work on the passed context
}];
```

PERFORMANCE TIP If you find yourself inserting many new entities at once, then the asynchronous pattern presented in this section might still cause noticeable pauses in the UI because Core Data locks all contexts while it's writing to the persistent store. This means that the main MOC—used for updating the UI—has to wait to retrieve information. In this case, you should change the approach to save the worker context every couple of rows, and also save the main MOC more often. Saving smaller chunks will make these context locks less noticeable.

The temporary creation of child MOCs is a very lightweight process. Another interesting use for them is as a way to implement transactions in Core Data. Any modifications to the context are only "committed" if you call the save method. If the context is discarded without saving, the changes are "rolled back" (they never make it to the parent MOC). In a Core Data–driven app, you could implement the save/cancel functionality with that approach. If users tap the Save button, the child context is saved; if they tap Cancel, it's discarded.

You'll see this asynchronous update method put to good use in the next section, where you'll use it to update scanned barcodes with metadata from Discogs.

6.1.4 Presenting the barcode scanner modally

When the user wants to add a new CD or LP to their collection, they tap the plus button in the upper-left corner of the app. There you present the barcode scanner view controller you created in chapters 2 and 3. Two things will lead to the scanner's dismissal: the user either scans a barcode or taps the Cancel button.

One minimal change is required to `DTCameraPreviewController` for using it modally. You need to stop it from detecting barcodes while it's being dismissed. You only want the first barcode detection to trigger the dismissal, whereas the detection delegate could be called multiple times during the dismissal animation, which would cause iOS to emit warnings about you trying to dismiss one view controller multiple times.

If you inspect the sample source, you'll find the addition of an `_isDisappearing` instance variable that's set to `YES` in `viewWillDisappear:`. This allows you to ignore barcode detection callbacks from AV Foundation during the dismissal.

The source code reused from earlier projects is grouped within the Copied Code group in the sample project. The main storyboard embeds the scanner view controller inside a navigation controller, as shown in figure 6.3. A modal presentation segue leads from the plus button on the root view controller to the barcode scanner. The simplest way to get this into a new project is to copy and paste it from an existing project's storyboard editor to the storyboard editor of the new project.

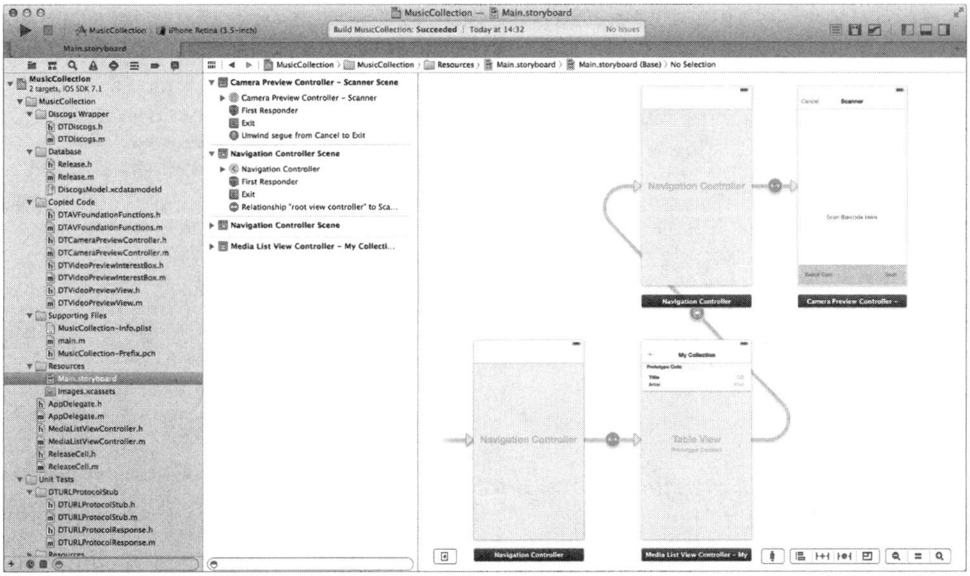

Figure 6.3 Music Collection storyboard

Set the identifier of the modal segue to `showScanner` because you need to set the scan delegate when it's shown. This is done in `MediaListViewController`, which governs the main app view with the list of music media in your collection:

```
- (void)prepareForSegue:(UIStoryboardSegue *)segue sender:(id)sender {
   if ([segue.identifier isEqualToString:@"showScanner"]) {
      UINavigationController *nav =  (UINavigationController *)
                                        segue.destinationViewController;
      DTCameraPreviewController *preview = (DTCameraPreviewController *)
                                              nav.viewControllers[0];
      preview.delegate = self;
   }
}
```

The `destinationViewController` of this segue is a navigation controller that has the scanner view controller at the first position of its `viewControllers`. This lets you retrieve a reference to `DTCameraPreviewController` and set the delegate to `self`.

Dismissing a presented view controller is also called *unwinding*. You can add a dummy unwind action method to the same view controller to enable the creation of an unwind segue in the storyboard editor:

```
- (IBAction)unwindFromScannerViewController:(UIStoryboardSegue *)segue {
   // intentionally left black
}
```

Having a method with such a signature enables the creation of unwind segues. Back in the storyboard editor you can now Ctrl-drag from the Cancel Bar Button Item onto the Exit option, as shown in figure 6.4. A popup menu lets you select the dummy method.

Making this connection creates a new unwind segue that appears underneath the green Exit symbol. Click on it and set the identifier to `unwind`, as shown in figure 6.5. This allows you to trigger it from code as well.

At this point you can already cancel the scanner by tapping the Cancel button, with no extra code required.

In the next section we'll create a wrapper class for the Discogs search API to fill in some more interesting information on the scanned item.

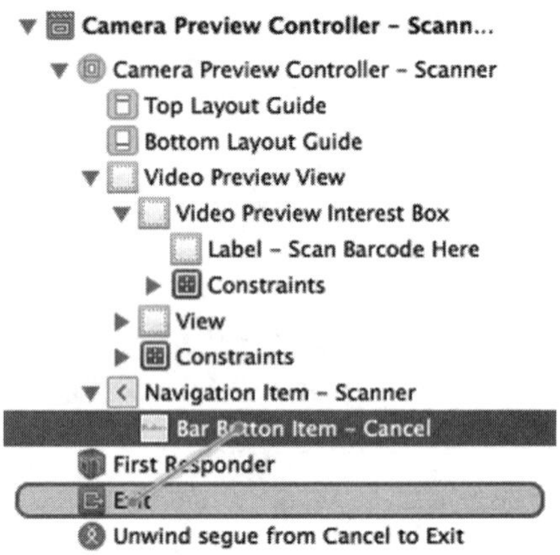

Figure 6.4 Connecting the unwind segue

6.1.5 Using NSURLSessionDataTask to call RESTful web APIs

Representational State Transfer (REST) is the name-child of Roy Fielding, who coined the term in 2000 for his doctoral dissertation. There's a lot of boring theory behind it, but for our purposes, you only need to know that web services are said to be *RESTful* if they adhere to these conventions:

- Methods share a common base URI (API endpoint).
- Entities and methods have distinct paths relative to the API endpoint.
- Standard HTTP methods are used for interacting with entities (`GET`, `PUT`, `POST`, `DELETE`).
- Data is represented in a common internet media type, such as JSON.

RESTful web APIs are ideally suited for mobile applications because they make use of the same mechanisms used for retrieving web pages in your mobile browser or uploading a file to a website. You don't need to encode/decode between specific transport formats; you just need to perform simple HTTP requests. When data is returned to you—for example, as a result of doing a search—it's most commonly in

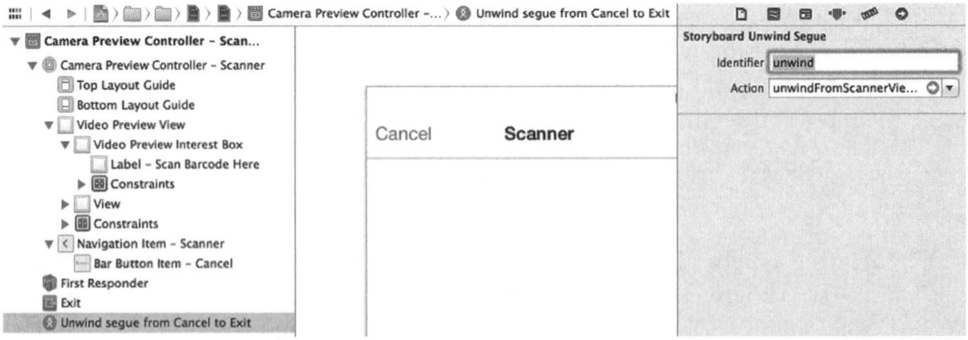

Figure 6.5 Setting the unwind segue identifier

JavaScript Object Notation (JSON). As you'll see in this section, all the building blocks for calling RESTful web APIs are provided for you since iOS 7.

For the purposes of the Music Collection app, you'll create a `DTDiscogs` wrapper around the Discogs search method (http://www.discogs.com/developers/#page:database,header:database-search). The wrapper's method will abstract the calling of the web API, verify the response, and call a completion handler. The `DTDiscogs` class (whose interface definition is shown in the following code snippet) will represent Discogs, and it will have a search method that searches by GTIN. (There are other search options offered by Discogs, but we're only interested in finding items by barcode.)

```
typedef void (^DTDiscogsCompletion)(id result, NSError *error);

@interface DTDiscogs : NSObject

- (void)searchForGTIN:(NSString *)gtin
          completion:(DTDiscogsCompletion)completion;

@end
```

Define type for the completion handler (annotation on the `typedef` line)

Search for releases on Discogs database by GTIN (annotation on the `searchForGTIN:completion:` method)

The `DTDiscogs` wrapper class abstracts away the network request that performs the actual calling of the web API, as illustrated in figure 6.6—you don't want to have to create data tasks and the associated checking code for every individual API method. The

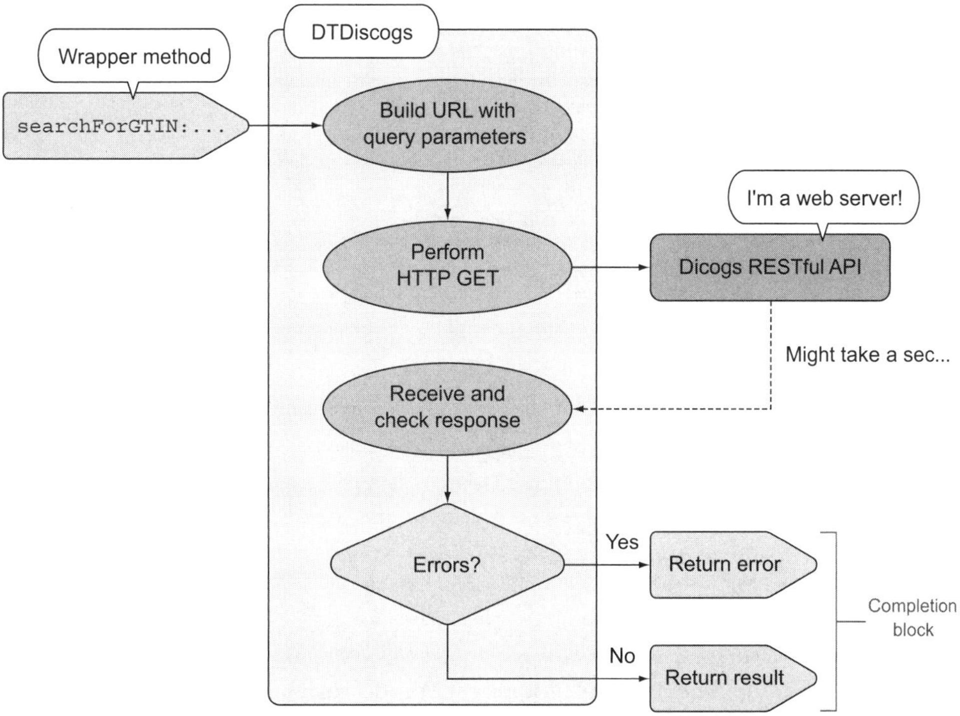

Figure 6.6 Discogs wrapper flow

paradigm communicated by the method signature is that you pass a GTIN, and in a short while your completion block will be called. Then you'll get either a `nil` error and an object passed as `result`, or if something went wrong there will be an `NSError` with details about what went wrong.

Let's dive into the implementation of the `DTDiscogs` wrapper class, which you'll find in DTDiscogs.m in the Music Collection app.

At the top, there are a couple of definitions:

```
#define API_ENDPOINT @"http://api.discogs.com"
#define URLENC(string) [string \
   stringByAddingPercentEncodingWithAllowedCharacters:\
    [NSCharacterSet URLQueryAllowedCharacterSet]];
NSString * const DTDiscogsErrorDomain = @"DTDiscogs";
```

Common base URI of all Discogs API operations

Macro to shorten code needed to URL-encode a parameter

Error domain string for returning result-checking errors

All operations on the Discogs web API are reachable through URLs relative to the Discogs API endpoint. Parameters need to be added to the URL as a query. The following helper method constructs the full method URL, adding and URL-encoding parameters as needed:

```
- (NSURL *)_methodURLForPath:(NSString *)path
                  parameters:(NSDictionary *)parameters {
   NSURL *endpointURL = [NSURL URLWithString:API_ENDPOINT];

   if ([parameters count]) {
      NSArray *sortedKeys =
               [[parameters allKeys]
                sortedArrayUsingSelector:@selector(compare:)];
      NSMutableArray *tmpArray = [NSMutableArray array];

      for (NSString *key in sortedKeys) {
         NSString *value = parameters[key];
         NSString *encKey = URLENC(key);
         NSString *encValue = URLENC(value);

         NSString *tmpStr = [NSString stringWithFormat:@"%@=%@",
                             encKey, encValue];
         [tmpArray addObject:tmpStr];
        }
        path = [path stringByAppendingFormat:@"?%@",
              [tmpArray componentsJoinedByString:@"&"]];
    }
   }
   return [NSURL URLWithString:path
                 relativeToURL:endpointURL];
}
```

Convert endpoint URI string to URL

Sort parameter dictionary keys to get consistent ord

URL-encode parameter name and value

Add key/value pairs to temp array

Append combined query string to path

Return constructed method URI

In case of errors, you'll want to return an `NSError` with a message describing what went wrong. The following helper method creates such an error with the suitable error domain, code, and message:

```
- (NSError *)_errorWithCode:(NSUInteger)code
                    message:(NSString *)message {
   NSDictionary *userInfo;
   if (message) {
      userInfo = @{NSLocalizedDescriptionKey : message};
   }
   return [NSError errorWithDomain:DTDiscogsErrorDomain
                              code:code
                          userInfo:userInfo];
}
```

> **URL encoding**
>
> You can only have certain characters inside a website address, because characters like the equal sign, question mark, and ampersand are imbued with specific meanings. You have to escape such characters if you want to pass them via the query portion of the URL.
>
> Prior to iOS 7, you had to go down to the Core Foundation level and call `CFURLCreateStringByAddingPercentEscapes` to make strings URL-safe. Apple listened to developers who wished for a more elegant solution and added the `URLQueryAllowedCharacterSet` class method to `NSCharacterSet`, as well as a suitable category method to `NSString` for escaping all characters in a string that are not part of the passed character set.
>
> These "percent escapes" consist of a percent sign followed by two hex digits. For example, a space (ASCII code 32) is represented as %20, with hex 20 being the same as decimal 32. This process of substituting characters with escape sequences—to make them URL-safe—is also commonly referred to as *URL encoding*.

The implementation for `searchForGTIN:completion:` is relatively short because the grunt work is performed in another internal method. This division allows you to easily add additional wrapper methods to the `DTDiscogs` class. All you have to do is specify the method path and suitable parameters:

```
- (void)searchForGTIN:(NSString *)gtin
           completion:(DTDiscogsCompletion)completion {
   NSParameterAssert(gtin);
   NSParameterAssert(completion);

   if ([gtin length]==13 && [gtin hasPrefix:@"0"]) {
      gtin = [gtin substringFromIndex:1];
   }

   NSString *functionPath = @"/database/search";
   NSDictionary *params = @{@"type": @"release",
                            @"barcode": gtin};

   [self _performMethodCallWithPath:functionPath
                         parameters:params
                         completion:completion];
}
```

Assert that all parameters are non-nil

Path of the search function relative to API endpoint URI

GTIN-13 converted to UPC if applicable

Create dictionary with function parameters

Call the method that does actual work

For the purposes of the Music Collection app, you're searching releases by GTIN. Discogs defines a "release" as "a particular physical or digital object released by one or more Artists." This is why the type parameter is `release`, and the barcode search parameter is the GTIN you're looking for.

> **Barcode guru tip**
>
> Many web services—including Discogs—might not find items if you're searching for GTIN-13 barcodes. In particular, if they're U.S.-centric or have data from a time before the *grand unification*, you'll have to search for UPCs instead.
>
> A UPC (12 digits) is represented as GTIN-13 by appending a leading 0. So if you see a 13-digit barcode with a leading zero, you can trim it off and search for the UPC instead. This approach is compatible with barcodes from outside the U.S. because there numbers other than zero are used as leading digits.

The `NSURLSession` for the data task comes from a property accessor. The session object is instantiated "lazily" as soon as the accessor method is accessed the first time. The designated initializer, `-init`, calls the secondary initializer, taking a configuration parameter passing the standard ephemeral configuration. This is the ideal session configuration for API calls, which usually have no use for local caching:

```
@implementation DTDiscogs {
   NSURLSession *_session;
   NSURLSessionConfiguration *_configuration;
}

- (instancetype)initWithSessionConfiguration:
                               (NSURLSessionConfiguration *)configuration {
   self = [super init];

   if (self) {
      _configuration = configuration;
   }

   return self;
}

- (instancetype)init {
   // use ephemeral config, we need no caching
   NSURLSessionConfiguration *config =
             [NSURLSessionConfiguration ephemeralSessionConfiguration];
   return [self initWithSessionConfiguration:config];
}

- (NSURLSession *)session {
   if (!_session) {
```

Annotations:
- Private instance variables
- Secondary initializer taking configuration
- Store-passed configuration reference in ivar
- Default initializer for normal operation
- Ephemeral configuration used by default
- Lazy creation method for session

```
      _session = [NSURLSession sessionWithConfiguration:_configuration];
   }

   return _session;
}
```

Having a secondary initializer will allow you to customize the URL session configuration for unit testing later in this chapter. But for now you can use the default initializer with the default ephemeral configuration.

The method doing the actual work is too long to display in a single listing, so we'll first look at the overall structure and then zoom in on the processing code. The method first gathers the necessary ingredients to make the network request, and then it processes the response inside the request's completion block:

```
- (void)_performMethodCallWithPath:(NSString *)path
                        parameters:(NSDictionary *)parameters
                        completion:(DTDiscogsCompletion)completion {
   NSURL *methodURL = [self _methodURLForPath:path
                                   parameters:parameters];
   NSURLRequest *request = [NSURLRequest requestWithURL:methodURL];
   NSURLSessionDataTask *task = [[self session]
                          dataTaskWithRequest:request
                          completionHandler:^(NSData *data,
                                  NSURLResponse *response,
                                      NSError *error) {

      NSError *retError = error;
      id result = nil;

      if (retError) {
         completion(nil, retError);
         return;
      }

      //


      completion(result, retError);
   }];

   [task resume];
}
```

Construct calling URL with helper method
Create URL request; default HTTP verb is GET
Create data task for the URL session
Check for transport error, such as no network connection
Insert processing and error-checking of response here
Call completion block, passing result or error
Task is created suspended, so this starts it

`NSURLRequest` embodies the method, headers, timeout, and other values relevant to the HTTP request. To specify a different HTTP method than the default `GET`, you would instead create an `NSMutableURLRequest`, which offers `setHTTPMethod:` for changing it.

The first error checked for is the one reported in the data task's `completionHandler`. Those errors always relate to networking problems. For example, the internet connection might be down or the API endpoint URL might not be resolving.

After various processing and error-checking steps, the completion block is called, passing the result or error. Because all URL session tasks are created in a suspended state, you need to resume the task to have it perform the network request.

The following listings are all inserted into the marked location in the previous listing. Note that all these code snippets use the previously defined helper method for creating an `NSError` before calling the completion block, passing it, and then bailing out of the block via `return`.

First you check if the response came from the correct host. If you use OpenDNS for your network, you'll get a status 200 response coming from www.website-unavailable.com, which is in lieu of a DNS resolution error. Granted that's a rather unlikely occurrence, but it doesn't hurt to have this check in place:

```
NSString *calledHost = [methodURL host];
NSString *responseHost = [response.URL host];

if (![responseHost isEqualToString:calledHost]) {
   NSString *msg = [NSString stringWithFormat:
                    @"Expected result host to be '%@' but was '%@'",
                    calledHost, responseHost];
   retError = [self _errorWithCode:999 message:msg];
   completion(nil, retError);
   return;
}
```

The URL-loading system also supports dealing with protocols other than HTTP. Because of this, the `response` parameter is of class `NSURLResponse`. To make sure that you got an HTTP response—including HTTP status code and headers—you perform the following check:

```
if (![response isKindOfClass:[NSHTTPURLResponse class]]) {
   NSString *msg = @"Response is not an NSHTTPURLResponse";
   retError = [self _errorWithCode:999 message:msg];
   completion(nil, retError);
   return;
}
```

`NSHTTPURLResponse` is a subclass of `NSURLResponse`, providing these HTTP-specific properties for your inspection. You want to be certain that the response has the correct class before you typecast the response object to `NSHTTPURLResponse` and access properties.

You always expect the response to be in JSON format, and Discogs will always return a JSON dictionary containing the results or an error message. If the content type isn't "application/json" or can't be parsed, then something must have gone wrong:

```
NSHTTPURLResponse *httpResp = (NSHTTPURLResponse *)response;
NSDictionary *headers = [httpResp allHeaderFields];
NSString *contentType = headers[@"Content-Type"];

if ([contentType isEqualToString:@"application/json"]) {
```

```
    result = [NSJSONSerialization JSONObjectWithData:data
                                             options:0
                                               error:&retError];
}
```

You parse the JSON response in any case. When you inspect the HTTP headers, you have to consider the HTTP status code. Only codes below 400 mean that you got a successful method result. Otherwise the parsed JSON will contain the error message:

```
if (httpResp.statusCode >= 400) {
    NSString *message = result[@"message"];      <-- Error message is in parsed JSON dictionary

    retError = [self _errorWithCode:httpResp.statusCode
                            message:message];
    result = nil;                                <-- Reset result after getting the error message
}

completion(result, retError);    <-- Call completion block, passing result or error
```

The final statement calling the external completion block concludes this extensive error checking and processing. Note that this code just forwards the parsed JSON response as opposed to creating custom model objects from it. For a larger app, you might want to do this as part of your API wrapper, but for this small example I prefer this form, as it simplifies filling in the Core Data fields in the next section.

6.1.6 Authenticating API requests with OAuth

Initially Discogs didn't require authentication on their search endpoint. But by far the largest group of applications using the Discogs API were MP3-tagging applications that would hammer the Discogs search API with mostly nonsensical search terms found in pirated music filenames and metadata, resulting in an extraordinary waste of resources. So the decision was made to require user authentication on calls to the search function. Discogs chose OAuth 1.0a for their authentication.

OAuth has these main goals:

- To know which *application* is making API requests
- To know on behalf of which *user* these requests are made
- To know if the user has *authorized* the application to make those requests
- To ensure that the requests have *not been spoofed* or otherwise tampered with
- To facilitate an authentication flow where the application doesn't have to save the username and password

There are two common versions of OAuth that you may encounter. Version 1.0a is the original standard, with the appended *a* denoting that it was slightly modified to work around a security problem.

> **What is OAuth 2.0?**
>
> OAuth 1.0 requires elaborate construction of an authorization header that contains a cryptographic signature. The community found that this requirement was a big hassle and difficult to get right. The HTTPS protocol already provides end-to-end encryption, so it was felt that there was no longer a need for a signature.
>
> OAuth 2.0 is different from OAuth 1 in many ways, and these versions are not compatible with each other. This is why versions 1 and 2 continue to coexist. That's all you need to know about OAuth 2.0 at this point.

The "classic" OAuth 1.0 authentication flow has three steps, or legs, which is why it's also referred to as *three-legged OAuth* (see figure 6.7).

Of these three steps, the first and last are HTTP POST requests that you can perform without user interaction. The second leg presents a web view by loading a page from the website. There the user has to log into the service and authorize your app. The web service will then redirect to a callback URL that you can catch so you know when the web view is no longer needed.

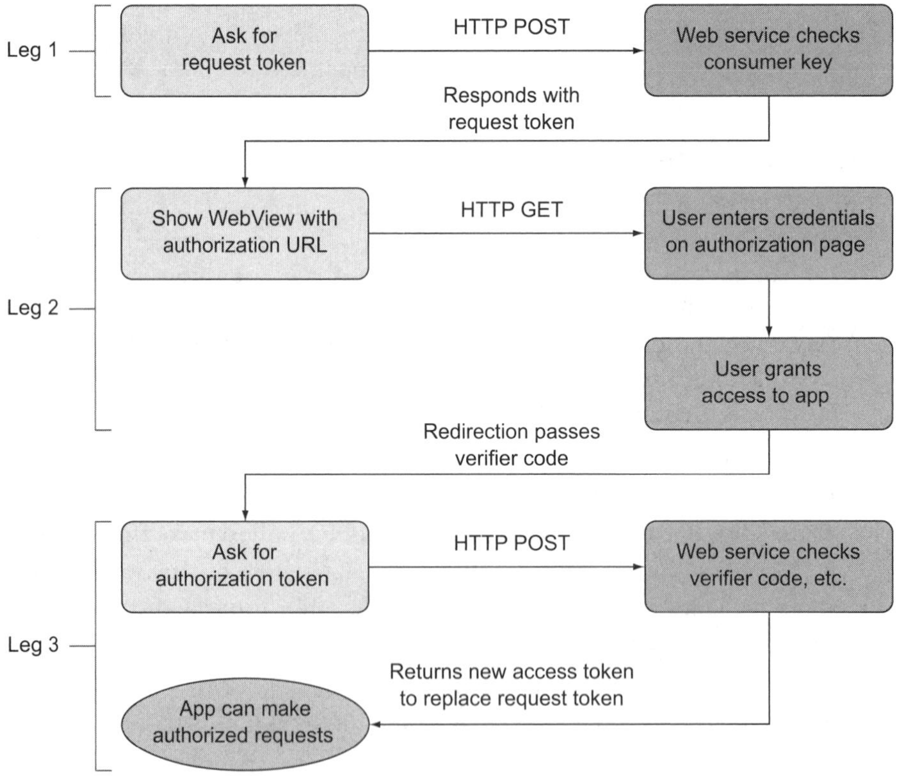

Figure 6.7 Three-legged OAuth flow

How to get rid of the dreaded web view

OAuth was designed to work in the scenario where website A wanted to access user data on website B, so the designers saw nothing wrong with redirecting the user to a web page on B for the authorization step, and having the successful authorization redirect back to A. But this requirement to present the authorization page in a web view feels anachronistic when modern apps have great native user interfaces.

One attempt at a solution was the invention of xAuth by Twitter, which sticks with OAuth 1.0a for requests made on behalf of users. In xAuth, the username and password are simply added to the first leg's authorization header. But this presents a trust problem, because any app that gets hold of the user's credentials could impersonate the user. This is why Twitter now only grants xAuth privileges to a very few and select app vendors, like Apple.

So the general answer is that you can't get rid of the web view in the second leg of OAuth 1 unless somebody at the service you're trying to access owes you a favor.

6.1.7 Adding DTOAuth to your project

Because Discogs uses OAuth 1.0a for their authentication, you'll need to implement this in your `DTDiscogs` wrapper. DTOAuth is an open source project (available on GitHub: https://github.com/Cocoanetics/DTOAuth) that contains all the code necessary to add OAuth 1.0a support to your app.

Due to the complexity of the cryptographic signature, I'm providing the DTOAuth component with the Music Collection sample code in the Externals folder. You'll include it as a subproject and link the static library target from it into your app binary to access its functionality.

Create an Externals subfolder in your project structure, and copy the contents of the DTOAuth project there. Then add a reference to `DTOAuth.xcodeproj` in the app project. Figure 6.8 shows the referenced Xcode subproject inside the Music Collection project.

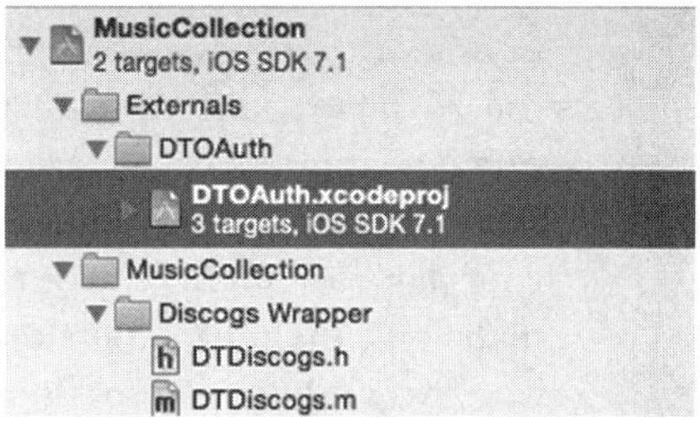

Figure 6.8 DTOAuth subproject

Having an Xcode project referenced as a subproject gives you access to all its targets. Add the static library target both as a dependency and in the linker build phase, as shown in figure 6.9. This tells Xcode that your app needs to be rebuilt if there's a change in the DTOAuth project. The linker build phase merges the compiled object code from inside the libDTOAuth_iOS.a static library with your app binary.

To enable Xcode to find the DTOAuth headers inside the subproject, you need to add the folder where you put the DTOAuth source code to your User Header Search Paths build setting: `${SOURCE_ROOT}/Externals/DTOAuth`. Choose the `recursive` option so that the indexer will also look in subfolders of this location.

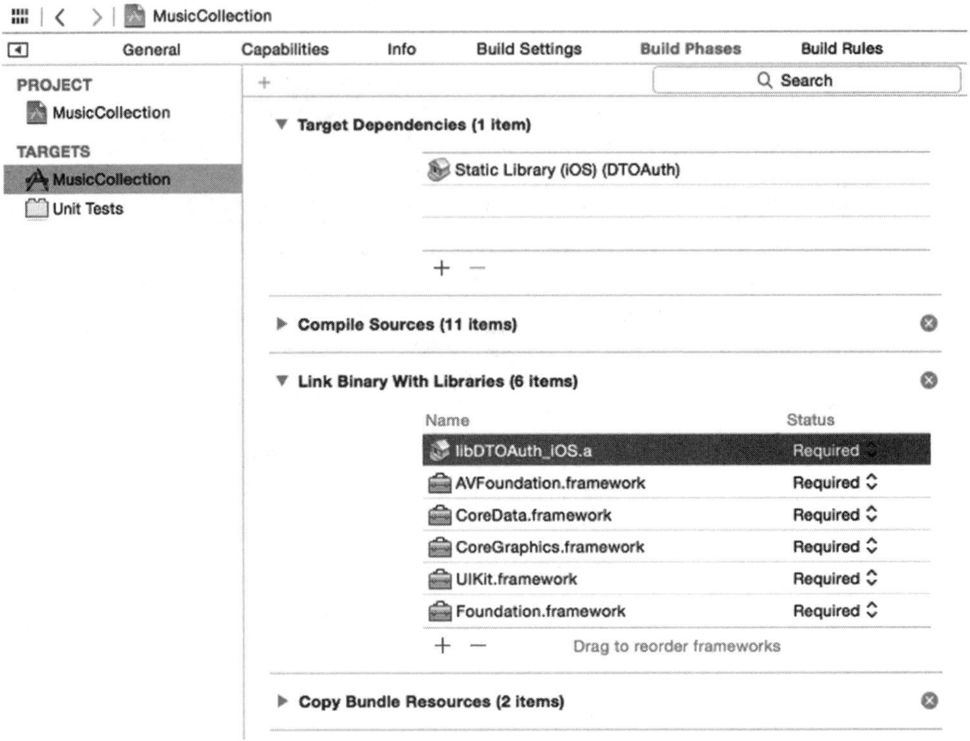

Figure 6.9 DTOAuth added as dependency

6.1.8 Configuring the OAuth consumer

To participate in OAuth, you need to create an application on the Discogs developer website (https://www.discogs.com/settings/developers). Your app is referred to as the *consumer*; take note of the *consumer key* and *consumer secret* values. In terms of nomenclature, the key is generally public and will be passed around, whereas the secret is kept private and is used for signing stuff. You should take care to never post your pair to a public source code repository, because this would enable somebody with malicious intent to impersonate your app when talking to the service.

The authentication flow state information is encapsulated in `DTOAuthClient`; `DTDiscogs` requires an instance of it for signing web API HTTP requests. This instance will be created in a lazy property accessor method.

First up, you need a property definition in the `DTDiscogs` header. Here are the two additions you have to make:

```
extern NSString * const DTDiscogsErrorDomain;

@class DTOAuthClient;

typedef void (^DTDiscogsCompletion)(id result, NSError *error);
```

Tells compiler that DTOAuthClient is a valid type name without having to import the header

```
@interface DTDiscogs : NSObject

- (instancetype)initWithSessionConfiguration:(NSURLSessionConfiguration *)
    configuration;
- (void)searchForGTIN:(NSString *)gtin completion:(DTDiscogsCompletion)
    completion;

@property (nonatomic, strong) DTOAuthClient *oauthClient;

@end
```

Lazily initialized property for the OAuth client object

Moving on to the DTDiscogs implementation, you need an import for DTOAuthClient.h, and then you can create a lazy property initializer (shown in the following code) that takes care of setting up the consumer the first time the property is accessed. When initializing the OAuth client object, you have to pass the consumer key and secret to it. It also needs to know the base URLs for the three legs, as these can be different from service to service:

```
- (DTOAuthClient *)oauthClient {
    if (!_oauthClient) {
        _oauthClient = [[DTOAuthClient alloc]
                        initWithConsumerKey:@"mDOtjNkiAPSklsVSIrbF"
                        consumerSecret:@"UvXUCTOgyHKCFEnZpzDUhOofaDsZQMyA"
                        ];
        _oauthClient.requestTokenURL = [NSURL URLWithString:
                             @"http://api.discogs.com/oauth/request_token"];
        _oauthClient.userAuthorizeURL = [NSURL URLWithString:
                             @"http://www.discogs.com/oauth/authorize"];
        _oauthClient.accessTokenURL = [NSURL URLWithString:
                              @"http://api.discogs.com/oauth/access_token"];
    }
    return _oauthClient;
}
```

Replace with your own consumer key

Replace with your own consumer secret

Base URL for first leg (request token)

Base URL for second leg (authorization)

Base URL for third leg (access token)

Now you need to add an Authorization header to all your Discogs API requests. At the beginning of the _performMethodCallWithPath:parameters:completion: method, add the following code, which adds the Authorization header if the OAuth client possesses a valid access token (that is, if isAuthenticated is true):

```
- (void)_performMethodCallWithPath:(NSString *)path
                       parameters:(NSDictionary *)parameters
                       completion:(DTDiscogsCompletion)completion
{
   NSURL *methodURL = [self _methodURLForPath:path
                                  parameters:parameters];
   NSMutableURLRequest *request =
                      [NSMutableURLRequest requestWithURL:methodURL];

   if ([self.oauthClient isAuthenticated])
```

Check if OAuth client object has valid access token

```
{
   NSString *authHeader =
         [self.oauthClient authenticationHeaderForRequest:request];
   [request addValue:authHeader forHTTPHeaderField:@"Authorization"];
}
...
```

Create contents for Authorization header

Add header to request

This is all you need to do within the DTDiscogs wrapper class to add OAuth. Next you need to hook up the search function to the barcode scanner and, if necessary, carry out the OAuth flow.

6.1.9 Implementing the UI for OAuth authorization

You want to show the OAuth authorization web view (second leg) at the latest possible moment—after the user has successfully scanned a barcode and before you execute the search on Discogs. The flowchart in figure 6.10 illustrates the decision about whether or not carrying out the OAuth flow is required.

When the scanner view controller finds a valid GTIN, it calls the delegate method and is dismissed with a slide-out animation. During this animation, you can't present any new view controller, such as the DTOAuthWebViewController provided for the second leg by DTOAuth. You have to delay handling the scanned code until the dismissal animation has ended.

Right after triggering the presentation or dismissal of a view controller, you can get a reference to the responsible transition coordinator. This coordinator offers a

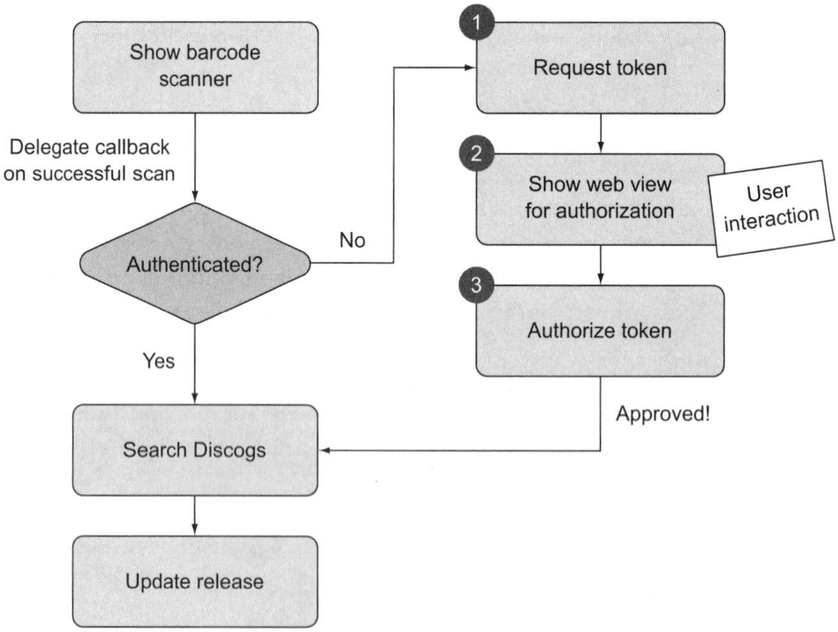

Figure 6.10 To OAuth or not to OAuth

method to animate something in parallel with the animation and also provides a handy completion block that you can use.

The following code is called by the `DTCameraPreviewController` when a new barcode is scanned, showing how the handling of the scanned code is delayed until the transition animation has completed:

```
- (void)previewController:(DTCameraPreviewController *)previewController
             didScanCode:(NSString *)code ofType:(NSString *)type {
   [previewController performSegueWithIdentifier:@"unwind" sender:self];
   [self.transitionCoordinator animateAlongsideTransition:NULL
          completion:^(id<UIViewControllerTransitionCoordinatorContext>
                          context) {
      [self _handleScannedCode:code];
   }];
}
```

- **Dismiss scanner via named unwind segue**
- **Nothing (NULL) to animate alongside the animation**
- **Handle code after transition is over**

You create a helper method that carries out the OAuth flow on the right side of the flowchart in figure 6.10. Each step has a completion handler, and if the step was successful, the next step is carried out. Interspersed are abort conditions that cancel the flow as soon as one step fails:

```
- (void)_authenticateAndThenPerformBlock:(void (^)(void))block {
   [_discogs.oauthClient requestTokenWithCompletion:^(NSError *error) {
      if (error) {
       NSLog(@"Error requesting token: %@",
              [error localizedDescription]);
         return;
      }

      dispatch_async(dispatch_get_main_queue(), ^{
         DTOAuthWebViewController *webView =
            [[DTOAuthWebViewController alloc] init];
         UINavigationController *nav =
            [[UINavigationController alloc]
                initWithRootViewController:webView];
         [self presentViewController:nav animated:YES completion:NULL];

         NSURLRequest *request = [_discogs.oauthClient
                                  userTokenAuthorizationRequest];
         [webView startAuthorizationFlowWithRequest:request
          completion:^(BOOL isAuthenticated, NSString *verifier) {
             [self dismissViewControllerAnimated:YES completion:NULL];

         if (!isAuthenticated) {
            NSLog(@"User did not authorize app");
            return;
         }

         [_discogs.oauthClient authorizeTokenWithVerifier:verifier
          completion:^(NSError *error) {
```

- **Start first leg**
- **Cancel flow if first leg failed**
- **Dispatch to main queue for following UIKit interaction**
- **Create web view controller for second leg**
- **Get HTTP request for second leg**
- **Start second leg**
- **Dismiss web view controller**
- **Cancel flow if second leg failed or user didn't authorize the app**
- **Start third leg**

```
                    if (error) {
                       NSLog(@"Unable to get access token: %@",
                             [error localizedDescription]);
                       return;
                    }

                    block();
                 }];
              }];
           });
        }];
    }
```

Cancel flow if third leg failed

At this point, all went well; execute the block

If you make it to the very bottom of the code, then all three legs were successful and the passed block can be executed. This is where you can execute the Discogs search following the OAuth authorization flow.

6.1.10 Connecting barcode scanning and metadata retrieval

You can now fill in the `_handleScannedCode:` method. This method first creates a new blank `Release` object in the database via the following helper method:

```
- (Release *)_insertNewReleaseWithGTIN:(NSString *)GTIN {

   // create a new Release object and fill in barcode
   Release *release = [NSEntityDescription
                        insertNewObjectForEntityForName:@"Release"
                        inManagedObjectContext:_managedObjectContext];
   release.barcode = GTIN;
   release.genre = @"Unknown";

   NSError *error = nil;
   if (![_managedObjectContext save:&error]) {
      NSLog(@"Unresolved error %@, %@", error, [error userInfo]);
      abort();
   }

   return release;
}
```

The error handling in this example is intentionally crude. Aborting the entire application is frowned on in real-life apps.

If the user is already authorized, then you can search Discogs and update the new `Release` object right away. If not, this will have to wait until after successful completion of the authorization flow:

```
- (void)_handleScannedCode:(NSString *)code {
   Release *release = [self _insertNewReleaseWithGTIN:code];

   if ([_discogs.oauthClient isAuthenticated]) {
      [self _performSearchAndUpdateRelease:release];
```

Create a new Release object and fill in barcode

Check if authentication is still required

Perform search and update right away

```
        } else {
            [self _authenticateAndThenPerformBlock:^{     // Execute authentication flow
                [self _performSearchAndUpdateRelease:release];   // Perform search, and update after authorization succeeds
            }];
        }
    }
```

The helper method `_performSearchAndUpdateRelease:` queries Discogs and—if there was a hit—updates the freshly inserted `Release` object:

```
- (void)_performSearchAndUpdateRelease:(Release *)release {
   [_discogs searchForGTIN:release.barcode completion:^(id result,    // Search Discogs for the GTIN.
                                                   NSError *error) {
      if (error || ![result isKindOfClass:[NSDictionary class]]) {    // Bail out if there was a problem.
         return;
      }

      NSDictionary *dict = (NSDictionary *)result;      // Check if there were search results.
      NSArray *results = dict[@"results"];
      if (![results count]) {
         return;
      }

      // always use first result
      NSDictionary *theResult = results[0];
      [self _updateRelease:release fromDictionary:theResult];   // Updated new Release from first search result
   }];
}
```

The update code is grouped in `_updateRelease:fromDictionary:`, and it uses the background-context update paradigm introduced earlier:

```
- (void)_updateRelease:(Release *)release
        fromDictionary:(NSDictionary *)dict {
   [self _performDatabaseUpdatesAndSave:
    ^(NSManagedObjectContext *context) {
       Release *updatedRelease = (Release *)           // Get version of the Release for temp context
          [context objectWithID:release.objectID];

       NSString *title = dict[@"title"];
       NSString *artist = nil;
       NSRange rangeOfDash = [title rangeOfString:@"-"];

       if (rangeOfDash.location != NSNotFound) {
          artist = [[title substringToIndex:rangeOfDash.location]     // Split title field into title and artist
                     stringByTrimmingCharactersInSet:
                     [NSCharacterSet whitespaceAndNewlineCharacterSet]];
          title = [[title substringFromIndex:rangeOfDash.location+1]
                    stringByTrimmingCharactersInSet:
                    [NSCharacterSet whitespaceAndNewlineCharacterSet]];
       }
```

```
        updatedRelease.title = title;
        updatedRelease.artist = artist;
        updatedRelease.genre = [dict[@"genre"] firstObject];
        updatedRelease.style = [dict[@"style"] firstObject];
        updatedRelease.format = [dict[@"format"] firstObject];
        updatedRelease.year = @([dict[@"year"] integerValue]);
        updatedRelease.uri = dict[@"uri"];
    }];
}
```

Update values in the Release object

NSManagedObjects—like the Release object passed as a parameter here—can only be used with the managed object context they came from. But you can get a copy of the object suitable for another context via the MOC's objectWithID: method. The managed object's objectID property is the only one you can safely access from another thread. Inside the block of the update method, you're on the private queue of the worker context.

Discogs returns album title and artist behind the "title" key of the result dictionary. You then need to separate the values at the dash character and trim off any remaining whitespace. The genre, style, and format values are arrays from which you always take the first value.

_performDatabaseUpdatesAndSave takes care of saving the changes. It first saves the worker context and then also saves the main MOC. This, in turn, triggers an update on the fetched results controller, which then configures the table view row for this entity with the new values.

MediaListViewController configures cells with incomplete information to display the GTIN and "No info found." As soon as the title property of the shown Release object becomes non-nil, the labels are populated accordingly. Figure 6.11 shows this progression from prototype cell to complete entry.

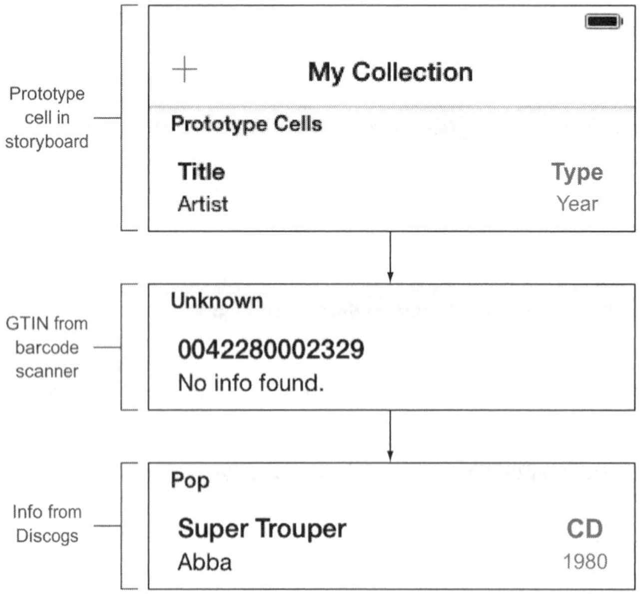

Figure 6.11 Filling in the blanks from Discogs

We haven't gone into how the table view rows are configured for every `Release`—that's typical boilerplate code that you're likely very familiar with. Please refer to the MediaListViewController.m sample code to see how this is set up.

6.2 Unit-testing network operations

In the previous section, you created a class that wraps the Discogs web service API. In pro parlance, such a class is also referred to as a *unit*, because it has a minimum of external dependencies. Really, the only things it depends on, outside of the networking code, are classes and types defined in Apple's frameworks. In other words, it's a perfect candidate for *unit testing*.

Generally speaking, you want to create a sufficient number of tests to make sure that assumptions made about a unit hold true even if code inside the unit is changed. The header of a class is like a contract you make with people who use the class, so I like to keep the headers as simple as possible and also to add lots of commentary about what parameters are valid. Unit tests are a form of such comments that can be automatically tested by a machine.

Imagine that your API wrapper class is used by a larger team of developers and that you refactor some crucial bits, accidentally changing some behavior that another team member is relying on. A unit test that tests such an assumption would flag this change and save you from the embarrassment of checking faulty code into the shared source repository.

Manually testing all areas of an app under development grows tedious even for the most patient human being. Unit tests are usually performed by a machine—a build server or your own Mac—with unfaltering precision and endurance.

Now let's get down to brass tacks and create some unit tests for `DTDiscogs`.

6.2.1 Introducing NSURLProtocol

The difficult part of testing anything to do with networking is that network connectivity might change from one run of unit tests to the next. This presents a bit of a problem. If your unit tests work one time because the remote server is reachable, but they fail subsequently because the internet connection is down, this can be a source of stress for you as a developer. You don't want unit tests to fail just because the environment changed.

> **NOTE** Testing how a unit interacts with the environment is a different kind of test: an *integration test*. This might also be an interesting thing to test, but in this section we're exclusively looking at ensuring that a unit is and will keep working flawlessly.

The actual network operation happens deep under the hood of Apple's URL-loading system. Even with modern networking via `NSURLSession`, Apple is building on the tried and true networking foundations that remain the same. In the flowchart in figure 6.12, the `DTDiscogs` piece is the system under test, but triggering a search will

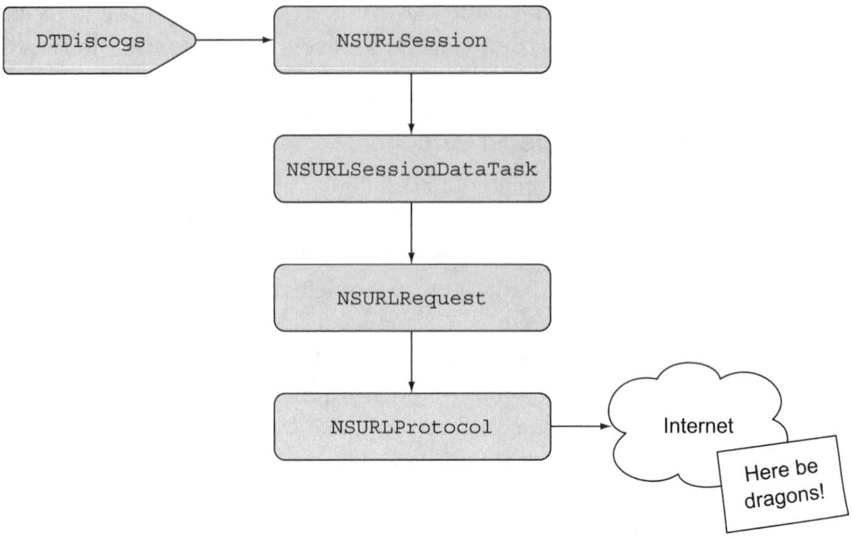

Figure 6.12 The internet as a variable

cause an execution cascade through several system classes. The part where there's communication via the internet is where it becomes fragile.

An `NSURLRequest` represents a request to be made via any TCP/IP-based network connection. It can be for any kind of protocol as expressed by the request's URL scheme. When the connection is to be established, the operating system will query all installed `NSURLProtocol` subclasses to find one that's willing and able to accommodate the request. The system provides only two: `NSAboutURLProtocol`, which handles requests for the `about:` URL scheme, and `NSCFURLProtocol`, which handles all `http:` and `https:` requests. The default behavior is that the system-provided `NSCFURLProtocol` will win the fight and be the one to perform the actual communication with the internet.

The great thing is that this system can be adapted and extended by developers. You can install a protocol for your own `foobar:` scheme or replace the system's handling of HTTP requests.

6.2.2 *Implementing a custom URL scheme with NSURLProtocol*

Let's create a custom NSURLProtocol. In this section we'll implement one to handle the `foobar:` URL scheme. Whenever there's an image referenced by a URL like foobar://oliver.jpg, our app should load this from the app bundle instead of the internet. This `LocalImageProtocol` example project will implement the `foobar:` custom URL scheme for use with a `UIWebView`.

First you need to create an `NSURLProtocol` subclass and name it `LocalImage-Protocol`. You need to implement the class method by which the system will ask your class if it's interested in handling requests:

```
+ (BOOL)canInitWithRequest:(NSURLRequest *)request {
   if ([request.URL.scheme isEqualToString:@"foobar"]) {   <- Only interested in foobar: requests
      return YES;
   }

   return NO;   <- iOS should try other protocol handlers
}
```

The second class method you need to implement is one that makes requests canonical. The point of it is to transform multiple variations of a URL, which all refer to the same resource, into the same canonical URL. This is only really used if you allow caching, because you'd want to cache each retrieved resource only once, with the canonical URL being the cache key. In our example, we won't worry about this cache deduplication, so we can simply return the original request:

```
+ (NSURLRequest *)canonicalRequestForRequest:(NSURLRequest *)request {
   return request;
}
```

If your class responded to the `+canInitWithRequest:` affirmatively, the system will create an instance of your class to handle the specific request. On this instance, you have a property referencing the `request`, as well as a `client` property that more or less represents the `NSURLConnectionDelegate`. You implement the `-startLoading` method to carry out the actual work, and communicate with this delegate, informing it about the various stages as you carry them out.

Note the use of `NSURL`'s `resourceSpecifier` in the following code for retrieving the filename. Because you don't have any host and path components in the foobar URL, the entire string after the scheme becomes the resource specifier:

```
- (void)startLoading {
   NSString *fileName = [self.request.URL resourceSpecifier];   <- Get requested filename
   NSBundle *bundle = [NSBundle mainBundle];
   NSString *imagePath = [bundle pathForResource:fileName
                                          ofType:nil];   <- Determine image filename in app bundle; type is part of name

   if (imagePath) {
      [self _sendImageAtPath:imagePath];   <- Send image to the client
   }
   else {
      [self _sendError];   <- Inform client about the error
   }
}
```

If there's no image in the app bundle with this resource name, you'll send an error to the object that has been registered as being interested in progress and status updates from the loading process, also called the *URL-loading client*. In this case, you also have to implement the `-stopLoading` method, even if it does nothing. Without this dummy implementation, there will be an exception stating that this method is only implemented in the abstract superclass:

```
- (void)stopLoading {
   // nothing to do, but still needs to be implemented
}
```

The method to handle the error case is just as simple:

```
- (void)_sendError {
   NSDictionary *info = @{NSLocalizedDescriptionKey:
                           @"Cannot find file in app bundle"};
   NSError *error = [NSError
                     errorWithDomain:NSStringFromClass([self class])
                     code:999 userInfo:info];

   [self.client URLProtocol:self didFailWithError:error];
}
```

Create an error

Send error to URL-loading client

Finally, you implement the `_sendImageAtPath:` helper method that sends the found image to the URL-loading client and messages the appropriate methods of the `NSURLProtocolClient` protocol to inform the client about the start, received data, and finish of the loading process:

```
- (void)_sendImageAtPath:(NSString *)imagePath {
   NSHTTPURLResponse *response = [[NSHTTPURLResponse alloc]
                                  initWithURL:self.request.URL
                                  statusCode:200
                                  HTTPVersion:@"1.1"
                                  headerFields:nil];
   [self.client URLProtocol:self
         didReceiveResponse:response    )
         cacheStoragePolicy:NSURLCacheStorageNotAllowed];

   NSData *data = [NSData dataWithContentsOfFile:imagePath];
   if ([data length]) {
      [self.client URLProtocol:self didLoadData:data];
   }

   [self.client URLProtocolDidFinishLoading:self];
}
```

Simulate an HTTP response.

The URL is reused.

Success is communicated with status code 200.

Doesn't matter, so use 1.1

You don't need to send any HTTP headers as part of the response.

Send response to URL-loading client.

Load file data and send it to client.

Inform client about end of loading.

If you wanted to, you could also add HTTP headers, such as to specify a content type, but this example works fine without them.

The protocol implementation is now finished. To install it for use by the URL-loading system, add this line to your app delegate:

```
[NSURLProtocol registerClass:[LocalImageProtocol class]];
```

If you run the `LocalImageProtocol` sample app, you'll see a web view loading an HTML string with an embedded image (see figure 6.13). This image is loaded from the app bundle via the foobar:Oliver.jpg URL because now there's a protocol to handle it.

This technique can be used to implement any kind of URL protocol. In the following section, we'll build a mechanism for stubbing network requests with it.

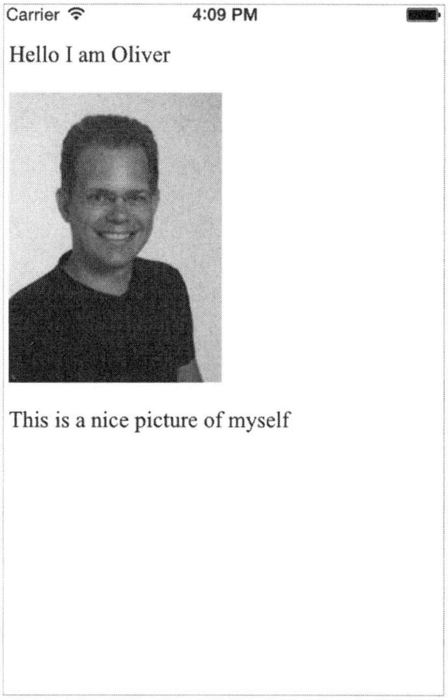
Carrier
4:09 PM
Hello I am Oliver
This is a nice picture of myself

Figure 6.13 `LocalImageProtocol` **sample app**

6.2.3 Stubbing NSURLRequest responses with DTURLProtocolStub

In the Music Collection app, you'll find `DTURLProtocolStub`, which works much like `LocalImageProtocol` but with a few more bells and whistles. Like the app in the previous section, it's a simple subclass of `NSURLProtocol`. Instead of repeating the explanation of how it works, let's do something more exciting: eliminate the internet as a variable by simulating network requests.

Test stubs are programs that simulate the behavior of components that a module undergoing tests depends on. In this case the tested module is the `DTDiscogs` wrapper class, and the component it depends on is the Discogs web service. By specifying a variety of canned answers, you can create unit tests covering all sorts of scenarios, including those that are extremely rare in real life.

The `DTURLProtocolStub` class, which is provided as part of the Music Collection sample app, lets you stub HTTP network requests. To use this class in your own unit tests, copy the headers and implementation files for `DTURLProtocolStub` and `DTURLProtocolResponse` to your project, and make sure that the .m files are compiled for the unit test target.

FINDING THE UNIT TEST SOURCE CODE All the code mentioned in this section—along with a few more tests—can be found in DiscogsQueryTests.m, which contains the Music Collection app unit tests.

Let's assume you have a component that depends on a GET request to www.apple.com. You want to test one scenario where the response works with an HTTP status code of 200 (OK). Then you want to see that your code works correctly if—however unlikely—you get a code of 404 (Not Found).

The stubbing class is designed to provide canned responses based on criteria you define. Those criteria are specified in a test block that receives a reference to the `NSURLRequest` object for which the loading should occur. The test block can inspect properties of the URL request, like the URL, and if it returns `YES` the response should be returned. Specify a `NULL` test block to have the response always be delivered.

Having imported the stub header, you can add code to simulate the successful request. Response tests are executed for each request in the same order they were registered with the `DTURLProtocolStub` class. The following example installs a stub for requests to the Apple domain:

```
- (void)testFakeApple {
   NSString *string = @"Hello, I am Apple. Really! ;-)";
   [DTURLProtocolStub addPlainTextResponse:string statusCode:200
    forRequestPassingTest:^BOOL(NSURLRequest *request) {
                        NSString *host = request.URL.host;
                        if ([host isEqualToString:@"www.apple.com"]) {
                           return YES;
                        }
                        return NO;
    }];

   NSURL *URL = [NSURL URLWithString:@"http://www.apple.com"];
   NSURLRequest *request = [NSURLRequest requestWithURL:URL];
   NSHTTPURLResponse *response;
   NSError *error;
   NSData *data = [NSURLConnection sendSynchronousRequest:request
                                   returningResponse:&response
                                               error:&error];
   NSString *responseString =
      [[NSString alloc] initWithData:data
                          encoding:NSUTF8StringEncoding];
   NSString *contentType = response.allHeaderFields[@"Content-Type"];

   XCTAssertEqualObjects(string, responseString,
                         @"wrong response string");
   XCTAssertEqual(response.statusCode, 200,
                  @"Status should be 200");
   XCTAssertEqualObjects(contentType, @"text/plain",
                         @"wrong content type");
}
```

Provide canned response with content type "text/plain"

Return this response only for calls to domain www.apple.com

Execute synchronous URL request

Convert response data to string

Get content type from response headers

Assertions to determine if all went as expected

This unit test uses a convenience method of `DTURLProtocolStub` that provides a plain text response for all requests to the www.apple.com URL. A complete test case method incorporates several unit test assertions to determine if the result is indeed what was expected.

All methods on `DTURLProtocolStub` are class methods, because you have no reference to the individual protocol object instance that the system will create for the `NSURLRequest`. You need to install the stubbing protocol class in the `-setUp` method of your test case class:

```
- (void)setUp {
   [super setUp];

   [NSURLProtocol registerClass:[DTURLProtocolStub class]];
   [DTURLProtocolStub removeAllResponses];

   [DTURLProtocolStub setMissingResponseBlock:^(NSURLRequest *request) {
      XCTFail(@"No response configured for request to %@", request.URL);
      return (NSError *)nil;
   }];
}
```

Registers the stub handler for URL-loading system

Remove responses left over from previous test case setUp

Install warning for missing responses

This setup method is called before each individual test case method. Because of this, you need to remove the responses left over from the previous test. The `+setMissingResponseBlock:` method warns you if you forgot to provide a response for a specific scenario. Figure 6.14 shows the `testFakeApple` unit test passing because all assertions on the URL response object are passing.

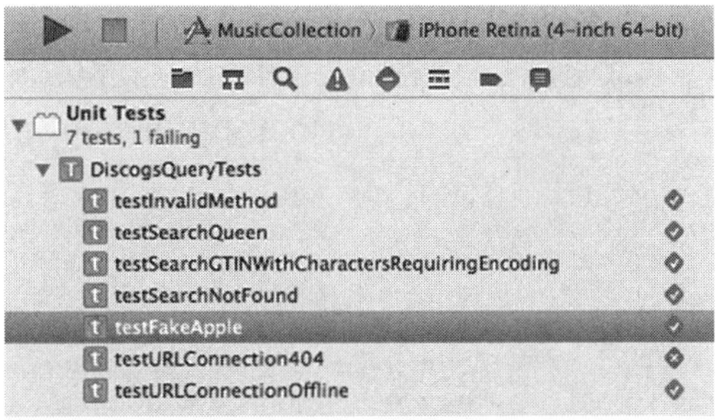

Figure 6.14 Fake Apple unit test passing

For the scenario where the call to Apple needs to return a 404 instead, you specify the appropriate response:

```
NSString *string = @"404 Not Found";
[DTURLProtocolStub addPlainTextResponse:string statusCode:404
                 forRequestPassingTest:NULL];
```

If you pass `NULL` for the test block, this 404 response is sent for all requests. This is more convenient if you only have a single stubbed response. You have both tools at your disposal: the fine chisel (fine-grained test blocks) to target a variety of requests all getting different responses, or the heavy hammer (a `NULL` test block) that responds with the same content regardless of the request. Use the one that best suits the task at hand.

Another good test to have is one that checks how the URL connection (and your error handling) would deal with an offline internet connection:

```
NSError *offlineError = [NSError errorWithDomain:@"NSURLErrorDomain"
                                            code:-1009
                                        userInfo:nil];
[DTURLProtocolStub addErrorResponse:offlineError
             forRequestPassingTest:NULL];
```

In real life—outside of unit testing—iOS messages the `connection:didFailWithError:` delegate method for a variety of transport errors, including -1009 for an offline connection. The preceding convenience method lets you specify the `NSError` that will be returned to the delegate. Which error this is doesn't usually matter unless your error-checking code relies on a specific error code or message.

> **NOTE** Don't confuse *HTTP errors* with connection/transport errors. Even an HTTP status code 404—for a web page that can't be found—is considered to be a *successful connection*. Connection or transport errors, on the other hand, occur if there's no internet connection, if DNS can't resolve the host name, or if the connection times out. Successful connections result in `didFinishLoading` and unsuccessful ones in `didFailWithError:`.

`DTURLProtocolStub` has one more trick up its sleeve: you can record the individual `NSURLRequest` before it's treated with a response. This is useful if you want to make sure that the URL has been constructed in a certain way by your wrapper class.

Place the following code into your test case `setUp` to have subsequent requests added to an array. This enables you to inspect the requests after the simulated network operations to assert that only those that you expected were added:

```
_recordedRequests = [NSMutableArray array];
[DTURLProtocolStub setBeforeRequestBlock:^(NSURLRequest *request) {
   [_recordedRequests addObject:request];
}];
```

Fresh array for the recording is created each time setup is called

Add response to array

Block gets executed before stubbed response is sent

You've seen `DTURLProtocolStub` in action for "classic" `NSURLConnection`-based networking. Next we'll look at how to use it together with `NSURLSession`.

6.2.4 Stubbing NSURLSession requests with DTURLProtocolStub

Before iOS 7, installing a protocol handler would always affect all network connections. In iOS 7 and later, `NSURLSession` doesn't use the global protocol registry. Instead, the list of active `NSURLProtocol` classes is kept by `NSURLSessionConfiguration` instances.

In section 6.1.5 you used the default ephemeral session configuration to perform the Discogs query. You might also remember creating a secondary initializer for DTDiscogs that takes a session configuration as a parameter. This was done deliberately to allow you to modify the list of protocol handlers.

The `MusicCollection` unit tests implementation has the following helper method that modifies the session configuration to install your protocol stubbing class:

```
- (NSURLSessionConfiguration *)_testSessionConfiguration {
   NSURLSessionConfiguration *config =
      [NSURLSessionConfiguration ephemeralSessionConfiguration];
```

```
    config.protocolClasses = @[[DTURLProtocolStub class]];

    return config;
}
```

The test case `-setUp` creates a fresh instance of `DTDiscogs` in an instance variable that uses this configuration:

```
NSURLSessionConfiguration *config = [self _testSessionConfiguration];
_discogs = [[DTDiscogs alloc] initWithSessionConfiguration:config];
```

This causes all subsequent `searchForGTIN:completion:` calls to be handled by the protocol stubber, allowing you to specify a variety of responses for all the test cases you can dream up. Because the responses coming from Discogs are JSON, there's a convenience method to have the response data come from a file path. Having the JSON come from files is much more convenient than having to specify the JSON as long strings in your unit test code.

Instead of configuring a single cover-all response like in the previous section, we'll now set up a cascade of tests and responses where each subsequent test is broader than the previous one. The following three code snippets form the `_setupProtocolStubForSearch` setup method, which can be reused for several test cases.

The first code snippet configures a successful response to a search for a specific Queen album by GTIN. The response data comes from a JSON file inside the unit test bundle:

```
NSString *path = [self _pathForResource:@"search_success"
                                 ofType:@"json"];
[DTURLProtocolStub addResponseWithFile:path statusCode:200
 forRequestPassingTest:^BOOL(NSURLRequest *request) {
if (![request.URL.path isEqualToString:@"/database/search"]) {
    return NO;
}

NSArray *queryParams = [request.URL.query
                        componentsSeparatedByString:@"&"];
if (![queryParams containsObject:@"barcode=077774620420"]) {
    return NO;
}

return YES;
 }];
```

Get path of JSON file inside test bundle via helper method

Request must be for the search function of the API

Request must contain a query parameter with the correct GTIN

If the test for the first response doesn't match, then a second test returns a "not found" response to a search request:

```
path = [self _pathForResource:@"search_not_found"
                       ofType:@"json"];
[DTURLProtocolStub addResponseWithFile:path statusCode:200
 forRequestPassingTest:^BOOL(NSURLRequest *request) {
```

Get path of JSON file inside test bundle via helper method

```
    if ([request.URL.path isEqualToString:@"/database/search"]) {
       return YES;
    }

    return NO;
 }];
```

Request must be for the search function of the API

If the API function URL points to an incorrect path on the Discogs server, it will respond with a "resource not found" error, with status code 404. We'll use this as the final response for all requests not handled by the previous two tests. This way you can also test whether the code can deal with this occurrence:

```
path = [self _pathForResource:@"resource_not_found"
                       ofType:@"json"];
[DTURLProtocolStub addResponseWithFile:path statusCode:404
 forRequestPassingTest:NULL];
```

All three JSON files can be found in the Music Collection project. They were created by saving the responses Discogs sent for these scenarios. Having them as files is much more convenient than constructing `NSDictionary` instances and then encoding these as JSON.

6.2.5 How to test asynchronous completion handlers

The `DTDiscogs` wrapper is constructed so that when you call the search method, you pass a completion block. This block will be called after the networking operations and subsequent validation are finished. That means it will be executed on a separate background queue and might also take a short while to complete.

Unit tests are executed on the main queue, so you need a way to pause execution until the completion block is called. Otherwise the test case would continue on and finish while the completion block is still executing. This pause mechanism is provided by Grand Central Dispatch (GCD) in the form of *semaphores.*

You create a semaphore in `-setUp` amongst the other initialization code you want to execute for each test:

```
_requestSemaphore = dispatch_semaphore_create(0);
```

Two helper methods call two semaphore functions. Their only purpose is to provide a name describing what they're used for:

```
- (void)_waitForRequestToFinish {
   dispatch_semaphore_wait(_requestSemaphore, DISPATCH_TIME_FOREVER);
}

- (void)_signalThatRequestIsDone {
   dispatch_semaphore_signal(_requestSemaphore);
}
```

Halt current thread until request signals that it's done

Call at end of async block to unlock the semaphore

In practice, you wait on the semaphore right after the call to the search function. Inside the completion block, you unlock the semaphore as a last action.

Here's the unit test for the scenario where a Queen album is found:

```
- (void)testSearchQueen {
   [self _setupProtocolStubForSearch];

   [_discogs searchForGTIN:@"077774620420"
      completion:^(id result, NSError *error) {
         XCTAssertNil(error, @"There should be no error");
         XCTAssertNotNil(result, @"There should be a response");
         XCTAssertTrue([result isKindOfClass:[NSDictionary class]],
                       @"Result should be a dictionary");
         NSArray *results = result[@"results"];
         XCTAssertEqual([results count], 1, @"One result expected");
         NSDictionary *lastResult = [results lastObject];
         NSString *title = lastResult[@"title"];
         XCTAssertEqualObjects(title, @"Queen - Queen",
                              @"Title is wrong");

         [self _signalThatRequestIsDone];
      }];

   [self _waitForRequestToFinish];
}
```

Helper method for setting up the cascade of search results

Various assertions that should be met for test to pass

Unlock semaphore when the completion block is done

Main thread execution waits here until semaphore is released

6.2.6 *Shifting to test-driven development*

In this chapter we first developed the DTDiscogs *unit*, and then we implemented unit tests for it. I can't give you more than a few thoughts on the broad subject of unit testing, but I wanted to show you how to deal with the tricky bits relevant to our subject matter: eliminating the internet as a variable in your test setup, and testing asynchronous code.

The basic approach to unit testing—which I demonstrated in this chapter—is to create the implementation first and then create unit tests for it. The unit tests nail down the assumptions you make about your code's output. Should you ever change your implementation to give different output, you'd notice this through failing unit tests. Unit tests serve as coal mine canaries in this regard.

Another approach I often take is to implement new unit tests for bugs I fix. This makes sure that I'll never undo a fix for an already-fixed bug while fixing a new one. As apps grow more complex, you're bound to lose the ability to foresee all the side effects that new code or changes will have on all other areas.

The reverse approach is to write the test first, knowing full well that it's failing. Then you implement the minimum behavior that will allow the test to pass. Then write another failing test, rinse, and repeat. This approach is referred to as *test-driven* because the creation of tests drives the implementation of features.

The main advantage of test-driven development (TDD) is that you don't have to think up appropriate unit tests for all branches in your implementation code after the fact. Once you have a working program, you'll most likely also have a reasonable set of unit tests.

Whichever of these styles better suits your taste is up to you. But however you decide, unit tests will help you create better code—you can never have too many of them.

6.3 Summary

You now know that your users can scan barcodes on mobile devices that are connected to the internet by means of 3G cellular data or WiFi networking. Now you can start thinking about interesting usage scenarios. Can you think of a situation where it would be orders of magnitude more convenient to scan a product barcode than to enter multiple bits of information?

This chapter's sample app demonstrated how you can use barcode scanning to let a user add music media to a collection. As a Core Data–based app, it displayed the music collection in a table list view, governed by a fetched-results controller. It introduced modern networking embodied by `NSURLSession` and demonstrated how to create a convenient wrapper class around the Discogs web service API.

You've learned a method for offloading Core Data updates to a temporary worker context, and you've also seen how unwinding segues are created and used. These are two skills that are tangential to the main goal of this chapter—retrieving metadata for scanned barcodes—but they're nevertheless quite useful to know.

In the section on unit testing, we explored a technique for stubbing server responses for `NSURLConnection` and `NSURLSession`. For both of them, you can install a custom `NSURLProtocol` to dish out responses. Then you saw how to synchronize test execution and asynchronous completion handlers by using a dispatch semaphore.

These are the key takeaways for this chapter:

- `NSURLSession`-based networking and barcode scanning were both introduced in iOS 7.
- You can create a URL session with the most suitable of three default configurations: default, ephemeral, or background.
- Use `NSURLSessionDownloadTask` for downloading files and `NSURLSessionUploadTask` for uploading.
- Avoid performing update operations on a main-queue-based managed object context. This can lead to UI stuttering.
- `NSURLSessionDataTask`, in combination with the ephemeral configuration, is ideal for web API calls because you typically don't need any result caching there.
- You should abstract the network operations for interacting with a RESTful service into a wrapper class.
- You should check for all possible kinds of errors when dealing with the result of a web API call.
- You should unit test any networking wrapper code you write. Whether you prefer to code first and then formulate tests or follow TDD is up to you. But you can never have too many unit tests.
- Simulating network responses eliminates the internet as a variable and also lets you test how your code can deal with a greater variety of responses.

This chapter elaborated on using the always-on internet of modern smartphones to retrieve metadata based on scanned barcodes. In the next and final chapter of this book, you'll see how you can use the user's current geographic and semantic context to further enhance your barcode-scanning apps.

7 Putting barcodes in context

This chapter covers

- Taking advantage of your user's context to create "magic"
- Geofencing locations with Core Location
- Determining semantic location with iBeacons

Modern smartphones are uniquely aware of the current context a user is in. Whether you're moving or standing still, or whether you're inside a moving car—it feels totally natural to be able to open the Maps app and see your current position on the planet indicated by a pulsating blue dot.

Apple has an uncanny ability to pick the most beneficial technological advancements to be added in each new iOS version, for users as well as developers. The Core Location framework has been part of the iPhone operating system since the first version, but it was originally limited to getting user location by means of WiFi and cell tower triangulation. A three-axis accelerometer was also on board to allow the device to detect its own orientation so that it could rotate the UI to match.

On the second-generation iPhone 3G, Apple added a GPS receiver that further increased the accuracy of Core Location. But because Core Location beautifully abstracts determining the device location, there were almost no changes to the public APIs. The same can be said about the third-generation iPhone 3GS, which added a magnetometer allowing iOS to rotate maps to face the direction the user is looking.

Another generation later, with the iPhone 4, Apple added a three-axis digital gyroscope sensor, providing additional accuracy when detecting rotation. *Are you beginning to see the trend?*

As more sensor chips are added to the device, it knows more about the user and about the surroundings the user is in. This is commonly referred to as the *user context.* On your Mac, a context menu is a popup menu showing only activities that make sense in the context you point the arrow at. On mobile devices, apps can (and should) provide similar functionality and only present users with information or actions that are relevant to the context they're presently in.

This chapter introduces the two major functionalities found in *Core Location*: *geographic context* from the user's geolocation and *semantic context* from tracking and ranging iBeacons. The difference between these two will soon become clear as we look at how you can use these to better serve your customers.

7.1 Understanding multiple layers of context

Let's assume for a moment that you're inside an Apple Store. Your iPhone can infer this from your geographic location, because you're within a certain radius of the store. Your iPhone is strongly receiving the signal from an iBeacon, which indicates that you must be standing close to the table displaying iPads.

I'd like to point out two further levels of context that are provided by barcodes. First, the Apple Store app lets you scan barcodes found on various products, such as an accessory cable. This indicates that you have a specific interest in such a product, which is another piece of context. In the case of Apple, you can pay for the cable with your iTunes account and walk out of the store without ever having to talk to a genius. This is a great feature to offer to customers who are either shy or in a hurry.

Most electronic products have a second barcode—besides the GTIN product code—showing the device's serial number. If you scan a MacBook's GTIN, your context would be "any such model of MacBook." But if you scanned the serial number on the MacBook's box, your context would be a single unique device. This specific device has unique properties, like tech specs or when AppleCare runs out. You could build an inventory-tracking app that maintains a database of all the serial numbers of your company's devices. Then you could assign specific pieces of equipment to individual employees, and track who in your company is using what.

In the sample app for this chapter, we'll look at three of the four levels of context (depicted in figure 7.1), because both barcode-related contexts work the same way,

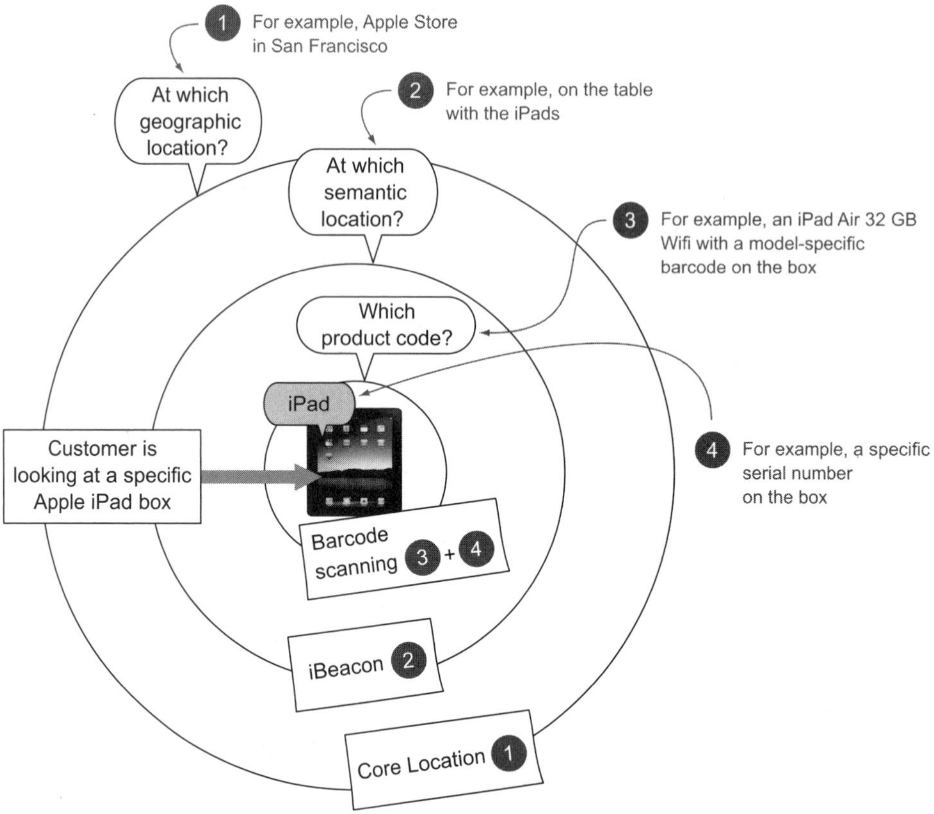

Figure 7.1 Multiple layers of context

technically speaking. Besides, several previous chapters have already taught you how to add a modal view controller with a barcode scanner to your apps.

As British writer Arthur C. Clarke put it, "Any sufficiently advanced technology is indistinguishable from magic." (*Profiles of the Future*, 1962) The situational awareness emerging from the iPhone's built-in sensors is the main ingredient you can use to delight your users and create "magic" in your apps. You might not be able to anticipate *all* your user's needs, but anticipating a few more than your competitor's apps might make a big difference to your bottom line.

7.2 Building a YardSale app

Until now, people selling off things they don't need anymore have done so the "traditional way"—yard sales, garage sales, and the like. Those one-person flea markets often have a treasure trove of goodies, but interested buyers might never know about them if they don't happen to pass by the home of the seller at the right time. There has to be an app for that.

Let's assume that you're working for a startup that aims to establish "yard sales as a service" to conquer this untapped market. People having a yard sale would sign up with your company as sellers, submit the dates they're holding a sale, and enter a list of products and the prices they're offering those items at. A free app, which you're tasked to develop, should be put on the App Store to help drive prospective customers to those sellers.

Your company could sell packs of iBeacon devices to your users or guide them to one of the many companies that sell iBeacons. Any beacon adhering to Apple's iBeacon standard can be used for this purpose, including virtual (software) iBeacons. Apps running on devices capable of Bluetooth LE can emit an iBeacon. We'll use this software-based option for testing the sample app so that you don't have to rush out to buy a hardware iBeacon.

The finished YardSale app will have these features:

- The app will feature a list of currently active yard sale locations and show them on a map.
- If a user taps on one of the location pins, they'll see the sale's name in a callout bubble.
- Tapping on the callout accessory will show the in-store UI for this yard sale.
- The user can easily "leave" the store by tapping a Close button.
- If the app is inactive and the user walks into the vicinity of a yard sale, they will get a notification about the sale.
- When the app is active or becomes active because of the user tapping on the notification action, the in-store UI will also be shown.
- The in-store UI shows a list of products grouped by the table they're on (to enable multitable yard sales).
- If an iBeacon is received more strongly than any others, only the table associated with this beacon is shown.
- The in-store UI displays a button allowing the user to scan a barcode on an item for sale, and after scanning an alert will show the layers of context.

In contrast to our previous sample apps, this one doesn't just have just one interface, but two: one for outside of stores and one for inside, as shown in figure 7.2. Plus, there will be notifications outside of the app, which could be counted as a sort of minimalistic UI for your app. The purpose of the YardSale app is to demonstrate how you can take advantage of the user's context to decide which of these user interfaces will most benefit the user.

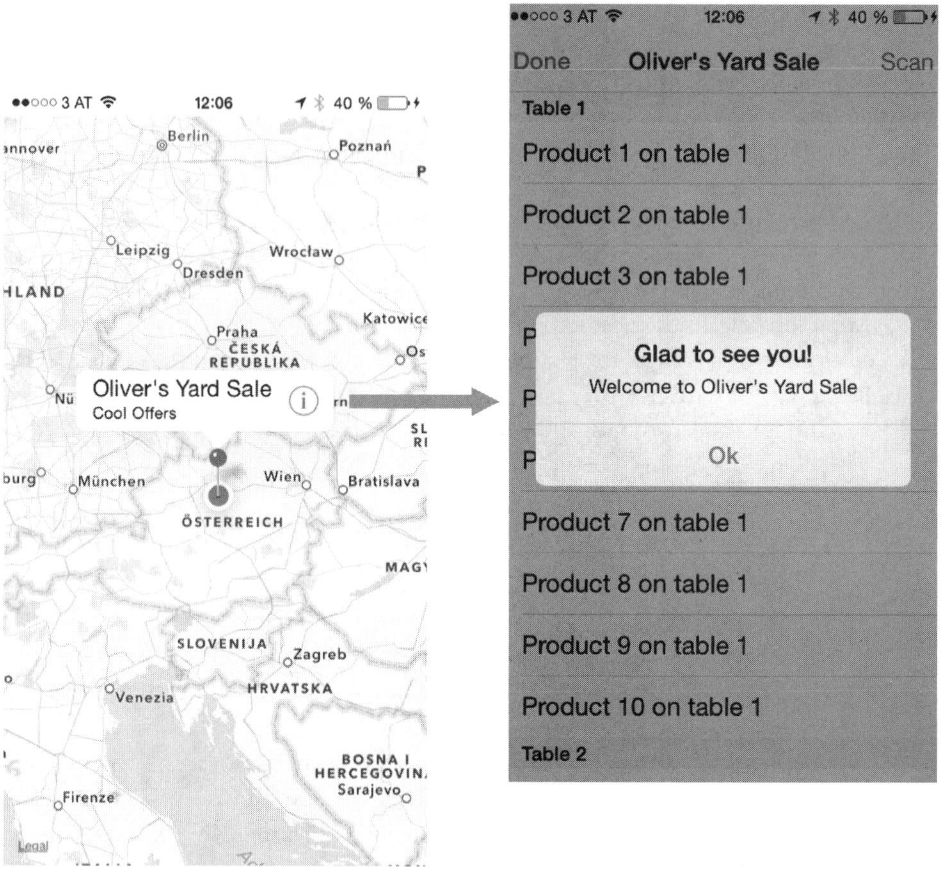

Figure 7.2 The finished YardSale app

7.2.1 *Creating the outside-the-store experience*

No matter how many physical store locations you have, there will always be a "whole world" outside of the stores. The user interface you'll develop in this section will aim to provide information to your users that's beneficial when they're out and about. At its simplest, the UI will show a map with pins showing the locations of yard sales. This will allow the user to look up the closest sale locations.

Let's get started building this part of the YardSale app.

Create a new app project using the Single View Application template, and call it "YardSale." Using the refactor tool, rename the `ViewController` class with a more descriptive name: `MapViewController`. This will be both the root view controller of your application and the controller for the map.

For showing the map and pins, you'll use `MKMapView` provided by the MapKit framework. In the main storyboard, add a new map view as a subview of the previous root view that the Xcode template set up for you. Add constraints to pin the sides of the subview flush with the sides of its superview. The top should be aligned with the

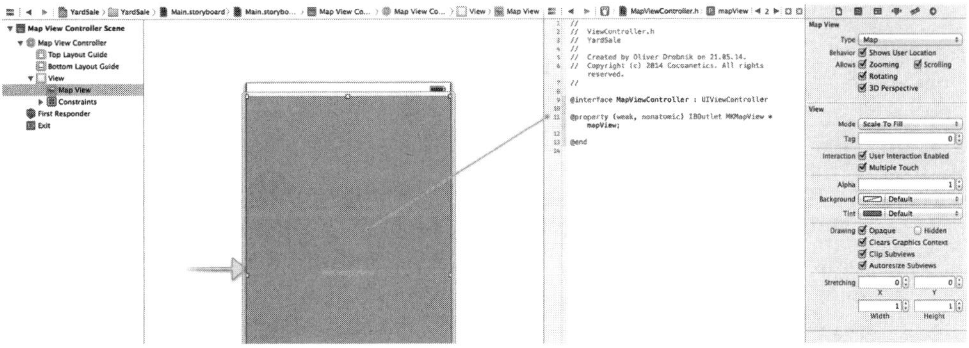

Figure 7.3 Adding an outlet for the map view

top layout guide so that the map doesn't extend under the status bar. This way the map will always resize correctly if you rotate the device.

For setting the annotations on the map, you need an outlet. Open MapViewController.h in the assistant editor and Ctrl-drag the map view onto it to create an `IBOutlet`, as shown in figure 7.3.

In order to reference methods and classes from the MapKit framework, add it to your target's Link Binary With Libraries build phase. I recommend that you add the main headers for Apple frameworks to the precompiled header file (PCH). This speeds up compilation and makes all symbols available for all your source files. For `MapKit.framework` the header to add is MapKit.h. You can look at the YardSale sample app contained in this book's sample code to see this.

For this demo, the locations will come from a property list that has the following four values for each sale:

- The geolocation of the yard sale, coded as *latitude* and *longitude*
- The *name* of the yard sale
- A unique *identifier* to identify each yard sale

In the plist, those yard sale locations are represented as dictionaries, but inside the app you'll want to convert them into proper objects of type `SalePlacemark`. By deriving from `MKPlacemark`, you can directly use the `SalePlacemarks` as map view annotations.

The `SalePlace` class extracts these values from the surrounding dictionary and puts them into the appropriate instance variables. Because `MKPlacemark` already has a property to take on the location, you can pass it through to the dedicated initializer:

Create location struct from dictionary values

Call superclass's existing initializer taking the geocoordinate

```
- (instancetype)initWithDictionary:(NSDictionary *)dictionary {
   CLLocationCoordinate2D coord;
   coord.latitude = [dictionary[@"Latitude"] floatValue];
   coord.longitude = [dictionary[@"Longitude"] floatValue];
   self = [super initWithCoordinate:coord
                  addressDictionary:nil];
```

```
    if (self) {
       _name = dictionary[@"Name"];
       _identifier = dictionary[@"Identifier"];
    }
    return self;
}
```

Set additional instance variables

You're using the existing placemark subclasses in the API. CLPlacemark in Core Location is a place with a radius and an address dictionary. MKPlacemark—found in the MapKit framework—is a subclass of CLPlacemark, adding the methods of the MKAnnotation protocol. This means you can use those placemarks as model objects for adding annotations to a map view.

In the YardSale app, the handling of the plist is encapsulated in the YardSaleManager class. A private helper method loads the list of sale locations from the plist, converting them to SalePlace instances:

```
- (void)_loadAnnotations {
   NSString *path =[[NSBundle mainBundle] pathForResource:@"Locations"
                                                  ofType:@"plist"];
   NSArray *locs = [NSArray arrayWithContentsOfFile:path];
   NSMutableArray *tmpArray = [NSMutableArray array];
   for (NSDictionary *oneLoc in locs) {
      SalePlace *place = [[SalePlace alloc] initWithDictionary:oneLoc];
      [tmpArray addObject:place];
   }
   _annotations = [tmpArray copy];
}
```

Get path to plist file in app bundle

Convert places dictionaries into sale places

Store immutable copy of the array in ivar

It's very tempting—especially in a small app like this one—to place such model-related code in the view controller where you're using it. But as you'll see, you'll also need to access those placemarks from the app delegate, so it's smarter to have a dedicated model controller class like YardSaleManager. Once it's instantiated, you can pass a reference to it to all objects needing to interact with the sales places.

This instantiation of the yard sale manager instance is done in the first method that's called when your app launches. The storyboard has no reference to the app delegate, which would allow you to set an outlet on the MapViewController. But because you know that the map view controller will be set as the rootViewController of the app's window, you can get the reference from there:

```
- (BOOL)application:(UIApplication *)application
      didFinishLaunchingWithOptions:(NSDictionary *)launchOptions {
   _saleManager = [YardSaleManager new];
   MapViewController *vc =
     (MapViewController *)self.window.rootViewController;
   NSAssert([vc isKindOfClass:[MapViewController class]],
           @"Root VC is not a MapViewController!");
   vc.yardSaleManager = _saleManager;
   return YES;
}
```

Create model controller instance

Get reference to map view controller

Assert your assumption that root VC is what you expect

Hand model controller reference to map view controller

You can now place your pins on the map, ideally right before the MapViewController's view will become visible. But you can't put it in viewWillAppear:, because this method will also be called if the in-store UI is being dismissed. In real life you'd need further logic to prevent double-setting the same annotations and to handle updating. But for this sample app we're foregoing such complexities:

```
- (void)viewDidLoad {
   [super viewDidLoad];
   NSArray *annotations = _yardSaleManager.annotations;              <-- Get all annotations from manager
   [self.mapView addAnnotations:annotations];                        <-- Add annotations to map
   [self.mapView showAnnotations:annotations animated:YES];          <-- Zoom to fit all annotations
}
```

With this code in place, your app should load the placemarks from the app bundle and show them as red pins on the map.

If you tap on one of the red pins, a callout bubble is shown. Its contents stem from the values of the title and subtitle properties returned from SalePlace:

```
- (NSString *)title {
   return [NSString stringWithFormat:@"%@'s Yard Sale", _name];
}

- (NSString *)subtitle {
   return @"Cool Offers";
}
```

You also want to be able to enter a sale location via an accessory button in the form of an info button on the right side of the callout bubble (see figure 7.4). Tapping this button should show the in-store UI with information and actions specific to this particular site.

Figure 7.4 Apple's yard sale

Getting your home coordinates

Please replace the "Oliver" sale place and coordinates in Locations.plist with your own location. For your testing, you can also add a few places near your current location. The locations in the YardSale app's property list are almost certainly too far away from you for reasonable testing.

A quick way to find an address's geographic coordinates is to search for them on Google Maps. Note the decimal numbers in the address bar—those are the latitude and longitude degrees of the address. Copy them to the latitude and longitude fields in the property list.

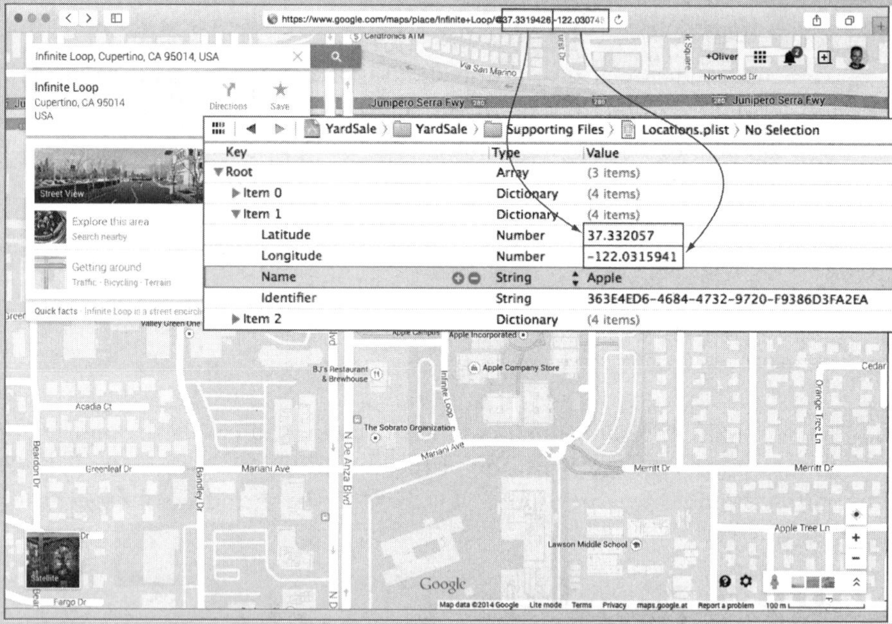

Getting coordinates with Google Maps

Another way to find geographic coordinates, which is slightly more involved but also more suitable for iOS developers, is to run the GetLocation sample app, which you can find with the book's source code. This displays your current geolocation together with a reverse-geocoded address for your present location.

Make the MapViewController the delegate of the map view by connecting the delegate outlet with the view controller in Interface Builder. The following MKMapViewDelegate method lets you customize the annotation pins:

```
- (MKAnnotationView *)mapView:(MKMapView *)mapView
          viewForAnnotation:(id<MKAnnotation>)annotation {
   if ([annotation isKindOfClass:[MKUserLocation class]]) {
      return nil;
   }
```

Preserve blue dot for the user location

```
    MKPinAnnotationView *pav =
       [[MKPinAnnotationView alloc] initWithAnnotation:annotation
                                     reuseIdentifier:nil];
    pav.canShowCallout = YES;

    UIButton *detailButton =
       [UIButton buttonWithType:UIButtonTypeDetailDisclosure];
    pav.rightCalloutAccessoryView=detailButton;
    return pav;
}
```

Enable showing of callout bubble from pin annotation

Create new default red pin annotation view

Create default info button

Set button as the right accessory of the callout bubble

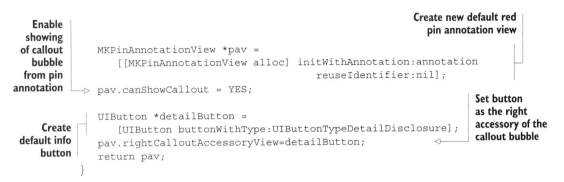

If you implement this delegate method, it's important to exclude the annotation representing the user's current location. Otherwise it would also get a red pin, confusing users who are expecting to seeing a blue pulsating dot for their current location.

Finally, to trigger the segue to the in-store UI, you need to implement another delegate method that's called as soon as the user taps on the info button for a callout:

```
- (void)mapView:(MKMapView *)mapView
 annotationView:(MKAnnotationView *)view
 calloutAccessoryControlTapped:(UIControl *)control {
   [mapView deselectAnnotation:view.annotation animated:YES];
   [self performSegueWithIdentifier:@"ShowSalePlace" sender:view];
}
```

Hide info bubble

Show in-store UI

The aforementioned segue doesn't exist yet. You'll implement the in-store view controller next.

7.2.2 Implementing the in-store user interface

You want to show users information relevant to yard sales they're visiting, whether virtually, when they tap on the callout, or physically, when they come close to the place of the sale. For this purpose, you'll implement a table view controller that shows in-store information.

The transition from map to in-store UI could either be a modal segue or push segue. I chose the modal option here because then the map remains underneath the sliding-in view controller. This gives the user a clue that in order to return to the map, they need to "exit" the store.

Add a new `UITableViewController` subclass to the project and call it `InStoreViewController`. In Interface Builder, add this new view controller embedded in a navigation controller. This will give you a navigation bar on which to mount the Close button (see figure 7.5).

There's no UI element in the `MapViewController` to which you could connect a segue, so instead you can connect it to the Manual option under Triggered Segues, as shown in figure 7.6. Doing so creates a new segue that you set to the "modal" segue type. To be able to call it from your code, give it an identifier of `ShowSalePlace`.

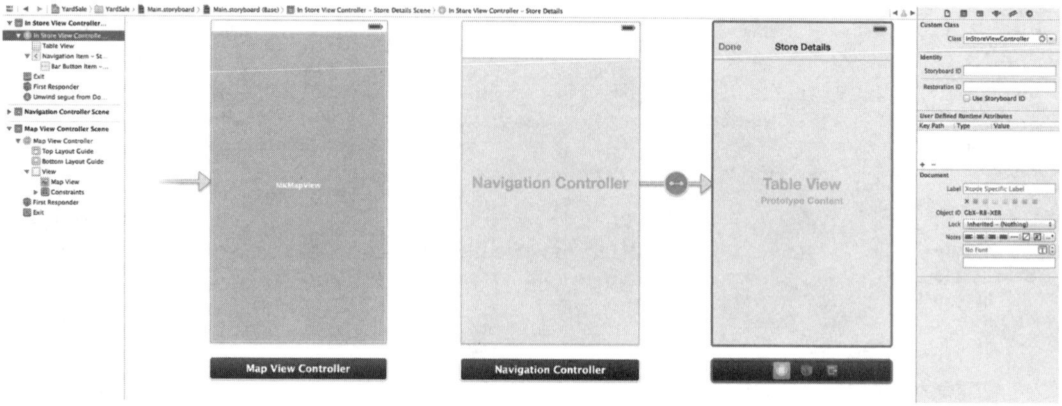

Figure 7.5 Adding the in-store UI

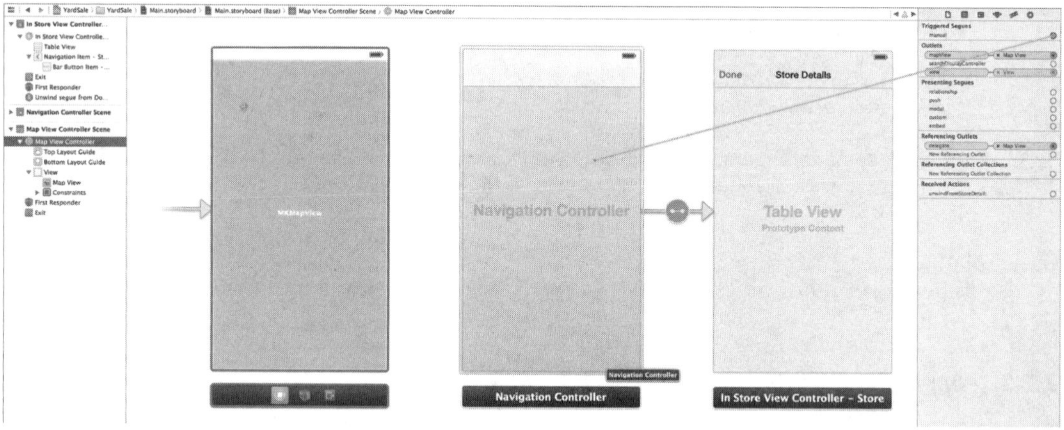

Figure 7.6 Adding the in-store UI segue

Add a dummy unwinding method to the `MapViewController`. This lets you connect the Close bar button to the green Exit icon. (Please refer to section 6.1.4 for an explanation of unwind segues.)

You've now created a segue that you can call programmatically via its identifier, and you've also set it up so that the modal view controller is dismissed when the Close button is tapped. In fact, you're already performing the segue in reaction to the callout bubble's accessory button being tapped.

You need to pass the relevant `SalePlace` to the `InStoreViewController`. This is done in `prepareForSegue:sender:`, which is called right before the segue animation happens. The in-store view controller has a `salePlace` property to receive it:

Destination is the navigation controller.

This is only relevant for the segue with the correct identifier.

```
- (void)prepareForSegue:(UIStoryboardSegue *)segue sender:(id)sender {
   if ([segue.identifier isEqualToString:@"ShowSalePlace"]) {
      UINavigationController *nav = [segue destinationViewController];
      InStoreViewController *vc = nav.viewControllers[0];
      vc.salePlace = [sender annotation];
   }
}
```

In-store UI is the first of the navigation controller's view controllers.

Set the annotation as the salePlace.

You're passing the `MKAnnotationView` as the sender of the segue when calling it from code (see the code snippet at the end of section 7.2.1). The annotation view object has an `annotation` property that references the `SalePlace` object belonging to it. Sometimes you see developers "abusing" the sender method to directly pass the model object, but I frown on this practice because in UIKit nomenclature the `sender` parameter is supposed to be the control triggering some activity, not a model object.

To demonstrate that you're showing the correct yard sale with your in-store view controller, you can set the title in `viewWillAppear:` to the `SalePlace` title:

```
self.navigationItem.title = self.salePlace.title;
```

This completes the UI work for both views that the YardSale app will provide. The app launches in "global view" showing the map of pins. If you tap on a pin, a callout shows more details and an info button. Tapping on this shows the in-store UI modally. Tapping on the Close button dismisses it.

The next step is to show the in-store UI if the user gets close to a yard sale.

7.3 Geofencing store locations

You want your app to alert users when they come close to a listed yard sale, even if the YardSale app isn't active. Apple's rule is that apps may not run in the background and use up the battery. There are exceptions to this rule that the developer can request for specific use cases. Receiving background location updates is one of them.

Fortunately, you don't need to manually monitor the current location to compare it with yard sale locations. In iOS 4, Apple introduced *region monitoring*, also often referred to as *geofencing*. You can register up to 20 circular regions, and iOS will wake your app to inform it if one of those regions has been entered or exited. iOS does this tracking at a fraction of the energy cost it would take if you were to do it manually.

7.3.1 Introducing region monitoring

A `CLCircularRegion`, used for monitoring, is defined by a geographic center (latitude/longitude) and a radius (in meters) around those coordinates. To monitor for one such region, you create a `CLLocationManager`, set a delegate to receive updates, and start monitoring for it:

```
_locationMgr = [[CLLocationManager alloc] init];
_locationMgr.delegate = self;
CLLocationCoordinate2D coord =
   CLLocationCoordinate2DMake(37.332057, -122.0315941};
CLCircularRegion *region =
   [[CLCircularRegion alloc] initWithCenter:coord
                                     radius:100
                                 identifier:@"Apple HQ"];
[_locationMgr startMonitoringForRegion:region];
```

Create location manager and store it in ivar

Set self to be recipient of delegate messages

Create coordinate struct for Apple HQ

Create circular region around coordinate

Tell location manager to monitor this region

It might take a while for iOS to determine the status of this region. But when it does, your delegate object receives a call to `locationManager:didDetermineState:forRegion:`. This state can be `CLRegionStateUnknown`, `CLRegionStateInside`, or `CLRegionStateOutside`. You can coerce the location manager to update the region state right away with the `requestStateForRegion:` method.

7.3.2 Monitoring an unlimited number of regions

In our yard sale scenario, you want to have thousands of sellers as clients. How can you work around Apple's limit of only monitoring 20 regions with a single app?

The trick is to only register for monitoring the 10 yard sale locations closest to the current location of the user. If the user moves by a certain distance, you can update the registrations. This achieves the same effect as if you were monitoring all yard sales at the same time, albeit much more efficiently.

To determine the 10 candidate regions, you need to sort the locations by distance from a given point, and then only return the 10 closest ones. `YardSaleManager` gets a new method for this purpose:

```
- (NSArray *)annotationsClosestToLocation:(CLLocation *)location {
   NSArray *sorted = [[self annotations] sortedArrayUsingComparator:
              ^NSComparisonResult(SalePlace *pl1, SalePlace *pl2) {
     CLLocationDistance dist1 =
        [location distanceFromLocation:pl1.location];
     CLLocationDistance dist2 =
        [location distanceFromLocation:pl2.location];
     return [@(dist1) compare:@(dist2)];
   }];
   NSRange range = NSMakeRange(0, MIN(10, [sorted count]));
   return [sorted subarrayWithRange:range];
}
```

Sort sale places by distance from given location

Return first 10 locations, or all if there are less than 10 items in array

The next several code pieces in this section are from the `_updateMonitoredRegionsForLocation:` method, which you can inspect in AppDelegate.m in the YardSale sample code.

The following helper method receives the current user's location and then updates the monitored regions according to plan. First, you check if region monitoring is supported at all:

```
if (![CLLocationManager isMonitoringAvailableForClass:
      [CLCircularRegion class]]) {
   NSLog(@"Monitoring not available for CLCircularRegion");
   return;
}
```

Then you retrieve the 10 closest yard sale places and get a list of their identifiers. Regions you're still interested in aren't touched because they're already being monitored. Monitoring is stopped for regions that are now too far away from the user:

```
NSArray *sales = [_saleManager annotationsClosestToLocation:loc];
NSMutableArray *identsToMonitor =
   [[sales valueForKeyPath:@"@unionOfObjects.identifier"] mutableCopy];

for (CLRegion *region in _locationMgr.monitoredRegions) {
   if ([identsToMonitor containsObject:region.identifier]) {
      [identsToMonitor removeObject:region.identifier];
   }
   else {
      [_locationMgr stopMonitoringForRegion:region];
   }
}
```

Get closest 10 yard sales

Get IDs to monitor via key-value coding (KVC) operator

Iterate over currently monitored regions

Already monitoring this; remove it from to-do list

Not interested in this any more

After this loop, you have a list of region IDs that you still need to start monitoring. You also need to determine the maximum distance that one of these regions is away from the user's location:

```
CLLocationDistance maxDistance = 0;
for (SalePlace *onePlace in sales) {
   CLLocationDistance dist =
      [loc distanceFromLocation:onePlace.location];
   maxDistance = MAX(dist, maxDistance);

   if (![identsToMonitor containsObject:onePlace.identifier]) {
      continue;
   }

   CLCircularRegion *region =
      [[CLCircularRegion alloc] initWithCenter:onePlace.coordinate
                                        radius:100
                                    identifier:onePlace.identifier];
   region.notifyOnExit = NO;
   [_locationMgr startMonitoringForRegion:region];
}
```

Increase max distance if this place is further away.

The region is no longer on your to-do list.

Create circular region for yard sale place.

You don't care about exit notifications.

Register monitoring for this region.

Knowing the maximum distance that a monitored region is away from the user allows you to defer location updates until the user has traveled a significant distance. This allows iOS to refrain from waking up your app for each minor movement. Half the distance between the user and the farthest away monitored region is a good compromise:

```
[_locationMgr
   allowDeferredLocationUpdatesUntilTraveled:maxDistance/2.0
                                     timeout:CLTimeIntervalMax];
```

You can specify a distance or a time interval or both for the preceding method. The `CLLocationDistanceMax` and `CLTimeIntervalMax` constants let you specify that you don't want to limit this dimension.

You don't want to wait too long before knowing the monitored regions' state, so you want to trigger a state update right after updating the regions to be monitored. As of iOS 7.1, there's an issue with requesting a state update too soon after removing monitored regions—the monitoring would fail altogether. A workaround for this issue is to wait for at least 0.1 seconds. The following code waits for 0.2 seconds just to be safe:

```
dispatch_after(dispatch_time(DISPATCH_TIME_NOW,
                             (int64_t)(0.2 * NSEC_PER_SEC)),
               dispatch_get_main_queue(), ^{
                  for (CLRegion *oneRegion in
                        _locationMgr.monitoredRegions) {
                     [_locationMgr requestStateForRegion:oneRegion];
                  }
               });
```

You now have a convenient method for updating the monitored regions. The next thing to do is call it if there's been movement by the user.

7.3.3 Updating monitored regions based on user location

Like other sensors, users need to authorize access to their location information. Up until iOS 7, the first time an app requested location updates, a dialog would ask the user for permission. As of iOS 8, the app has to explicitly request authorization, and Apple split the permission into two parts:

- Only when the app is active and showing its UI, dubbed "when in use"
- "Always," even when the app is in the background

This gives users the cozy feeling that they're in control of which apps get which level of access. For example, a POI search app would only ever require when-in-use authorization.

The user might deny this access, or location services might be disabled through settings or by company policy. You can add the following helper method to deal with those possible authorization scenarios—it's called right after the app launches:

```
- (void)_enableLocationUpdatesIfAuthorized {
   CLAuthorizationStatus authStatus =
      [CLLocationManager authorizationStatus];
```

Get current authorization status

```
    if (authStatus == kCLAuthorizationStatusRestricted ||
        authStatus == kCLAuthorizationStatusDenied) {

       [self _informUserAboutNoAuthorization];
       _locationMgr = nil;
       return;
    }

#if __IPHONE_OS_VERSION_MAX_ALLOWED > __IPHONE_7_1
    if (authStatus == kCLAuthorizationStatusAuthorizedWhenInUse) {
       [self _informUserAboutBackgroundAuthorization];
    }
#endif

    // initialize location manager
    if (!_locationMgr) {
       _locationMgr = [[CLLocationManager alloc] init];
       _locationMgr.delegate = self;

  if __IPHONE_OS_VERSION_MAX_ALLOWED > __IPHONE_7_1
       if ([_locationMgr
            respondsToSelector:@selector(requestAlwaysAuthorization)]) {
          [_locationMgr requestAlwaysAuthorization];
       }
#endif

       [_locationMgr startMonitoringSignificantLocationChanges];
    }
}
```

Device policy has disabled location services

User has specifically denied or disabled location services for this app

Only option is to inform user

On iOS 8, location updates may be too restricted

Create location manager if there is none yet

On iOS 8, always request; gets ignored if already authorized

Only interested if there's a significant change in location

If you encounter a denied or restricted authorization status, you should tell the user that you can't provide app functionality dependent on location. For the denied status, the user can simply enable location services for your app in the Privacy section of the Settings app. For the restricted status, the user can't do anything but complain to the IT department (or parents) who made this policy decision.

Compiling with iOS 7 and iOS 8 SDKs

This code compiles with both the iOS 7 and iOS 8 SDKs because the `__IPHONE_OS_VERSION_MAX_ALLOWED` precompiler macro hides all code that the earlier SDK would complain about. This technique is particularly useful if you want to support new SDK features without breaking the build for your colleagues who might still use an older Xcode version.

Apps that were built with the iOS 8 SDK can still execute on iOS 7 devices if the deployment target build setting permits it. In order to prevent an "unrecognized selector" crash from calling a nonexistent method, you should ask if the object `respondsToSelector:`.

Your app requires access to the user's location while the app is not active in order to update the monitored regions, so you can tell the user that if you only have when-in-use authorization. The helper methods showing the respective `UIAlertViews` aren't shown here.

You get one chance to state your reason for needing location access when the authorization alert pops up (see figure 7.7). iOS 7 appends the contents of your `NSLocationUsageDescription` info.plist key to the dialog. You can also localize your message by putting it into the localized InfoPlist.strings files instead. iOS 8 adds two new such keys for the two kinds of authorization: `NSLocationWhenInUseUsageDescription` and `NSLocationAlwaysUsageDescription`. For backward compatibility with iOS 7, all three strings should be present. The iOS 7 authorization is equivalent to the "always" authorization in iOS 8.

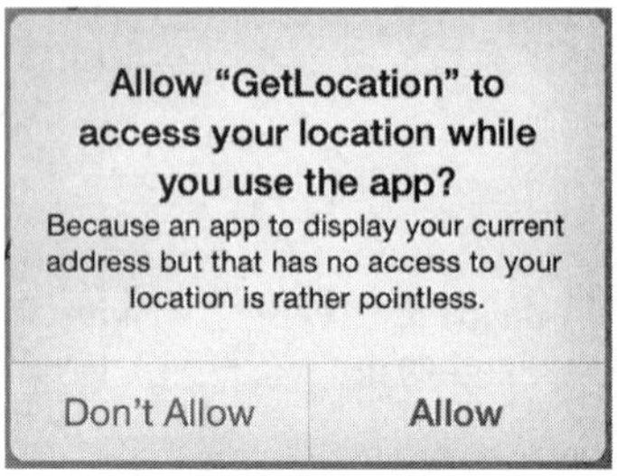

Figure 7.7 Location access dialog with custom reason

Monitoring significant location changes instead of normal location updates also reduces unnecessary battery drain. This works fine on physical devices, but I found that there are some problems with getting the iOS simulator to report those. As a work-around—while testing your app on Simulator—you can replace the `startMonitoringSignificantLocationChanges` line with the following to get a similar update profile:

```
_locationMgr.distanceFilter = 1000;
_locationMgr.desiredAccuracy = kCLLocationAccuracyKilometer;
[_locationMgr startUpdatingLocation];
```

Regardless of which kind of location updates you choose (normal, significant, or deferred), they always get reported to the same `CLLocationManagerDelegate` method:

```
- (void)locationManager:(CLLocationManager *)manager
    didUpdateLocations:(NSArray *)locations {
  CLLocation *location = [locations lastObject];
  if (location.coordinate.longitude
      != _mostRecentLoc.coordinate.longitude ||
      location.coordinate.latitude
      != _mostRecentLoc.coordinate.latitude) {
    _mostRecentLoc = [locations lastObject];

    [self _updateMonitoredRegionsForLocation:location];
  }
}
```

Get most recent location

Compare with previous location

Update monitored regions for this location

A location might be reported multiple times, so you keep the most recent one stored in the `_mostRecentLoc` ivar and only update regions if a newly reported location is different.

In addition to updating the monitored regions when the location changes, you also want to update whenever the app becomes active. This occurs if it returns from being backgrounded and also after the user reacts to the authorization dialog. If there's a most recent location stored in the ivar, you can also call the update method:

```
- (void)applicationDidBecomeActive:(UIApplication *)application {
   [self _enableLocationUpdatesIfAuthorized];
   if (_mostRecentLoc) {
      [self _updateMonitoredRegionsForLocation:_mostRecentLoc];
   }
}
```

If the user leaves the app via the home button and changes the authorization in the privacy settings, this delegate method is where you should react to this. This method is also called following the app's launch. This is why you call `_enableLocation-UpdatesIfAuthorized` here. This enables location updates if you have sufficient authorization, or it outputs the appropriate warning alerts to tell the user that certain app features won't work until "always" authorization is granted.

By monitoring significant location changes in combination with deferred updates, you keep battery drain to a minimum while keeping the list of monitored yard sale locations updated. This creates the effect of being able to monitor a virtually unlimited number of circular regions with only minimal battery drain.

7.3.4 Notifying users when entering a monitored region

The main purpose of this app is to alert users if they enter the vicinity of a yard sale, even when the YardSale app isn't running. You can achieve this by sending a location notification as soon as a region's state changes to "inside." You need to be able to get the `SalePlace` to correspond to a given identifier, so `YardSaleManager` gets another helpful method:

```
- (SalePlace *)salePlaceForIdentifier:(NSString *)identifier {
   NSPredicate *predicate =
      [NSPredicate predicateWithFormat:@"identifier == %@", identifier];
   NSArray *matches =
      [[self annotations] filteredArrayUsingPredicate:predicate];
   return [matches firstObject];
}
```

There should only ever be a single `SalePlace` with a given identifier. Because the method for filtering an array using a predicate returns an array, you return only the first object.

Before iOS 8, users couldn't prevent local notifications from appearing. Some apps, particularly games, abused this free reign to annoy users. Thankfully, Apple is unifying the privacy settings for remote and local notifications. As of iOS 8, your app gets its own privacy section in Settings where the user can modify location authorization as well as notification settings.

But you still have to support iOS 7 devices, so some extra code is necessary to avoid crashing when calling methods defined in the iOS 8 SDK. The following helper method should be called right after app launch to let iOS know the kinds of notifications you plan to send:

```
- (void)_authorizeLocalNotifications {
#if __IPHONE_OS_VERSION_MAX_ALLOWED > __IPHONE_7_1
   UIApplication *app = [UIApplication sharedApplication];
   if ([app respondsToSelector:
        @selector(registerUserNotificationSettings:)])
   {
      UIUserNotificationSettings *settings =
      [UIUserNotificationSettings settingsForTypes:
       UIUserNotificationTypeAlert|
       UIUserNotificationTypeSound categories:nil];
     [app registerUserNotificationSettings:settings];
   }
#endif}
```

Avoid crashing on iOS 7 devices where this selector doesn't exist.

Only include this code if building with iOS 8 SDK.

Build notification settings to include text alerts and sounds.

Register the notification settings with iOS.

The first time the app is launched on iOS 8, it takes a few seconds for the user to approve of your app sending notifications. The first-ever call to `registerUserNotificationSettings:` causes an authorization alert to pop up. You get a chance to react to the given authorization inside the following app delegate method:

```
#if __IPHONE_OS_VERSION_MAX_ALLOWED > __IPHONE_7_1
 - (void)application:(UIApplication *)application
        didRegisterUserNotificationSettings:
        (UIUserNotificationSettings *)notificationSettings {
   if (!notificationSettings.types) {
      // nothing allowed
      return;
   }

   if (_mostRecentLoc) {
      [self _updateMonitoredRegionsForLocation:_mostRecentLoc];
   }
}
#endif
```

Only include this code if building with iOS 8 SDK

User denied all notification types

Some action that was waiting for the user's decision

This delay only occurs the first time. Subsequent calls to the registration method cause an immediate callback. So—on iOS 8—this is the best place to put all code requiring knowledge of the user's authorization choices. In the YardSale app, you want to update the monitored regions' state and notify the user of any nearby yard sales.

The next helper method constructs and sends a local notification. Those work and look much like remote push notifications. Depending on the user's preference, they're either shown as a top banner or an alert. The user can also opt to include or exclude them in the Notification Center.

Because of the notification unification in iOS 8, this helper method contains some code that modifies the local notification based on the current notification settings. Failure to do so causes the notification to be ignored by the system, and the resulting log message scolds you for it.

The parameter for specifying a delay is useful when testing the code for simulating a user triggering the notification action:

```
- (void)_sendLocalNoteForSalePlace:(SalePlace *)place
                     afterDuration:(NSTimeInterval)duration {
   if ([_lastNotifiedSaleID isEqualToString:place.identifier]) {
      return;
   }
   UIApplication *app = [UIApplication sharedApplication];
   BOOL shouldAddMsg = YES;
   BOOL shouldAddSound = YES;
# if __IPHONE_OS_VERSION_MAX_ALLOWED > __IPHONE_7_1
   if ([app respondsToSelector:
        @selector(currentUserNotificationSettings)]) {
      UIUserNotificationSettings *settings =
         [app currentUserNotificationSettings];

      if (!settings.types) {
         return;
      }
      if (!(settings.types & UIUserNotificationTypeAlert)) {
         shouldAddMsg = NO;
      }
      if (!(settings.types & UIUserNotificationTypeSound)) {
         shouldAddSound = NO;
      }
   }
#endif
   NSString *msg = [NSString stringWithFormat:@"%@ is closeby!",
                    place.title];
   UILocalNotification *note = [[UILocalNotification alloc] init];
   note.alertAction = @"Visit";
   if (shouldAddMsg) {
      note.alertBody = msg;
   }
   if (shouldAddSound) {
      note.soundName = UILocalNotificationDefaultSoundName;
   }
   note.fireDate = [[NSDate date] dateByAddingTimeInterval:duration];
   note.userInfo = @{@"SaleID": place.identifier};
   _lastNotifiedSaleID = place.identifier;
   [app scheduleLocalNotification:note];
}
```

- **Bail out if user has been notified for this region.**
- **Default is to include sound and text alert.**
- **This code is only included if building with iOS 8 SDK.**
- **Check that iOS 8 methods exist before executing it.**
- **Retrieve current user-notification settings.**
- **Bail out because no notification types are specified.**
- **Toggle text alert if not permitted.**
- **Toggle alert sound if not permitted.**
- **Create new local notification.**
- **Build the notification message text with the sale place title.**
- **Set name of button when shown in alert style.**
- **Set the notification message if desired.**
- **Use system default sound if desired.**
- **Set the fire date of the notification.**
- **Add sale place identifier for later reference.**
- **Remember place identifier to prevent duplicate notification.**
- **Hand the configured notification off to the system.**

You'll need the `SalePlace` identifier later on for identifying which yard sale the user wants to execute the action for, so you put it in the location notification's `userInfo` dictionary. Instead of using the standard system sound, you can also specify the name of a CAF sound file contained in your app bundle. How about the sound of a cash register?

Apple provides instructions for how to convert sound files into a format appropriate for use as notification sounds.[1]

In the following method, which gets called when the state of a monitored region is updated, you want to avoid sending the same notification multiple times. A new ivar, `_lastNotifiedSaleID`, keeps track of the last sale place you sent a location notification for. You'll send the notification as soon as the region-monitoring callback method tells you about the boundary crossing:

```
- (void)locationManager:(CLLocationManager *)manager
     didDetermineState:(CLRegionState)state
             forRegion:(CLRegion *)region {
   switch (state) {
      case CLRegionStateUnknown: {
         NSLog(@"Unknown %@", region.identifier);
         break;
      }
      case CLRegionStateInside: {
         NSLog(@"Inside %@", region.identifier);
         SalePlace *salePlace =
            [_saleManager salePlaceForIdentifier:region.identifier];
         [self _sendLocalNoteForSalePlace:salePlace
                            afterDuration:0];
         _lastNotifiedSaleID = region.identifier;
         break;
      }
      case CLRegionStateOutside: {
         NSLog(@"Outside %@", region.identifier);
         break;
      }
   }
}
```

Only log identifier if a region's state is unknown

Get sale place object via the region's identifier

Send local notification after specified delay

Only log identifier of regions the user is outside of

To test this contraption, make sure that you have your current home location set up in the locations file. Set the duration to 5 seconds. This way you can launch the app and press the home button to send it to the background. When it sees that you're already inside your home location, it will schedule a local notification 5 seconds in the future, as shown in figure 7.8. The notification style for this screenshot has been switched to alert style because the banner style doesn't show the action button text.

If the user taps on the Visit button in the alert-style notification or taps on the notification banner, iOS will return control to your app. If it was suspended in the background, then it gets awoken; if it was terminated, it gets relaunched. In both cases, a method on the application delegate is called, which gives you an opportunity to react to the user's response.

Figure 7.8 Alert-style local notification

[1] See "Registering, Scheduling, and Handling User Notifications" in the "Local and Remote Notification Programming Guide": http://developer.apple.com/library/ios/documentation/NetworkingInternet/Conceptual/RemoteNotificationsPG/Chapters/IPhoneOSClientImp.html.

You add a new method to the `MapViewController` so that you can trigger the showing of the in-store UI from the app delegate:

```
- (void)showInStoreUIForSalePlace:(SalePlace *)place {
   MKAnnotationView *view = [self.mapView viewForAnnotation:place];    <- Get the annotation view for the pin belonging to the sale place's annotation object.
   [self performSegueWithIdentifier:@"ShowSalePlace" sender:view];    <- Pretend to have triggered the segue from this pin.
}
```

The preceding method simulates tapping on the annotation pin accessory button, allowing the `prepareForSegue:sender:` method to retrieve the annotation from the `sender` parameter and pass it to the in-store view controller. With this method you can trigger the "visit" from within the app delegate.

In the app delegate, the following helper method presents the in-store UI for a given store ID. This also makes sure that you're not trying to present the modal view controller twice. A friendly message welcomes the user to the store:

```
- (void)_showSalePlaceForIdentifier:(NSString *)identifier {
   MapViewController *vc =
                  (MapViewController *)self.window.rootViewController;
   if (vc.presentedViewController) {
      // In-Store VC already showing                 <- Bail out if there's already a store showing.
      return;
   }
   SalePlace *salePlace =                            <- Get SalePlace instance matching identifier parameter.
      [_saleManager salePlaceForIdentifier:identifier];
   NSString *msg = [NSString stringWithFormat:@"Welcome to %@",   <- Show welcome message.
                  salePlace.title];
   UIAlertView *alert = [[UIAlertView alloc]
                        initWithTitle:@"Glad to see you!"
                        message:msg
                        delegate:nil
                        cancelButtonTitle:@"Ok"
                        otherButtonTitles:nil];
   [alert show];
   [vc showInStoreUIForSalePlace:salePlace];          <- Present the store UI.
}
```

Once you've scheduled the location notification, it will "fire" at the given time. What happens then depends on whether or not the app is currently active in the foreground and whether it's running on an iOS 7 or 8 device (see table 7.1).

Table 7.1 Receiving a location notification

App state	iOS 7 (and earlier)	iOS 8
Foreground	Receive `application: didReceiveLocalNotification:` immediately	Receive `application: didReceiveLocalNotification:` immediately

Table 7.1 Receiving a location notification *(continued)*

App state	iOS 7 (and earlier)	iOS 8
Background	Receive `application: didReceiveLocalNotification:` after user taps on action and app becomes active	Receive `application: handleActionWithIdentifier: forLocalNotification: completionHandler:` after user taps on action and app becomes active

To cover all four scenarios, you need to implement the two application delegate methods, as follows:

```
- (void)application:(UIApplication *)application
    didReceiveLocalNotification:(UILocalNotification *)notification {
    NSString *saleID = notification.userInfo[@"SaleID"];
    [self _showSalePlaceForIdentifier:saleID];
}

#if __IPHONE_OS_VERSION_MAX_ALLOWED > __IPHONE_7_1
- (void)application:(UIApplication *)application
     handleActionWithIdentifier:(NSString *)identifier
     forLocalNotification:(UILocalNotification *)notification
     completionHandler:(void(^)())completionHandler {
    NSString *saleID = notification.userInfo[@"SaleID"];
    [self _showSalePlaceForIdentifier:saleID];
    completionHandler();
}
#endif
```

Annotations: **Get sale place identifier from notification userInfo payload** (on `NSString *saleID = ...`); **Show in-store UI** (on `[self _showSalePlaceForIdentifier:saleID];`); **This code is only included if building with iOS 8 SDK** (on `#if`); **Get sale place identifier from notification userInfo payload**; **Show in-store UI**; **Call provided completion handler** (on `completionHandler();`).

If the app is already in the foreground while sending this local notification, no alert or banner is shown. Instead, iOS calls the `application:didReceiveLocalNotification:` delegate method right away. This means that if you're entering a yard sale region while walking around with the map showing, the app will also move into the in-store UI. One might frown on such unexpected activity by the app, but it's quite likely that users would rather see information about the yard sale they just stumbled on. For the rare case that a user still wants to peruse the map—to find other nearby sales—there's the Close button.

You've now covered all scenarios inside and outside the app. Whether users react to a local notification or navigate to a yard sale by means of the map, they'll still end up seeing the in-store UI.

7.4 Enhancing the in-store UI with iBeacons

The framework in charge of everything related to a user's location is Core Location. Over the years, Apple has enhanced it and also made the technology backing it faster, more energy-efficient, and more accurate. The location on Earth is put together by triangulating cell towers and WiFi networks and—where the data can be received—with meter-accurate geopositioning from GPS and GLONASS satellites.

The dangers of using local notifications for UI flow

In the method that deals with monitored region state updates, you're always sending a local notification regardless of application state. This allows you to specify a delay so that you can press the home button and see the notification arrive for testing. It also allows you to demonstrate various scenarios of your app reacting to local notifications.

In a production app, you should only send the local notification if the app is in the background. If a user of iOS 8 hasn't authorized your app to send notifications, this would disable the functionality of showing the in-store UI while the app is in the foreground. To avoid this problem, you want to show the in-store UI without detouring via the local notification. The YardSale app features this modification.

But those technologies aren't able to help users navigate inside a store or shopping mall. Without the aid of satellites, location accuracy is within hundreds of meters. For this scenario, some genius at Apple invented *iBeacons.*

7.4.1 Introducing the iBeacon system

Rather than trying to supplement the accuracy of geolocation, iBeacons provide a *semantic context* to your app. They piggyback on top of Bluetooth Low Energy (BTLE) advertisements. BTLE, also known as Bluetooth 4.0, has only its name in common with earlier Bluetooth versions. It's a brand new standard aiming to be extremely power efficient. BTLE peripherals send out advertisement packets with identifiers telling interested listeners what kinds of services they offer. Those listening devices can then establish a connection to transfer bursts of data.

Ingeniously, iBeacon doesn't need any connection to work, because all necessary information is transmitted inside the advertisement packet: a beacon UUID, and a minor and major value. Thanks to this trick, it's extremely energy efficient to listen for iBeacon advertisements. For the same reason, you can get hardware iBeacons for around $30 each that run on a button battery for more than a year. All these need to do is send the iBeacon advertisement packet every couple of seconds. Very little energy is used for these transmissions because their range is only a couple of meters(see figure 7.9).

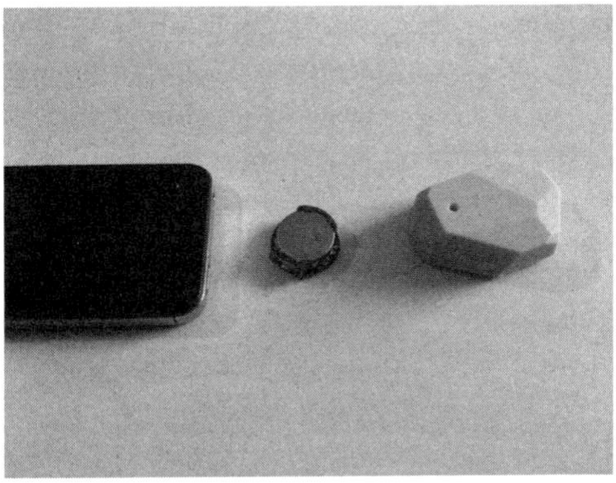

Figure 7.9 Two hardware iBeacons compared to iPhone

One interesting iBeacon usage scenario has to do with Passbook. Imagine a bus company sticking an iBeacon device next to the front doors of all their buses. If they add the beacon identifier as a relevancy criteria to their Passbook tickets, then iPhones can show the bus ticket on the lock screen when you get close to entering the bus. Passbook supports semantic and geographic locations as relevancy criteria.

For the YardSale app, you could use iBeacons to find out which table at a yard sale the user is closest to. That's assuming that you want to support multitable yard sales or flea markets.

There are two styles of interaction with iBeacons:

- *Monitoring*—This is eerily similar to monitoring geolocations, which was demonstrated in the previous section. It uses the same methods—the only difference is how you construct the region to be monitored.
- *Ranging*—This measures the signal strength being received from individual beacons to determine an approximate distance between them and the user.

7.4.2 iBeacon monitoring at a glance

For monitoring, instead of using a `CLCircularRegion` you use a `CLBeaconRegion`:

```
NSUUID *uuid = [[NSUUID alloc] initWithUUIDString:
                @"C70EEE03-8E77-4A57-B462-13CB0A3ED97E"];
CLBeaconRegion *beacon = [[CLBeaconRegion alloc]
                           initWithProximityUUID:uuid
                                      identifier:@"YardSale Beacon"];
[_locationMgr startMonitoringForRegion:beacon];
```

If you build with the iOS 7 SDK, you'll always be able to construct a beacon region, but that doesn't mean that the current device is able to monitor for beacon regions. Use the `isMonitoringAvailableForClass:` class method of `CLLocationManager` to determine if monitoring is available for `CLBeaconRegion`.

There are three variants of the initializer method available, depending on how narrowly you want to specify the beacon to be monitored. The primary beacon identifier is a universally unique identifier (UUID). In addition, you have two 16-bit integer values—the major and minor values. For example, if all Apple Stores shared the same UUID, the major value could identify the store location and the minor value could identify a semantic location inside each store. The preceding code only monitors for beacons with a particular UUID, regardless of the major and minor values, but those other variants will let you restrict to a specific major value or a specify a major and minor combination.

Generating a UUID

If you ever need to generate a UUID for your own purposes, there's a simple solution: in Terminal, just type `uuid` and press Enter. You'll get a freshly generated UUID.

iBeacons aren't monitored via the traditional Core Location technologies. Instead, they require that Bluetooth be active. If you try to monitor a beacon region with Bluetooth turned off, the user will get an alert from the system recommending that they turn on Bluetooth "for greater accuracy."

The 20-region limitation of Core Location doesn't differentiate between circular georegions and beacon regions. You could be monitoring 10 yard sale locations and 10 different beacon regions. For the purposes of the YardSale app, you have no use for beacon monitoring because you want to know about a *nearby* sale place, even when the user is 100 meters away. Bluetooth doesn't reach that far. Instead of beacon monitoring, we'll implement iBeacon ranging for the times when the user is already inside a yard sale area.

7.4.3 Making any app emit an iBeacon

Any app can act as an iBeacon while it's in the foreground. Remember when you built a ticket-verifier app in chapter 4? If you'd made this app an iBeacon emitter and added the beacon's UUID to the movie ticket passes, those tickets would have popped up on your guests' lock screens as soon as they came close to the person at the door wanting to check their tickets.

I'm assuming that you haven't bought a bunch of hardware beacons yet, so creating a software iBeacon is very useful when testing app scenarios involving iBeacon monitoring or ranging. The BeaconEmitter app included in this book's source code contains an implementation for you to use.

Emitting a beacon is slightly complicated because Core Bluetooth requires separate authorization. Also, you should only try to trigger actions with Bluetooth powered on. You can see the relevant code in the BeaconEmitter app's ViewController.m. The `_startAdvertising` method also constructs a `CLBeaconRegion`, but only for generating the peripheral data dictionary:

```
- (void)_startAdvertising {
    NSString *UUIDString = self.UUIDTextField.text;
    NSInteger major = [self.majorTextField.text integerValue];
    NSInteger minor = [self.minorTextField.text integerValue];
    NSUUID *UUID = [[NSUUID alloc] initWithUUIDString:UUIDString];
    CLBeaconRegion *region =
       [[CLBeaconRegion alloc] initWithProximityUUID:UUID
                                               major:major
                                               minor:minor
                                          identifier:@"FooBar"];

    NSDictionary *beaconPeripheralData =
       [region peripheralDataWithMeasuredPower:nil];
    [_peripheralManager startAdvertising:beaconPeripheralData];
}
```

Get UUID, major, and minor values from text fields

Create NSUUID object from UUID string

Create beacon region with these values

Identifier can't be nil, but is inconsequential

Use region's helper method to construct peripheral data dictionary

Start advertising this iBeacon

The beacon region object isn't needed after calling `peripheralDataWithMeasuredPower:`. The power parameter on this method will allow you to specify a custom RSSI value, and setting it to `nil` uses a reasonable default. The peripheral data dictionary contains Apple's iBeacon service ID, your UUID, the major and minor values, and the RSSI value. Nothing more to see there.

iOS will automatically pause these beacon advertisements a few seconds after the user sends the app into the background via the home button. Unfortunately, this can't be changed, even by specifying any of the two background modes related to Bluetooth. Apple is rather stubborn when it comes to conserving power. Using such a software iBeacon requires the app to remain running in the foreground.

7.4.4 Determining distance to iBeacons with ranging

Geofencing via geographic coordinates reliably informs you about nearby yard sale locations. But when on the premises or inside the store, you want to show the information that's relevant to semantic locations at this sale place. Imagine that your yard sale location has multiple tables or participants, and you put a hardware beacon on each table. *Ranging* is the process whereby iOS will report to you the relative signal strength at which iBeacons are currently being received. If you're closer to one beacon than another, you'll be receiving it at a greater signal strength.

Various kinds of hardware beacons might emit their signals at different strengths, so some allow you to calibrate by giving you a Received Signal Strength Indication (RSSI) value. This value—measured in decibels—is the strength at which a device would receive the signal at a given distance. But to keep things simple, let's assume that all your software beacons are sending at the same strength.

The iPhone 4S and later versions, and iPad 3 and later, have Bluetooth 4.0 chipsets. Run the provided BeaconEmitter app on a few of your older iOS devices for testing iBeacon ranging. Leave the UUID and major values as they are, and modify the minor value to be the table number. Minor 1 would be table number 1; minor 2, table number 2; and so on.

There's always the possibility that Bluetooth isn't available because either the user's device is too old or it's disabled. The default in-store view shows five sections, one for each table. In these sections there will be 10 products each. If the `_filteredTable` ivar is `-1`, then you want to show all table view sections. Otherwise, you show only the corresponding section. This way, iBeacon causes the list of products to be filtered down to the ones that are currently relevant for the user's semantic location.

The contents of the table view are intentionally very simple. Their sole goal is to show you that the data changes as you come close to different beacons:

```
- (NSInteger)numberOfSectionsInTableView:(UITableView *)tableView {
   return NUMBER_TABLES;
}

- (NSInteger)tableView:(UITableView *)tableView
      numberOfRowsInSection:(NSInteger)section {
```

```
    if (_filteredTable == -1 || section == _filteredTable) {
        return 10;
    }
    return 0;
}
```

Show 10 rows in table view section if this section index is equal to the filter variable or if no filter is active (-1)

Otherwise, hide this section's rows

The same technique shows section headers only when needed:

```
- (NSString *)tableView:(UITableView *)tableView
            titleForHeaderInSection:(NSInteger)section {
    if (_filteredTable == -1 || section == _filteredTable) {
        return [NSString stringWithFormat:@"Table %ld", (long)section+1];
    }
    return nil;
}
```

The row cells only show a sequential product number and which section they belong to:

```
- (UITableViewCell *)tableView:(UITableView *)tableView
                    cellForRowAtIndexPath:(NSIndexPath *)indexPath {
    UITableViewCell *cell = [[UITableViewCell alloc]
                             initWithStyle:UITableViewCellStyleDefault
                             reuseIdentifier:nil];
    cell.textLabel.text =
        [NSString stringWithFormat:@"Product %ld on table %ld",
                                   (long)indexPath.row+1,
                                   (long)indexPath.section+1];
    return cell;
}
```

Now that we've got the boring part out of the way, you can implement a location manager to take care of beacon ranging. You can have as many `CLLocationManager` instances as you like, so it's quite practical to have one dedicated to in-store beacon ranging that's only activated while `InStoreViewController` is showing:

```
- (void)viewDidLoad {
    [super viewDidLoad];
    NSUUID *uuid = [[NSUUID alloc]
            initWithUUIDString:@"C70EEE03-8E77-4A57-B462-13CB0A3ED97E"];
    _inStoreRegion = [[CLBeaconRegion alloc]
                      initWithProximityUUID:uuid
                                 identifier:@"In-Store"];
    _filteredTable = -1;
}
```

Specify same UUID as the BeaconEmitter sample app is configured with

Beacon region will be needed in multiple places, so it's stored in an instance variable

Default is to show all sections of table view

Right before the view controller's view appears, you create a dedicated location manager and start ranging, if available:

```
- (void)viewWillAppear:(BOOL)animated {
    [super viewWillAppear:animated];
    self.navigationItem.title = self.salePlace.title;
```

Set title to show that this is a specific store

```
    if (![CLLocationManager isRangingAvailable]) {
        NSLog(@"Ranging not available");
        return;
    }
    _beaconManager = [[CLLocationManager alloc] init];
    _beaconManager.delegate = self;
    [_beaconManager startRangingBeaconsInRegion:_inStoreRegion];
}
```

Continue only if ranging is available on this device

Create dedicated beacon-ranging manager

The preceding code starts the ranging for all iBeacons belonging to the given CLBeaconRegion. Let me stress again that how narrowly you define this region determines which beacons are considered to be part of it. For this example, all beacons sharing the UUID make up the in-store beacon region, regardless of major and minor values.

What goes up must come down. So you stop ranging and tear down the ranging manager if the view controller is going away:

```
- (void)viewWillDisappear:(BOOL)animated {
    [super viewWillDisappear:animated];
    [_beaconManager stopMonitoringForRegion:_inStoreRegion];
    _beaconManager.delegate = nil;
    _beaconManager = nil;
}
```

Clean up beacon ranging

Continue only if ranging is available on this device

Create dedicated beacon-ranging manager

A helper method groups the actions you need to do when the filter for your product table view changes:

```
- (void)setFilteredTable:(NSInteger)table {
    if (table != _filteredTable) {
        _filteredTable = table;
        // refresh table sections with animation
        NSIndexSet *indexSet =
            [NSIndexSet indexSetWithIndexesInRange:
                NSMakeRange(0, NUMBER_TABLES)];
        [self.tableView reloadSections:indexSet
                      withRowAnimation:UITableViewRowAnimationAutomatic];
    }
}
```

If there are any problems with ranging the beacons, a CLLocationManagerDelegate method is called. You want to deal with any errors gracefully and reset the filter on your table:

```
- (void)locationManager:(CLLocationManager *)manager
rangingBeaconsDidFailForRegion:(CLBeaconRegion *)region
                     withError:(NSError *)error {
    NSLog(@"%@", [error localizedDescription]);
    [self setFilteredTable:-1];
}
```

CORE BLUETOOTH HANGING IN IOS 7.1 On iOS 7.1 there are some circumstances that can cause Core Bluetooth to hang internally, effectively causing all ranging to fail. The only fix is to restart the device.

More often than not, ranging works perfectly and iOS calls another delegate method, passing it an array of `CLBeacon` objects. Those possess the raw RSSI value and also a `CLProximity` value specifying whether the distance is unknown, near, immediate, or far. This array also contains beacons that have recently disappeared with no distance info. Those you need to filter out. The remaining beacons get sorted by signal strength and the minor value is what you'll filter the table by:

```
- (void)locationManager:(CLLocationManager *)manager
       didRangeBeacons:(NSArray *)beacons
              inRegion:(CLBeaconRegion *)region {
   NSPredicate *pred =
      [NSPredicate predicateWithFormat:@"rssi < 0 AND proximity > 0"];
   beacons = [beacons filteredArrayUsingPredicate:pred];
   if (![beacons count]) {
      [self setFilteredTable:-1];
      return;
   }
   NSSortDescriptor *sort =
      [NSSortDescriptor sortDescriptorWithKey:@"rssi" ascending:NO];
   beacons = [beacons sortedArrayUsingDescriptors:@[sort]];
   CLBeacon *beacon = [beacons firstObject];
   NSInteger closestTableNumber = [beacon.minor integerValue];
   [self setFilteredTable:closestTableNumber];
}
```

Remove beacons that have disappeared.

No beacons being received; show all tables.

Sort beacons by signal strength.

Get first beacon; this is the closest.

This beacon's minor value is table index.

Filter products to only show this table.

For testing the beacon ranging functionality, you can place two iOS devices with the BeaconEmitter app running at opposite corners of a room. Have one configured to minor value `0` and the other to minor value `1`. While no beacon is active, the YardSale app will show five table view sections. Once you start a software iBeacon, you'll only see this one. If you have multiple iBeacons active, the YardSale app will always show the table view section corresponding to the closer beacon.

iBeacon ranging supposedly consumes more power than monitoring because iOS needs to determine the signal strengths. Also, it doesn't work in the background, unlike beacon monitoring. If you send the YardSale app into the background by pressing the home button, the ranging updates are paused. But ranging is more useful when the app is active anyway. You wouldn't want to bother your user with push notifications every time they got to a different shelf in your store.

7.4.5 *Adding an in-store barcode scanner*

The final feature we'll add to the YardSale app brings us back to barcode scanning. Section 6.1.4 explained how to add a modal barcode scanner view controller to your app. Here we'll repeat the process to let the user get information about a specific product.

You've done this before, and you can look at the YardSale app's code to see it fully implemented. Here's the list of steps involved in adding the barcode scanner to the YardSale app:

1. Open the MusicCollection app project.
2. Copy all classes from the Copied Code group into your YardSale app project.
3. Copy the navigation controller and camera preview controllers to your storyboard.
4. Add a scan button as the right bar button item of the in-store view controller.
5. Connect a modal segue from this button to the copied navigation controller.
6. Give this new segue the `ShowScanner` identifier.
7. Add a dummy unwind method to InStoreViewController.m.
8. Connect the scanner view controller's Cancel button to the unwind method.
9. Set the identifier for the new unwind segue to `unwind`.
10. Set the `scannerDelegate` property of the scanner in `prepareForSegue:sender:`.
11. Implement the delegate method for when a barcode has been scanned.

The two methods mentioned in steps 7 and 10 look like this:

```
- (IBAction)unwindFromScannerViewController:(UIStoryboardSegue *)segue {
   // intentionally left black
}

- (void)prepareForSegue:(UIStoryboardSegue *)segue sender:(id)sender {
   if ([segue.identifier isEqualToString:@"ShowScanner"]) {
      UINavigationController *nav = [segue destinationViewController];
      DTCameraPreviewController *vc = nav.viewControllers[0];
      vc.delegate = self;
   }
}
```

The dummy unwind method only serves the purpose of allowing you to create an unwind segue in Interface Builder and to give it an identifier for calling it programmatically. The complete YardSale app storyboard is shown in figure 7.10.

Finally, the implementation for reacting to a scanned barcode dismisses the modal barcode scanner and shows an alert giving details about the context:

```
- (void)previewController:(DTCameraPreviewController *)previewController
            didScanCode:(NSString *)code ofType:(NSString *)type {
   [previewController performSegueWithIdentifier:@"unwind" sender:self];
   NSString *msg;
   if (_filteredTable>=0) {
      msg = [NSString stringWithFormat:@"Scanned '%@' "
             "from table %ld "
             "%@", code, (long)_filteredTable+1,
             _salePlace.title];
   }
```

Dismiss scanner by calling the unwind segue by identifier

Filter is active; mention table in message

```
    else {
        msg = [NSString stringWithFormat:@"Scanned '%@' "
                "at %@", code,
                _salePlace.title];
    }
    UIAlertView *alert = [[UIAlertView alloc] initWithTitle:@"Scanned!"
                                                    message:msg
                                                   delegate:nil
                                          cancelButtonTitle:@"Ok"
                                          otherButtonTitles:nil];
    [alert show];
}
```

No filter active; just mention sale place title

Show alert

While this example just shows an alert, a real-life app could do something more interesting with the multiple layers of context information. You know which store the user is in, which semantic location inside the store the user is next to, and which specific item the user is interested in.

Apple trusts their customers enough to let them purchase small value accessories this way from within the Apple Store app while at a physical Apple store. As more developers become aware of these context-sensing capabilities, there are many more "magical" uses waiting to be discovered.

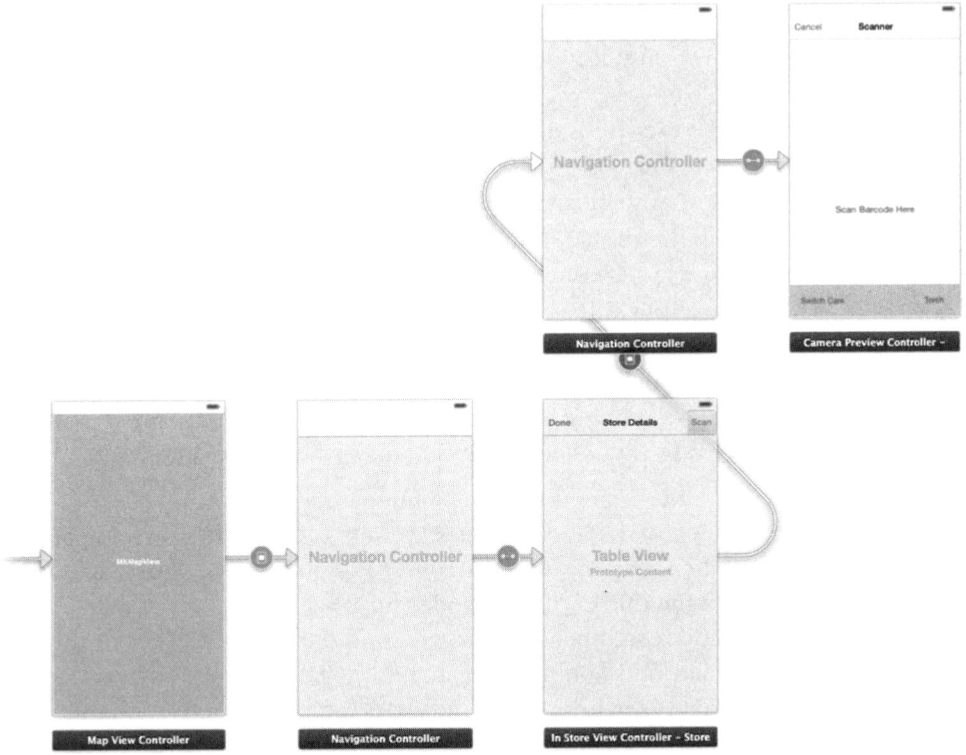

Figure 7.10 Complete YardSale app storyboard

7.5 Summary

Core Location lets you monitor two kinds of regions: geographic regions defined by a center and radius, and semantic regions defined by iBeacons. You can't monitor more than 20 regions at one time. The technique presented in this chapter allows you to monitor a virtually unlimited number of yard sale locations by dynamically updating the monitored georegions if the user moves significantly.

In additional to region *monitoring* for iBeacons, you can also request *ranging* for them. This uses more energy than beacon region monitoring, but it also gives you an indication about how far individual beacons are away from the user. This information can be useful in determining different contexts that you can present information and actions for as the user moves around the store.

Additional context information can come from allowing the user to scan barcodes in your store. Combining these multiple levels of context can give you insight into what the user might currently be most interested in. If your users get a sense that your app is "smarter" than others, they'll be more delighted to use it. Ask yourself, what information or actions would be most useful to me in this context?

These are the key takeaways for this chapter:

- Use geographic region monitoring to make your app aware of nearby physical stores.
- Local push notifications are a good way to alert the user, even if your app is inactive.
- While the user is inside a physical store, employ iBeacon ranging to determine a semantic location.
- Let the user interact with physical products by providing a barcode scanner.
- Optimize the displayed information and possible actions for a combination of multiple levels of context.
- Deal gracefully with disabled authorization, non-available monitoring or ranging, and errors.
- Apple introduced several authorization changes for background location updates and sending local notifications. Unless you choose to only support iOS 8, make sure you test your solution under both iOS 7 and iOS 8.

You've reached the end of this book, but hopefully not the end of your exploration of barcodes. You learned about barcodes, as well as several iOS technologies that are of great utility when working with barcodes. Possessing this knowledge, you can now rightfully claim the title of "iOS Barcode Guru."

I love barcodes so much there's even one on the back cover of this book! Keep your eyes peeled and you'll begin to notice barcodes everywhere, metaphorically screaming at you to create apps so your users can put them to good use.

appendix A
History of the UPC

When getting acquainted with barcodes used for tagging products, you'll come across a plethora of abbreviations. Some of these are names of barcode symbologies, and others are names of companies or organizations. Barcodes representing product numbers have had several different names over the course of their history, and multiple organizations have developed and maintained the related standards. Most people find this quite confusing initially.

This section provides an overview of the development of the very first barcode, the Universal Product Code (UPC). This brief history includes several informative as well as amusing lessons, and it also reveals the connections between several actors, standards, and organizations.

While your colleagues will still be confused as to the difference between UPC-A, EAN-13, and GTIN, you'll be able to confidently play the part of the *barcode guru* when discussing barcodes for use in your company or apps.

A.1 Bull's-eye origins

An old saying goes "war is good for business." Indeed, the United States experienced an unprecedented economic upturn during the Second World War (1939–1945) as soldiers were removed from their normal workplace to fight abroad, and jobs at home were filled by the formerly unemployed.

The grocery industry was forced to take a hard look into how it could scale its processes to cope with the increased demand. One day in 1940, an enterprising grocery executive visited the Engineering College at Drexel University in Philadelphia. He hoped to challenge them to develop a method for automating product identification at checkout, possibly gaining a commercial advantage over his competitors, with academia doing the research at low cost.

Drexel University declined the challenge. But Bernhard Silver, a graduate student there at the time, overheard the request and brought the idea to his friend Joe

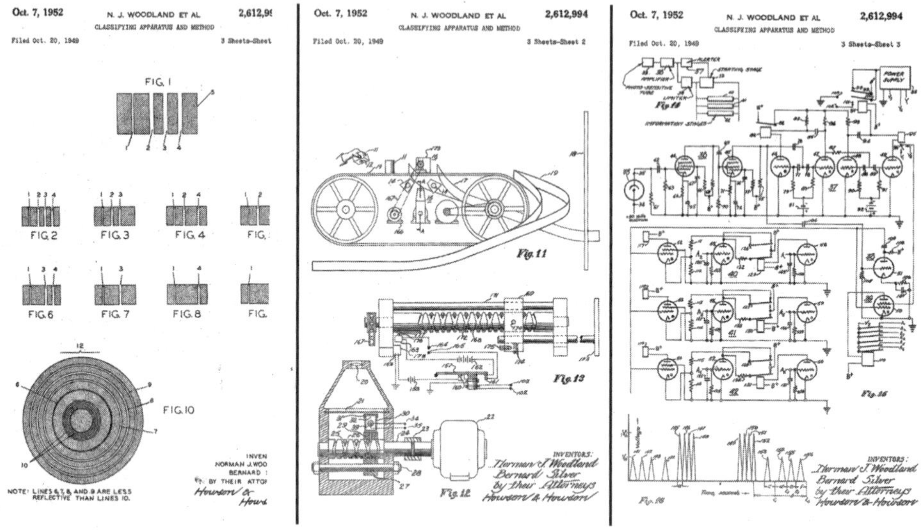

Figure A.1 Patent US 2612994 A is the earliest documented barcode.

(Norman J.) Woodland. Silver and Woodland saw an opportunity for inventing something revolutionary, and they went to work.

Automating anything in the middle of the twentieth century meant using physical machinery, so they needed to develop some marking scheme or identifier that could be affixed to products and that could be "read" by a machine. Once the item was identified, changing the price charged at the checkout counter would be an easy second step.

Joe Woodland had a stroke of genius when he absentmindedly ran his fingers through the sand on a beach. He realized that by varying the thickness of lines, he could represent different numbers, much like in Morse code but with more "symbols" than just a dot and a dash. Woodland had learned Morse code when he was a Boy Scout.

The two friends continued to work on their technology for nine more years. They applied for a US patent in 1949, and it was granted as US 2612994 A in 1952 (see figure A.1).

A.2 Startup story

The patented approach was to have circular lines around a center point printed in reflective ink. The reasoning behind this was that you could scan such symbols in any direction, always arriving at the same result. This design was reminiscent of a dart board, which earned it the unofficial name *bull's-eye symbol*.

Even though Woodland tried hard to find investors for this technology, he had no tangible success. The proof-of-concept experimental system that Silver and Woodland installed in the back room of a grocery store didn't convince anybody. Finally, the Philco company bought the patent from them for $15,000, equivalent to $132,000 in today's dollars.

It might have been a lack of marketing or the lack of practical applications for their solution, but the bull's-eye symbol remained unused for several decades.

Military efficiency improving the grocery industry

The US grocery industry continued to improve their distribution channels and became quite efficient in the early 1960s. Manual work remained the single most-limiting factor slowing their growth:

- The labor cost of retail checkout was a major cost factor. About 40% of labor expenditures went to checkers and baggers.
- Inventory tracking remained a manual process. Cash registers were only able to track the amount paid and which of five or six departments the item was from.
- The high rate of errors and slow transaction speed of humans caused a lot of problems. Retailers and manufacturers all had their own product codes, and these had to be manually copied and translated on invoices and other forms.

Several independent projects were started during the 1960s to address these issues and improve productivity at checkout. The US military employed many contractors to develop related technologies to increase efficiency. The Kroger Company of Cincinnati, Ohio, realized this and sponsored a high-tech conference in 1966. Their aim was to educate military contractors about the grocery distribution environment. Technologies originally developed for military logistics could also improve efficiency in the grocery industry and save costs.

Among the attendees of this conference was RCA, which had purchased the bull's-eye barcode patent from Philco a few years earlier. RCA formed a partnership with Kroger to develop a laser-based scanner prototype by 1968. This prototype was used to analyze the performance of various configurations of checkout machines in their Princeton, New Jersey, laboratory.

Confusion in numbers

Getting a grip on the basic technology of using a laser to read barcodes was the first hurdle. The second was the need to agree on a common scheme for identifying products. With individual retailers, grocery manufacturers, the National Association of Food Chains (NAFC), and the Grocery Manufacturers Association (GMA) all having ideas and concerns, there was no common ground nor leadership to establishing a standard.

Manufacturers, being the first in the product chain, already had case codes that they wanted to reuse as part of the code, resulting in rather wide barcode symbols with 11 or more digits. Retailers, on the other hand, worried about wasting too much packaging space with barcode symbols. They favored a standard of 7 digits or fewer.

With all this disagreement, the groups agreed on one thing: to form the Ad Hoc Committee on a Uniform Grocery Product Code in August 1970. The committee's goal was to create a standard for numbering as well as machine-readable representation.

CEO-driven development

Fortunately, the arguing trade association members had the wisdom take a back seat and let a dozen key grocery manufacture and retail executives form this committee themselves. The committee selected Burt Gookin, CEO of H.J. Heinz Company, to be chairman, and McKinsey and Company were hired to manage the project.

McKinsey took a rather scientific approach to the problem. They developed a model that allowed participants to measure and evaluate the economic impact of different proposals. Having a fact-based common evaluation framework allowed the industry see that this would eventually benefit everybody.

Airplane travel at this time still involved good food and lots of beverages, so the folk tale is that on a flight back from a West Coast brainstorming session, the members of the Ad Hoc Committee realized the solution to the numbering dilemma: a study done by the GMA had shown that 95% of products sold in the United States had five or fewer numerical characters in their case code, so they would assign a 5-digit prefix to each manufacturer, and let the manufacturer select another 5 digits, forming a 10-digit code. Later an 11th digit was added to distinguish between 10 different numbering ranges.

Another smart move was that no single executive from the committee claimed responsibility for this idea. Rather, McKinsey presented the approach to hundreds of companies, and all but two readily stated in writing that they'd support it. Had this approach come from a single person or company, there might have been severe backlash, due to fears that a competitor might gain an unfair advantage. Presenting it as the best-of-breed idea that the entire committee had come up with prompted an almost-universal "us too" response.

At the May 1971 Supermarket Industries trade show, the Ad Hoc Committee presented the general agreement on a coding format—a major milestone.

Making it machine-readable

The second part of this undertaking was still missing—the numbers of the coding format would have to be made readable by machines in order to allow for automation. Over the two years following the 1971 announcement, companies busily worked on their proposals for the committee. This ended in a three-day meeting held in January 1973, where each contender got a 20 minute slot to present its approach.

The two strongest contenders turned out to be RCA bull's-eye code and IBM's solution. The circular code still seemed to have the upper hand because of the omnidirectional readability and an existing laser-based scanning technology. Also, IBM—being extremely secretive about under-development projects—had not shown anything public before this time.

Originally, IBM had stated that it wasn't interested in participating. But IBM's George J. Laurer had recognized a fatal flaw in RCA's symbol. Printing it on product packages would often smear the circles in the direction of the paper feed. This rendered the code unreadable. Laurer's barcode design was linear, and you could orient the code such that the smearing during printing would elongate the lines slightly but preserve readability. Woodland, who was employed by IBM at this time, provided valuable input. When IBM's Senior VP Bob Evans made the presentation, he said this:

> *I know you may have concerns about what computer could keep up with scanning this symbol in a store checkout.*

He then reached into his pocket and produced a disk containing schematics for microcircuits and continued:

> *Each circuit on this disk is equivalent to a moderate size existing computer. If IBM were to develop a system, we would put one of these circuits in each checkstand.*

Evans spoke these words after Intel had created the 4004 processor in 1971 and 8008 processor in 1972. Intel's cofounder Gordon E. Moore had observed that the number of transistors in CPUs would double in number every two years. This statement was given the name "Moore's Law" in 1970.

The computer revolution had just begun and made IBM's barcode feasible.

And the winner is ...

As with the number format, the Ad Hoc Committee didn't want to make it sound like IBM was the winner of the contest, and conversely everybody else a loser. They slightly modified IBM's design by trimming off the tops of the code's longer marker lines. They also wanted somebody neutral to evaluate the proposal.

MIT in Cambridge performed the evaluation and recommended changing the numbers at the bottom to the OCR-B font. They argued that in a few years, the bars would not be needed any more, because computers would probably be able to read the numbers directly by then.

Finally, after three years, the *Universal Product Code* (UPC) was announced in a press release in April 1973. The winner was *everybody*.

The first UPC-marked item ever scanned was a 10-pack (50 sticks) of Wrigley's Juicy Fruit chewing gum, which is on display at the Smithsonian Institution's National Museum of American History in Washington, DC. This historic event took place on June 26, 1974.

Joe Woodland of IBM was honored with a National Medal of Technology in 1992 for "inventing the barcode."

A.3 UPC plus EAN equals GTIN

Shortly thereafter, the *Uniform Product Code Council* (UPCC) was formed to oversee the administration of the UPC system. It was founded as a not-for-profit standards organization.

Three years later, a European counterpart to the UPCC was formed, the European Article Numbering (EAN) Association based in Brussels, Belgium. To further increase the range of numbers the barcode could represent, a 13th digit (12 plus the check digit) was added. What followed was a meteoric rise in the adoption of the UPC/EAN code around the world.

At this point, the term *UPC* was colloquially used to refer to the UPC barcode, the UPC product number, and the UPC organization. The same happened in Europe, where the *EAN* abbreviation could refer to the EAN barcode, the EAN product number, or the EAN organization.

In 1978 Japan joined the EAN and adopted the EAN for use in Japan, calling it the *Japanese Article Number* (JAN). Originally founded by 12 European countries, the EAN was joined by many countries outside of the European continent. For many years, the European and US organizations worked alongside each other until in 1990 they signed a formal agreement to jointly manage the standard.

Fifteen more years passed before the UPCC and EAN Association decided to merge. EAN was renamed to *GS1 International*, and the UPCC became *GS1 US*. This merge greatly reduced the confusion over the many different organizations being in charge of the same numbering and barcode standards. The true origins of the *GS1* name are shrouded in mystery.

The second simplification step occurred in 2009 when the UPC/EAN/JAN codes were renamed to *Global Trade Item Number (GTIN)*. GS1 would love it if you'd only refer to their product barcodes as *GTIN*s from here on, but because the other names were in use for over 40 years, you'll still see UPC and EAN used colloquially.

As of the UPC's 40th anniversary in 2013, GS1 International has a presence in 111 countries, and it standardizes many other things—mostly related to commerce—besides the barcode.

Most barcode standards are actually being maintained by the International Standards Organization (ISO) at the lowest technical level. GS1 bases its standardization work on these ISO standards, but it adds the semantics necessary for using these barcodes in the context of commercial communication. This is why the GS1 tagline reads, "The global language of business."

BARCODE GURU TIP Use the name *GS1* to refer the standards organization. When referring to product numbers or barcodes, call them *GTIN*s.

A.4 Barcodes in the mobile age

Other industries had different needs, and this led to the development of barcode symbologies that could represent alphanumeric characters. Code 39 is the oldest among the barcode types supported by iOS; Code 93 and Code 128 are more-advanced symbologies.

The advancements in digital image processing gave rise to a new kind of barcode using more than one dimension. Small, inexpensive cameras on a chip, called CCDs, were able to scan 2D barcodes as well as the older 1D barcodes, which initially could only be scanned with a laser beam. As it became standard for smartphones to have built-in cameras, this put a potential barcode scanner in everyone's pocket.

Before the rise of the mobile phone, barcodes were only useful in places that had scanning equipment installed. Point of sale (POS) systems had bulky cash registers with built-in laser scanners and a database for looking up price information. But these technologies are now available in modern smartphones. Not only can users now scan barcodes with a device they're already carrying with them, but always-on internet connectivity and device sensors detect the user's current context and add degrees of utility that have never been possible before.

A.5 Summary

2013 marked the 40-year anniversary of the first widely used barcode, which eventually became the GTIN. Its original goal was to increase the efficiency of the grocery industry by enabling automatic product identification at the point of sale, and it fulfilled this goal many times over as the entire world adopted it. Most barcode symbologies are ISO standards at the lowest technical level; GS1 is in charge of defining the semantic meaning of content represented as GTINs and Code 128.

These are the key takeaways for this barcode overview:

- Barcodes are a tried-and-true technology, with the oldest commercial form—the UPC—being more than 40 years of age.
- Previously barcodes required laser-based scanners found in factories or at the point of sale. Today camera-equipped mobile phones are able to read them with ease. This opens up new usage scenarios where users can interact with the physical world.
- One-dimensional (1D) barcodes encode numbers or alphanumeric characters on a single line. Two-dimensional (2D) barcodes are able to encode arbitrary data on a grid forming a square.
- The international GS1 organization oversees the semantic implementations of barcodes in the context of commerce. See appendixes 2 and 3 for such semantics that they manage. GS1 unified the previously used UPC, EAN, and JAN codes and numbering schemes into the GTIN.

Apple began to integrate barcode technologies in iOS 7, adding only a few barcode-related APIs to iOS 8. Beginning with iOS 7, you don't need any third-party software for adding barcode scanning to your apps. This book equips you with all you need to know to create barcode-enabled apps.

appendix B
GTIN prefix ranges

Table B.1 shows the GTIN-13 prefix ranges related to 13-digit GTINs. An invisible leading zero is assumed for 12-digit UPCs. The countries mentioned in this table are not necessarily the country of manufacture, but the prefixes are assigned by the GS1 country organization to manufacturers from this country.

Ranges marked "restricted distribution"—defined by member organization (MO)—are valid in nonglobal contexts, such as the context of a store. For example, prefix 220 could be used for adding ad hoc barcodes to freshly packed produce.

Table B.1 GTIN-13 prefixes

Prefix range	Used by
000–019	United States and Canada
020–029	Restricted distribution (MO defined)
030–039	United States
040–049	Restricted distribution (MO defined)
050–059	Coupons
060–139	United States and Canada
200–299	Restricted distribution (MO defined)
300–379	France and Monaco
380	Bulgaria
383	Slovenia
385	Croatia
387	Bosnia and Herzegovina

Table B.1 GTIN-13 prefixes *(continued)*

Prefix range	Used by
389	Montenegro
390	Kosovo
400–440	Germany
450–459	Japan
460–469	Russia
470	Kyrgyzstan
471	Taiwan
474	Estonia
475	Latvia
476	Azerbaijan
477	Lithuania
478	Uzbekistan
479	Sri Lanka
480	Philippines
481	Belarus
482	Ukraine
484	Moldova
485	Armenia
486	Georgia
487	Kazakhstan
488	Tajikistan
489	Hong Kong SAR
490–499	Japan
500–509	United Kingdom
520–521	Greece
528	Lebanon
529	Cyprus
530	Albania
531	Macedonia
535	Malta

Table B.1 GTIN-13 prefixes *(continued)*

Prefix range	Used by
539	Ireland
540–549	Belgium and Luxembourg
560	Portugal
569	Iceland
570–579	Denmark, Faroe Islands, and Greenland
590	Poland
594	Romania
599	Hungary
600–601	South Africa
603	Ghana
604	Senegal
608	Bahrain
609	Mauritius
611	Morocco
613	Algeria
615	Nigeria
616	Kenya
618	Côte d'Ivoire
619	Tunisia
620	Tanzania
621	Syria
622	Egypt
623	Brunei
624	Libya
625	Jordan
626	Iran
627	Kuwait
628	Saudi Arabia
629	United Arab Emirates
630–639	Antarctica

Table B.1 GTIN-13 prefixes *(continued)*

Prefix range	Used by
640–649	Finland
690–699	China, The People's Republic
700–709	Norway
729	Israel
730–739	Sweden
740	Guatemala
741	El Salvador
742	Honduras
743	Nicaragua
744	Costa Rica
745	Panama
746	Dominican Republic
750	Mexico
754–755	Canada
759	Venezuela
760–769	Switzerland and Liechtenstein
770–771	Colombia
773	Uruguay
775	Peru
777	Bolivia
778–779	Argentina
780	Chile
784	Paraguay
786	Ecuador
789–790	Brazil
800–839	Italy, San Marino, and Vatican City
840–849	Spain and Andorra
850	Cuba
858	Slovakia
859	Czech Republic

Table B.1 GTIN-13 prefixes *(continued)*

Prefix range	Used by
860	Serbia
865	Mongolia
867	North Korea
868–869	Turkey
870–879	Netherlands
880	South Korea
884	Cambodia
885	Thailand
888	Singapore
890	India
893	Vietnam
894	Bangladesh
896	Pakistan
899	Indonesia
900–919	Austria
930–939	Australia
940–949	New Zealand
950	GS1 Global Office
951	Global Office (EPCglobal)
955	Malaysia
958	Macau
960–969	Global office (GTIN-8s)
977	Serial publications (ISSN)
978–979	Bookland (ISBN)
980	Refund receipts
981–984	Coupon identification for common currency areas
99	GS1 coupon identification

appendix C GS1-128 application identifiers

GS1 maintains the GS1-128 standard, which defines the semantics for use on top of Code 128 encoding. GS1-128 barcodes—found on more and more products—can contain a great variety of data. Each piece of information is tagged with an application identifier specifying its semantic meaning. Table C.1 lists the various application identifiers.

This list specifies the decimal position in numbers in an interesting way. For example, 310y is the application identifier for product net weight in kg. The *y* can be any digit from 0 to 9, and the integer that follows is to be divided by 10 to the power of *y*. For example, a net weight of 22.7 kg could be coded as 3101 000227, 3102 002270, 3103 022700, or 3104 227000.

Table C.1 GS1-128 application identifiers

AI	Description	Data format
00	Serial shipping container code (SSCC-18)	18 digits, numeric
01	Shipping container code (SSC)	14 digits, numeric
02	Number of containers	14 digits, numeric
10	Batch number	1–20 alphanumeric
11	Production date	6 digits: YYMMDD
13	Packaging date	6 digits: YYMMDD
15	Sell by date (quality control)	6 digits: YYMMDD
17	Expiration date	6 digits: YYMMDD
20	Product variant	2 digits

Table C.1 GS1-128 application identifiers *(continued)*

AI	Description	Data format
21	Serial number	1–20 alphanumeric
22	HIBCC quantity, date, batch, and link	1–29 alphanumeric
23x	Lot number	1–19 alphanumeric
240	Additional product identification	1–30 alphanumeric
250	Second serial number	1–30 alphanumeric
30	Quantity each	—
310y	Product net weight (kg)	6 digits
311y	Product length/1st dimension (meters)	6 digits
312y	Product width/diameter/2nd dimension (meters)	6 digits
313y	Product depth/thickness/3rd dimension (meters)	6 digits
314y	Product area (square meters)	6 digits
315y	Product volume (liters)	6 digits
316y	Product volume (cubic meters)	6 digits
320y	Product net weight (pounds)	6 digits
321y	Product length/1st dimension (inches)	6 digits
322y	Product length/1st dimension (feet)	6 digits
323y	Product length/1st dimension (yards)	6 digits
324y	Product width/diameter/2nd dimension (inches)	6 digits
325y	Product width/diameter/2nd dimension (feet)	6 digits
326y	Product width/diameter/2nd dimension (yards)	6 digits
327y	Product depth/thickness/3rd dimension (inches)	6 digits
328y	Product depth/thickness/3rd dimension (feet)	6 digits
329y	Product depth/thickness/3rd dimension (yards)	6 digits
330y	Container gross weight (kg)	6 digits
331y	Container length/1st dimension (meters)	6 digits
332y	Container width/diameter/2nd dimension (meters)	6 digits
333y	Container depth/thickness/3rd dimension (meters)	6 digits
334y	Container area (square meters)	6 digits
335y	Container gross volume (liters)	6 digits
336y	Container gross volume (cubic meters)	6 digits

Table C.1 GS1-128 application identifiers *(continued)*

AI	Description	Data format
340y	Container gross weight (pounds)	6 digits
341y	Container length/1st dimension (inches)	6 digits
342y	Container length/1st dimension (feet)	6 digits
343y	Container length/1st dimension (yards)	6 digits
344y	Container width/diameter/2nd dimension (inches)	6 digits
345y	Container width/diameter/2nd dimension (feet)	6 digits
346y	Container width/diameter/2nd dimension (yards)	6 digits
347y	Container depth/thickness/height/3rd dimension (inches)	6 digits
348y	Container depth/thickness/height/3rd dimension (feet)	6 digits
349y	Container depth/thickness/height/3rd dimension (yards)	6 digits
350y	Product area (square inches)	6 digits
351y	Product area (square feet)	6 digits
352y	Product area (square yards)	6 digits
353y	Container area (square inches)	6 digits
354y	Container area (square feet)	6 digits
355y	Container area (square yards)	6 digits
356y	Net weight (troy ounces)	6 digits
360y	Product volume (quarts)	6 digits
361y	Product volume (gallons)	6 digits
362y	Container gross volume (quarts)	6 digits
363y	Container gross volume (gallons)	6 digits
364y	Product volume (cubic inches)	6 digits
365y	Product volume (cubic feet)	6 digits
366y	Product volume (cubic yards)	6 digits
367y	Container gross volume (cubic inches)	6 digits
368y	Container gross volume (cubic feet)	6 digits
369y	Container gross volume (cubic yards)	6 digits
37	Number of units contained	1–8 digits
400	Customer purchase order number	1–29 alphanumeric
410	Ship to/deliver to location code (EAN13 or DUNS code)	13 digits

Table C.1 GS1-128 application identifiers *(continued)*

AI	Description	Data format
411	Bill to/invoice location code (EAN13 or DUNS code)	13 digits
412	Purchase from location code (EAN13 or DUNS code)	13 digits
420	Ship to/deliver to postal code (single postal authority)	1–9 alphanumeric
421	Ship to/deliver to postal code (multiple postal authority)	4–12 alphanumeric
8001	Roll products width/length/core diameter	14 digits
8002	Electronic Serial Number (ESN) for cellular phone	1–20 alphanumeric
8003	UPC/EAN number and serial number of returnable asset	14 digit UPC +1–16 alphanumeric serial number
8004	UPC/EAN serial identification	1–30 alphanumeric
8005	Price per unit of measure	6 digits
8100	Coupon extended code: number system and offer	6 digits, numeric
8101	8101 coupon extended code: number system, offer, end of offer	10 digits, numeric
8102	Coupon extended code: number system preceded by 0	2 digits, numeric
90	Mutually agreed between trading partners	1–30 alphanumeric
91	Company internal information	1–30 alphanumeric
92	Company internal information	1–30 alphanumeric
93	Company internal information	1–30 alphanumeric
94	Company internal information	1–30 alphanumeric
95	Company internal information	1–30 alphanumeric
96	Company internal information	1–30 alphanumeric
97	Company internal information	1–30 alphanumeric
98	Company internal information	1–30 alphanumeric
99	Company internal information	1–30 alphanumeric

index

Numerics

A

B

C

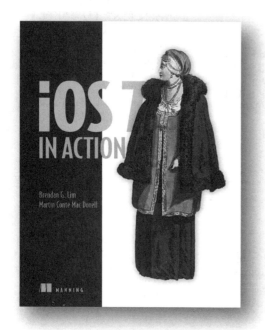

MORE TITLES FROM MANNING

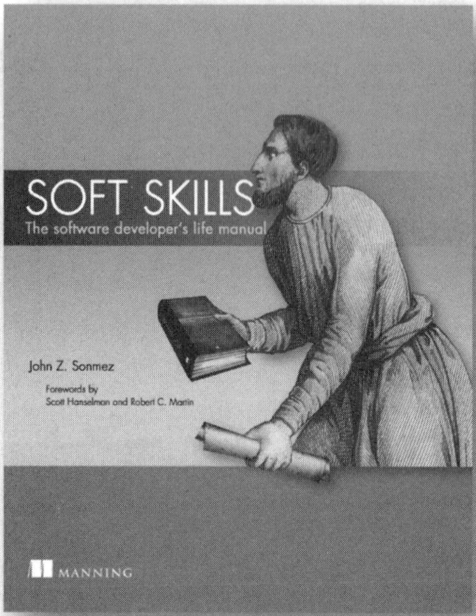

Soft Skills
The software developer's life manual
by John Z. Sonmez

ISBN: 9781617292392
504 pages
$34.99
December 2014

Programming for Musicians and Digital Artists
Creating music with ChucK
by Ajay Kapur, Perry Cook, Spencer Salazar, Ge Wang

ISBN: 9781617291708
344 pages
$44.99
December 2014

For ordering information go to www.manning.com